D1161072

Introduction to Bayesian Econometrics

This concise textbook is an introduction to econometrics from the Bayesian viewpoint. It begins with an explanation of the basic ideas of subjective probability and shows how subjective probabilities must obey the usual rules of probability to ensure coherency. It then turns to the definitions of the likelihood function, prior distributions, and posterior distributions. It explains how posterior distributions are the basis for inference and explores their basic properties. The Bernoulli distribution is used as a simple example. Various methods of specifying prior distributions are considered, with special emphasis on subject-matter considerations and exchange ability. The regression model is examined to show how analytical methods may fail in the derivation of marginal posterior distributions, which leads to an explanation of classical and Markov chain Monte Carlo (MCMC) methods of simulation. The latter is proceeded by a brief introduction to Markov chains. The remainder of the book is concerned with applications of the theory to important models that are used in economics, political science, biostatistics, and other applied fields. These include the linear regression model and extensions to Tobit, probit, and logit models; time series models; and models involving endogenous variables.

Edward Greenberg is Professor Emeritus of Economics at Washington University, St. Louis, where he served as a Full Professor on the faculty from 1969 to 2005. Professor Greenberg also taught at the University of Wisconsin, Madison, and has been a Visiting Professor at the University of Warwick (UK), Technion University (Israel), and the University of Bergamo (Italy). A former holder of a Ford Foundation Faculty Fellowship, Professor Greenberg is the coauthor of four books: *Wages, Regime Switching, and Cycles* (1992), *The Labor Market and Business Cycle Theories* (1989), *Advanced Econometrics* (1983, revised 1991), and *Regulation, Market Prices, and Process Innovation* (1979). His published research has appeared in leading journals such as the *American Economic Review*, *Econometrica*, *Journal of Econometrics*, *Journal of the American Statistical Association*, *Biometrika*, and the *Journal of Economic Behavior and Organization*. Professor Greenberg's current research intersts include dynamic macroeconomics as well as Bayesian econometrics.

Introduction to Bayesian Econometrics

EDWARD GREENBERG

Washington University, St. Louis

CAMBRIDGE
UNIVERSITY PRESS

CAMBRIDGE UNIVERSITY PRESS
Cambridge, New York, Melbourne, Madrid, Cape Town, Singapore, São Paulo, Delhi

Cambridge University Press
32 Avenue of the Americas, New York, NY 10013-2473, USA

www.cambridge.org
Information on this title: www.cambridge.org/9780521858717

First published 2008

Printed in the United States of America

A catalog record for this publication is available from the British Library.

Library of Congress Cataloging in Publication Data

Greenberg, Edward, 1936-
Introduction to Bayesian econometrics / Edward Greenberg.
p. cm.
Includes bibliographical references and index.
ISBN-13: 978-0-521-85871-7 (hardback)
ISBN-10: 0-521-85871-2 (hardback)
1. Econometrics.   2. Bayesian statistical decision theory.   I. Title.
HB139.G732   2008
330.01′519542–dc22   2007024630

ISBN   978-0-521-85871-7 hardback

Contents

List of Figures

List of Figures

List of Tables

Preface

To Instructors and Students

THIS BOOK IS a concise introduction to Bayesian statistics and econometrics. It can be used as a supplement to a frequentist course by instructors who wish to introduce the Bayesian viewpoint or as a text in a course in Bayesian econometrics supplemented by readings in the current literature.

While the student should have had some exposure to standard probability theory and statistics, the book does not make extensive use of statistical theory. Indeed, because of its reliance on simulation techniques, it requires less background in statistics and probability than do most books that take a frequentist approach. It is, however, strongly recommended that the students become familiar with the forms and properties of the standard probability distributions collected in Appendix A.

Since the advent of Markov chain Monte Carlo (MCMC) methods in the early 1990s, Bayesian methods have been extended to a large and growing number of applications. This book limits itself to explaining in detail a few important applications. Its main goal is to provide examples of MCMC algorithms to enable students and researchers to design algorithms for the models that arise in their own research. More attention is paid to the design of algorithms for the models than to the specification and interpretation of the models themselves because we assume that the student has been exposed to these models in other statistics and econometrics classes.

The decision to keep the book short has also meant that we have taken a stand on some controversial issues rather than discuss a large number of alternative methods. In some cases, alternative approaches are discussed in end of chapter notes.

Exercises have been included at the end of the chapters, but the best way to learn the material is for students to apply the ideas to empirical applications of their choice. Accordingly, even though it is not explicitly stated, the first exercise at the end of every chapter in Part III should direct students to formulate a model; collect data; specify a prior distribution on the basis of previous research design and, if necessary, program an algorithm; and present the results.

A link to the Web site for the course may be found at my Web site: http://edg. wustl.edu. The site contains errata, links to data sources, some computer code, and other information.

Acknowledgments

I would like to acknowledge and offer my sincere gratitude to some of the people who have helped me throughout my career. On the professional side, I start with my undergraduate years at the business school of New York University, where Abraham Gitlow awakened my interest in economics. My first statistics course was with F. J. Viser and my second with Ernest Kurnow, who encouraged me to continue my studies and guided me in the process.

At the University of Wisconsin–Madison, I was mentored by, among others, Peter Steiner and Guy Orcutt. Econometrics was taught by Jack Johnston, who was writing the first edition of his pathbreaking book, and I was fortunate to have Arthur Goldberger and Arnold Zellner as teachers and colleagues. My first mathematical statistics course was with Enders Robinson, and I later audited George Box's class, where I received my first exposure to Bayesian ideas. Soon afterward, Zellner began to apply the methods to econometrics in a workshop that I attended.

My interest in Bayesian methods was deepened at Washington University first by E. T. Jaynes and then by Siddhartha Chib. Sid Chib has been my teacher, collaborator, and friend for the last 15 years. His contributions to Bayesian statistics, econometrics, and MCMC methods have had enormous impact. I have been extremely fortunate to have had the opportunity to work with him. The students in my courses in Bayesian econometrics contributed to my understanding of the material by their blank stares and penetrating questions. I am most grateful to them.

My colleagues and the staff of the Economics Department at Washington University have always been extremely helpful to me. I am delighted to thank them for their support.

I am most grateful to my editor at Cambridge University Press, Scott Parris, for suggesting the book, and for his continuing encouragement and support, and to Kimberly Twist, Editorial Assistant at Cambridge, for her help in the publication process.

I am pleased to acknowledge the comments of Andrew Martin, James Morley, and two anonymous reviewers on various drafts of this book and, especially, those of Ivan Jeliazkov, who read it most carefully and thoughtfully and tested it on his students. All remaining errors are, of course, mine.

I am grateful to Professor Chang-Jin Kim for permission to utilize his software to compute some of the examples in Chapter 10.

On the personal side, I thank Arthur and Aida, Lisa and Howard, my grandchildren, and my colleagues and friends, particularly Sylvia Silver, Karen Rensing, Ingrid and Wilhelm Neuefeind, Maureen Regan and Sid Chib, Jasmine and Steve Fazzari, and Camilla and Piero Ferri.

In December 2005, my wife of more than 46 years passed away. I dedicate this book to Joan's memory.

Part I

Fundamentals of Bayesian Inference

Chapter 1

Introduction

THIS CHAPTER INTRODUCES several important concepts, provides a guide to the rest of the book, and offers some historical perspective and suggestions for further reading.

1.1 Econometrics

Econometrics is largely concerned with quantifying the relationship between one or more more variables y, called the response variables or the dependent variables, and one or more variables x, called the regressors, independent variables, or covariates. The response variable or variables may be continuous or discrete; the latter case includes binary, multinomial, and count data. For example, y might represent the quantities demanded of a set of goods, and x could include income and the prices of the goods; or y might represent investment in capital equipment, and x could include measures of expected sales, cash flows, and borrowing costs; or y might represent a decision to travel by public transportation rather than private, and x could include income, fares, and travel time under various alternatives.

In addition to the covariates, it is assumed that unobservable random variables affect y, so that y itself is a random variable. It is characterized either by a probability density function (p.d.f.) for continuous y or a probability mass function (p.m.f.) for discrete y. The p.d.f. or p.m.f. depends on the values of unknown parameters, denoted by θ. The notation $y \sim f(y|\theta, x)$ means that y has the p.d.f. or p.m.f. $f(y|\theta, x)$, where the function depends on the parameters and covariates. It is customary to suppress dependence on the covariates when writing the p.d.f. of y, so we write $y \sim f(y|\theta)$ unless it is necessary to mention the covariates explicitly.

The data may take the form of observations on a number of subjects at the same point in time – cross section data – or observations over a number of time periods – time series data. They may be a combination of cross-section and time-series observations: data over many subjects over a relatively short period of time

3

– panel data – or data over a fairly small number of subjects over long periods
of time – multivariate data. In some models, the researcher regards the covariates
as fixed numbers, while in others they are regarded as random variables. If the
latter, their distribution may be independent of the distribution of y, or there may
be dependence. All of these possibilities are discussed in Part III.

An important feature of data analyzed by econometricians is that the data are
almost always observational, in contrast to data arising from controlled experiments, where subjects are randomly assigned to treatments. Observational data
are often generated for purposes other than research, for example, as by-products
of data collected for governmental and administrative reasons. Observational data
may also be collected from surveys, some of which may be specially designed for
research purposes. No matter how collected, however, the analysis of observational
data requires special care, especially in the analysis of causal effects – the attempt
to determine the effect of a covariate on a response variable when the covariate is
a variable whose value can be set by an investigator, such as the effect of participating in a training program on income and employment or the effect of exercise
on health. When such data are collected from observing what people choose to do,
rather than from a controlled experiment in which they are told what to do, there is
a possibility that people who choose to take the training or to exercise are different
in some systematic way from people who do not. If so, attempting to generalize
the effect of training or exercise on people who do not freely choose those options
may give misleading answers. The models discussed in Part III are designed to deal
with observational data.

Depending on the nature of the data, models are constructed that relate response
variables to covariates. A large number of models that can be applied to particular
types of data have been developed, but, because new types of data sets may require
new models, it is important to learn how to deal with models that have not been
previously analyzed. Studying how Bayesian methodology has been applied to a
variety of existing models is useful for developing techniques that can be applied
to new models.

1.2 Plan of the Book

Part I of the book sets out the basic ideas of the Bayesian approach to statistical inference. It begins with an explanation of subjective probability to justify the
application of probability theory to general situations of uncertainty. With this background, Bayes theorem is invoked to define the posterior distribution, the central
concept in Bayesian statistical inference. We show how the posterior distribution
can be used to solve the standard problems of statistical inference – point and
interval estimation, prediction, and model comparison. This material is illustrated

with the Bernoulli model of coin tossing. Because of its simplicity, all relevant calculations can be done analytically.

The remainder of Part I is devoted to general properties of posterior distributions and to the specification of prior distributions. These properties are illustrated with the normal distribution and linear regression models. For more complicated models, we turn to simulation as a way of studying posterior distributions because it is impossible to make the necessary computations analytically.

Part II is devoted to the explanation of simulation techniques. We start with the classical methods of simulation that yield independent samples but are inadequate to deal with many common statistical models. The remainder of Part II describes Markov chain Monte Carlo (MCMC) simulation, a flexible simulation method that can deal with a wide variety of models.

Part III applies MCMC techniques to models commonly encountered in econometrics and statistics. We emphasize the design of algorithms to analyze these models as a way of preparing the student to devise algorithms for the new models that will arise in the course of his or her research.

Appendix A contains definitions, properties, and notation for the standard probability distributions that are used throughout the book, a few important probability theorems, and several useful results from matrix algebra. Appendix B describes computer programs for implementing the methods discussed in the book.

1.3 Historical Note and Further Reading

Bayesian statistics is named for the Rev. Thomas Bayes (1702–1761), and important contributions to the ideas, under the rubric of "inverse probability," were made by Pierre-Simon Laplace (1749–1827). Stigler (1986) is an excellent introduction to the history of statistics up to the beginning of the twentieth century. Another important approach to inference, the frequentist approach, was largely developed in the second half of the nineteenth century. The leading advocates of the approach in the twentieth century were R. A. Fisher, J. Neyman, and E. Pearson, although Fisher's viewpoint differs in important respects from the others. Howie (2002) provides a concise summary of the development of probability and statistics up to the 1920s and then focuses on the debate between H. Jeffreys, who took the Bayesian position, and R. A. Fisher, who argued against it.

The application of the Bayesian viewpoint to econometric models was pioneered by A. Zellner starting in the early 1960s. His early work is summarized in his highly influential book, Zellner (1971), and he continues to contribute to the literature. An important breakthrough in the Bayesian approach to statistical inference occurred in the early 1990s with the application of Markov chain Monte Carlo simulation to statistical and econometric models. This is an active area of research by statisticians, econometricians, and probabilists.

Several other recent textbooks cover Bayesian econometrics: Poirier (1995), Koop (2003), Lancaster (2004), and Geweke (2005). The book by Poirier, unlike the present book and the others mentioned earlier, compares and contrasts Bayesian methods with other approaches to statistics and econometrics in great detail. The present book focuses on Bayesian methods with only occasional comments on the frequentist approach. Two textbooks that emphasize the frequentist viewpoint – Mittelhammer et al. (2000) and Greene (2003) – also discuss Bayesian inference.

Several statistics books take a Bayesian viewpoint. Berry (1996) is an excellent introduction to Bayesian ideas. His discussion of differences between observational and experimental data is highly recommended. Another fine introductory book is Bolstad (2004). Excellent intermediate level books with many examples are Carlin and Louis (2000) and Gelman et al. (2004). At a more advanced level, the following are especially recommended: O'Hagan (1994), Robert (1994), Bernardo and Smith (1994), Lee (1997), and Jaynes (2003).

Although directed at a general statistical audience, three books by Congdon (2001, 2003, 2005) cover many common econometric models and utilize Markov chain Monte Carlo methods extensively. Schervish (1995) covers both Bayesian and frequentist ideas at an advanced level.

Chapter 2

Basic Concepts of Probability and Inference

2.1 Probability

SINCE STATISTICAL INFERENCE is based on probability theory, the major difference between Bayesian and frequentist approaches to inference can be traced to the different views that each have about the interpretation and scope of probability theory. We therefore begin by stating the basic axioms of probability and explaining the two views.

A probability is a number assigned to statements or events. We use the terms "statements" and "events" interchangeably. Examples of such statements are

- $A_1 =$ "A coin tossed three times will come up heads either two or three times."
- $A_2 =$ "A six-sided die rolled once shows an even number of spots."
- $A_3 =$ "There will be measurable precipitation on January 1, 2008, at your local airport."

Before presenting the probability axioms, we review some standard notation:

The *union* of A and B is the event that A or B (or both) occur; it is denoted by $A \cup B$.
The *intersection* of A and B is the event that both A and B occur; it is denoted by AB.
The *complement* of A is the event that A does not occur; it is denoted by A^c.

The probability of event A is denoted by $P(A)$. Probabilities are assumed to satisfy the following axioms:

Probability Axioms

1. $0 \leq P(A) \leq 1$.
2. $P(A) = 1$ if A represents a logical truth, that is, a statement that must be true; for example, "A coin comes up either heads or tails."
3. If A and B describe disjoint events (events that cannot both occur), then $P(A \cup B) = P(A) + P(B)$.

---

4. Let $P(A|B)$ denote "the probability of A, given (or conditioned on the assumption) that B is true." Then

$$P(A|B) = \frac{P(AB)}{P(B)}.$$

All the theorems of probability theory can be deduced from these axioms, and probabilities that are assigned to statements will be consistent if these rules are observed. By consistent we mean that it is not possible to assign two or more different values to the probability of a particular event if probabilities are assigned by following these rules. As an example, if $P(A)$ has been assigned a value, then Axioms 1 and 2 imply that $P(A^c) = 1 - P(A)$, and $P(A^c)$ can take no other value. Assigning some probabilities may put bounds on others. For example, if A and B are disjoint and $P(A)$ is given, then by Axioms 1 and 3, $P(B) \leq 1 - P(A)$.

2.1.1 Frequentist Probabilities

A major controversy in probability theory is over the types of statements to which probabilities can be assigned. One school of thought is that of the "frequentists." Frequentists restrict the assignment of probabilities to statements that describe the outcome of an experiment that can be repeated. Consider A_1: we can imagine repeating the experiment of tossing a coin three times and recording the number of times that two or three heads were reported. If we define

$$P(A_1) = \lim_{n \to \infty} \frac{\text{number of times two or three heads occurs}}{n},$$

we find that our definition is consistent with the axioms of probability.

Axiom 1 is satisfied because the ratio of a subset of outcomes to all possible outcomes is between zero and one. Axiom 2 is satisfied if the probability of a logically true statement such as $A_4 =$ "either $0, 1, 2,$ or 3 heads appear" is computed by following the rule since the numerator is then equal to n. Axiom 3 tells us that we can compute $P(A \cup B)$ as $P(A) + P(B)$ since, for disjoint events, the number of times A or B occurs is equal to the number of times A occurs plus the number of times B occurs. Axiom 4 is satisfied because to compute $P(A|B)$ we can confine our attention to the outcomes of the experiment for which B is true; suppose there are n_B of these. Then

$$P(A|B) = \lim_{n_B \to \infty} \frac{\text{number of times } A \text{ and } B \text{ are true}}{n_B}$$

$$= \lim_{n, n_B \to \infty} \frac{\text{number of times } A \text{ and } B \text{ are true}}{n} \div \frac{n_B}{n}$$

$$= \frac{p(AB)}{p(B)}.$$

This method of assigning probabilities, even to experiments that can be repeated in principle, suffers from the problem that its definition requires repeating the experiment an infinite number of times, which is impossible. But to those who believe in a subjective interpretation of probability, an even greater problem is its inability to assign probabilities to such statements as A_3, which cannot be considered an outcome of a repeated experiment. We next consider the subjective view.

2.1.2 Subjective Probabilities

Those who take the subjective view of probability believe that probability theory is applicable to any situation in which there is uncertainty. Outcomes of repeated experiments fall in that category, but so do statements about tomorrow's weather, which are not the outcomes of repeated experiments. Calling the probabilities "subjective" does not imply that they may be assigned without regard to the axioms of probability. Such assignments would lead to inconsistencies. de Finetti (1990, chap. 3) provides a principle for assigning probabilities that does not rely on the outcomes of repeated experiments, but is consistent with the probability axioms.

de Finetti developed his approach in the context of setting odds on a bet that are fair in the sense that, in your opinion, neither you nor your opponent has an advantage. In particular, when the odds are fair, you will not find yourself in the position that you will lose money no matter which outcome obtains. de Finetti calls your behavior *coherent* when you set odds in this way. We now show that coherent behavior implies that probabilities satisfy the axioms.

First, let us review the standard betting setup: in a standard bet on the event A, you buy or sell betting tickets at a price of 1 per ticket, and the money you receive or pay out depends on the betting odds k. (We omit the currency unit in this discussion.) In this setup, the price of the ticket is fixed and the payout depends on the odds. We denote the number of tickets by S and make the convention that

$S > 0$ means that you are betting that A occurs (i.e., you have bought S tickets on A from your opponent) and $S < 0$ means that you are betting against A (i.e., you have sold S tickets on A to your opponent). If you bet on A and A occurs, you receive the 1 that you bet plus k for each ticket you bought, or $S(1 + k)$, where k is the odds *against* A:

$$k = \frac{1 - P(A)}{P(A)}$$

(see Berry, 1996, pp. 116–119). If A occurs and you bet against it, you would "receive" $S(1 + k)$, a negative number because $S < 0$ if you bet against A.

In the de Finetti betting setup, the price of the ticket, denoted by p, is chosen by you, the payout is fixed at 1, and your opponent chooses S. Although you set p, the fact that your opponent determines whether you bet for or against A forces you to set a fair value. We can now show the connection between p and $P(A)$. If the price of a ticket is p rather than one as in the standard betting situation, a winning ticket on A would pay $p + pk = p(1 + k)$. But in the de Finetti setup, the payout is one; that is, $p(1 + k) = 1$, or $k = (1 - p)/p$, which implies $p = P(A)$. Accordingly, in the following discussion, you can interpret p as your subjective belief about the value of $P(A)$.

Consider a simple bet on or against A, where you have set the price of a ticket at p and you are holding S tickets for which you have paid pS; your opponent has chosen S. (Remember that $S > 0$ means that you are betting on A and $S < 0$ means you are betting against A.) If A occurs, you pay pS and collect S. If A does not occur, you collect pS. Verify that these results are valid for both positive and negative values of S. We summarize your gains in the following table, where the rows denote disjoint events and cover all possible outcomes:

Event	Your gain
A	$S - pS = (1 - p)S$
A^c	$-pS$

We can now show that the principle of coherency restricts the value of p you set. If $p < 0$, your opponent, by choosing $S < 0$, will inflict a loss (a negative gain) on you whether or not A occurs. By coherency, therefore, $p \geq 0$. Similarly, if you set $p > 1$, your opponent can set $S > 0$, and you are again sure to lose. Axiom 1 is therefore implied by the principle of coherency.

If you are certain that A will occur, coherency dictates that you set $p = 1$: you will have zero loss if A is true, and the second row of the loss table is not relevant, because A^c is impossible in your opinion. This verifies Axiom 2.

To examine the subjective assignment of $P(A_1 \cup A_2)$ if A_1 and A_2 are disjoint, consider the table of gains when you set prices p_1, p_2, p_3, and your opponent chooses S_1, S_2, and S_3, respectively, on the events A_1, A_2, and $(A_1 \cup A_2)$. A positive (negative) S_1 again means that you are betting on (against) A_1, and the same for S_2 and S_3.

Event	Your gain
A_1	$(1 - p_1)S_1 - p_2 S_2 + (1 - p_3)S_3$
A_2	$-p_1 S_1 + (1 - p_2)S_2 + (1 - p_3)S_3$
$(A_1 \cup A_2)^c$	$-p_1 S_1 - p_2 S_2 - p_3 S_3$

As before, the events listed in the first column are a disjoint set that cover all possible outcomes. Verify that the three rows in the second column of the table express your winnings (or your losses if the values are negative) as a function of the values of p_1, p_2, and p_3 that you choose and the values of S_1, S_2, and S_3 that your opponent chooses:

$$W_1 = (1 - p_1)S_1 - p_2 S_2 + (1 - p_3)S_3,$$
$$W_2 = -p_1 S_1 + (1 - p_2)S_2 + (1 - p_3)S_3,$$
$$W_3 = -p_1 S_1 - p_2 S_2 - p_3 S_3.$$

Your opponent can now set each of W_1, W_2, and W_3 to negative values and solve for the values of S_1, S_2, and S_3 that create those losses for you. But you can prevent this by choosing p_1, p_2, and p_3 in such a way that the equations cannot be solved. This requires that the determinant of the system be set to zero; that is,

$$\begin{vmatrix} 1 - p_1 & -p_2 & 1 - p_3 \\ -p_1 & 1 - p_2 & 1 - p_3 \\ -p_1 & -p_2 & -p_3 \end{vmatrix} = 0.$$

By computing the determinant, you will find that $p_1 + p_2 = p_3$, which is the third axiom.

Finally, consider Axiom 4: $P(A|B) = P(AB)/P(B)$. For this case, we assume that the bet on $A|B$ is cancelled if B fails to occur. Consider the three sets of events, prices, and stakes (AB, p_1, S_1), (B, p_2, S_2), and $(A|B, p_3, S_3)$. These imply the following payoff table in which the rows cover all possible outcomes and are disjoint:

Event	Your gain
AB	$(1 - p_1)S_1 + (1 - p_2)S_2 + (1 - p_3)S_3$
BA^c	$-p_1 S_1 + (1 - p_2)S_2 - p_3 S_3$
AB^c	$-p_1 S_1 - p_2 S_2$
$(A \cup B)^c$	$-p_1 S_1 - p_2 S_2$

Since the third and fourth payoffs are identical, we can consider only the three distinct equations. As above, to prevent your opponent from being able to win regardless of the outcome you will need to set

$$
\begin{vmatrix}
1 - p_1 & 1 - p_2 & 1 - p_3 \\
-p_1 & 1 - p_2 & -p_3 \\
-p_1 & -p_2 & 0
\end{vmatrix} = 0.
$$

It is easily verified that $p_1 = p_2 p_3$, which is Axiom 4.

The point of this discussion is that the assignment of subjective probabilities must follow the standard axioms if a person is to be coherent in the sense of not setting probabilities in a way that is sure to result in losses. As mentioned above, probability theory is about the consistent setting of probabilities. Calling probabilities "subjective" does not imply that they can be set arbitrarily, and probabilities set in accordance with the axioms are consistent.

We now turn to the statistical implications of the subjective view of probability.

2.2 Prior, Likelihood, and Posterior

In this section, we introduce the fundamental idea of the posterior distribution and show how it can be computed from the likelihood function and the prior distribution. In the next chapter, we explain how the posterior distribution can be used to analyze the central issues in inference: point estimates, interval estimates, prediction, and model comparisons.

To understand the implications for statistical inference of adopting a subjective view of probability, it is useful to consider a simple example. Let $y = 1$ if a coin toss results in a head and 0 otherwise, and let $P(y = 1) = \theta$, which is assumed to be constant for each trial. In this model, θ is a *parameter* and the value of y is the data. Under these assumptions, y is said to have the Bernoulli distribution, written as $y \sim \text{Be}(\theta)$. We are interested in learning about θ from an experiment in which the coin is tossed n times yielding the data $y = (y_1, y_2, \ldots, y_n)$, where y_i indicates whether the ith toss resulted in a head or tail.

From the frequentist point of view, probability theory can tell us something about the distribution of the data for a given θ because the data can be regarded as the outcome of a large number of repetitions of tossing a coin n times. The parameter θ is an unknown number between zero and one. It is not given a probability distribution of its own, because it is not regarded as being the outcome of a repeated experiment.

From the subjective point of view, however, θ is an unknown quantity. Since there is uncertainty over its value, it can be regarded as a random variable and assigned a probability distribution. Before seeing the data, it is assigned a *prior* distribution $\pi(\theta)$, $0 \leq \theta \leq 1$. Bayesian inference centers on the *posterior* distribution $\pi(\theta|y)$, which is the distribution of the random variable θ, conditioned on having observed the data y. Note that in the coin-tossing example, the data y_i are discrete – each is 0 or 1 – but the parameter θ is continuous.

All the models we consider in this book have one or more parameters, and an important goal of statistical inference is learning about their values. When there is more than one parameter, the posterior distribution is a joint distribution of all the parameters, conditioned on the observed data. This complication is taken up in the next chapter.

Before proceeding, we explain some conventions about notation for distributions.

Notation for Density and Distribution Functions

- $\pi(\cdot)$ denotes a prior and $\pi(\cdot|y)$ denotes a posterior density function of parameters; these densities are continuous random variables in the statistical models we discuss.
- $p(\cdot)$ denotes the probability mass function (p.m.f.) of a discrete random variable; $P(A)$ denotes the probability of event A.
- $f(\cdot)$ denotes the probability density function (p.d.f.) for continuous data. $F(\cdot)$ denotes the (cumulative) distribution function (d.f.) for continuous data; that is, $F(y_0) = P(Y \leq y_0)$.
- When the distinction between discrete and continuous data is not relevant, we employ the $f(\cdot)$ notation for both probability mass and density functions.

The posterior density function $\pi(\theta|y)$ is computed by Bayes theorem, which follows from Axiom 4: from $P(A|B) = P(AB)/P(B)$, we can infer $P(B|A) = P(BA)/P(A)$. But since $P(AB) = P(BA)$, we have Bayes theorem:

$$P(A|B) = \frac{P(B|A)P(A)}{P(B)}.$$

By setting $A = \theta$ and $B = y$, we have for discrete y

$$\pi(\theta|y) = \frac{p(y|\theta)\pi(\theta)}{p(y)}, \tag{2.1}$$

where $p(y) = \int p(y|\theta)\pi(\theta)\,d\theta$. The effect of dividing by $p(y)$ is to make $\pi(\theta|y)$ a normalized probability distribution: integrating Equation (2.1) with respect to θ yields $\int \pi(\theta|y)\,d\theta = 1$, as it should.

For continuous or general y, we rewrite (2.1) as

$$\pi(\theta|y) = \frac{f(y|\theta)\pi(\theta)}{f(y)}, \tag{2.2}$$

where $f(y) = \int f(y|\theta)\pi(\theta)\,d\theta$. Equation (2.2) is the basis of Bayesian statistics and econometrics. It is necessary to understand it thoroughly. The left-hand side has been interpreted as the posterior density function of $\theta|y$. Now consider the right-hand side. The first term in the numerator is $f(y|\theta)$, the density function for the observed data y when the parameter value is θ. Take the coin-tossing experiment as an example. Suppose the coin is tossed three times and (H, T, H) results, so that $y = (1, 0, 1)$. If the probability of a head is θ,

$$P(1, 0, 1|\theta) = P(1|\theta)P(0|\theta)P(1|\theta) = \theta(1 - \theta)\theta = \theta^2(1 - \theta).$$

From this expression, and in general, we see that $f(y|\theta)$ is a function of θ once the data are known. As a function of θ, $f(y|\theta)$ is called the *likelihood function*; it plays a central role in both frequentist and Bayesian statistics. It is important to note that the likelihood function is not a p.d.f. for θ; in particular, its integral over θ is not equal to one, although its integral (in this case, a sum) over y is.

The second term in the numerator of (2.2), the prior density $\pi(\theta)$, embodies our beliefs about the distribution of θ before seeing the data y. These beliefs are based on the researcher's knowledge of the problem at hand; they may be based on theoretical considerations or on previous empirical work. The prior distribution usually depends on parameters, called *hyperparameters*, which may either be supplied by the researcher or given probability distributions.

We have already remarked that the denominator of (2.2), $f(y)$, normalizes the posterior distribution. Since it is independent of θ, however, it is often convenient to write the posterior distribution as

$$\pi(\theta|y) \propto f(y|\theta)\pi(\theta), \tag{2.3}$$

that is, the posterior distribution is proportional to the likelihood function times the prior distribution. In this form, the right side of the equation does not integrate to one, but as a function of θ, it has the same shape as $\pi(\theta|y)$.

For the Bayesian, the posterior distribution is central to inference because it combines in one expression all the information we have about θ. It includes information about θ before the current data through the prior distribution and the information contained in the current data through the likelihood function.

It is useful to think of (2.3) as a method of updating information, an idea that is reinforced by the prior–posterior terminology. Before collecting the data y, our information about θ is summarized by the prior distribution $\pi(\theta)$. After observing y, our information about θ is summarized by the posterior distribution $\pi(\theta|y)$. Equation (2.3) tells us how to update beliefs after receiving new data: multiply the prior by the likelihood to find an expression proportional to the posterior.

We illustrate these ideas with the coin-tossing example. The likelihood function for a single toss of a coin can be written as $p(y_i|\theta) = \theta^{y_i}(1-\theta)^{1-y_i}$, which implies $P(y_i = 1|\theta) = \theta$ and $P(y_i = 0|\theta) = 1 - \theta$. For n independent tosses of a coin, we therefore have

$$p(y_1, \ldots, y_n|\theta) = \theta^{y_1}(1-\theta)^{1-y_1} \cdots \theta^{y_n}(1-\theta)^{1-y_n}$$
$$= \prod \theta^{y_i}(1-\theta)^{1-y_i}$$
$$= \theta^{\sum y_i}(1-\theta)^{n-\sum y_i}. \tag{2.4}$$

To complete the specification of the model, we need a prior distribution. Since $0 \le \theta \le 1$, the prior should allow θ to take on any value in that interval and not allow it to fall outside that interval. A common choice is the beta distribution Beta(α, β) discussed in Section A.1.9:

$$\pi(\theta) = \frac{\Gamma(\alpha + \beta)}{\Gamma(\alpha)\Gamma(\beta)}\theta^{\alpha-1}(1-\theta)^{\beta-1}, \quad 0 \le \theta \le 1, \quad \alpha, \beta > 0.$$

Note that α and β are hyperparameters. Why choose the beta distribution? First, it is defined in the relevant range. Second, it is capable of producing a wide variety of shapes, some of which are displayed in Figure 2.1. Depending on the choice of α and β, this prior can capture beliefs that indicate θ is centered at 1/2, or it can shade θ toward zero or one; it can be highly concentrated, or it can be spread out; and, when both parameters are less than one, it can have two modes.

The shape of a beta distribution can be understood by examining its mean and variance:

$$E(\theta) = \frac{\alpha}{\alpha + \beta}, \qquad \text{Var}(\theta) = \frac{\alpha\beta}{(\alpha + \beta)^2(\alpha + \beta + 1)}.$$

From these expressions you can see that the mean is 1/2 if $\alpha = \beta$, a larger α (β) shades the mean toward 1 (0), and the variance decreases as α or β increases. It is also useful to note that we may first specify $E(\theta)$, and Var(θ) and then find the α and β that correspond to the moments. These relationships may be found in (A.7).

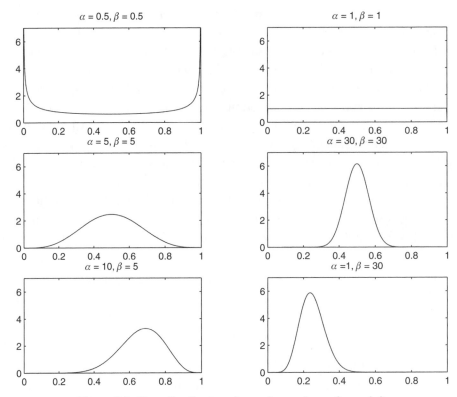

Figure 2.1. Beta distributions for various values of α and β.

A third reason for choosing this distribution is that the beta prior in combination with the likelihood function of (2.4) yields a posterior distribution that has a standard form, which is convenient for analyzing the properties of the posterior. In fact, we next show that the posterior distribution for a model in which data are generated by the Bernoulli distribution with a Beta(α_0, β_0) prior is also a beta distribution. This is an example of a *conjugate* prior, where the posterior distribution is in the same family as the prior distribution. From (2.3),

$$\pi(\theta|y) \propto p(y|\theta)\pi(\theta)$$
$$\propto \theta^{\sum y_i}(1-\theta)^{n-\sum y_i}\theta^{\alpha_0-1}(1-\theta)^{\beta_0-1}$$
$$\propto \theta^{(\alpha_0+\sum y_i)-1}(1-\theta)^{(\beta_0+n-\sum y_i)-1}.$$

In this expression, the normalizing constant of the beta distribution has been absorbed into the proportionality constant because the constant does not depend on θ. As promised, $\pi(\theta|y)$ is in the form of a beta distribution with parameters $\alpha_1 = \alpha_0 + \sum y_i$ and $\beta_1 = \beta_0 + n - \sum y_i$.

The way in which α_0 and β_0 enter this expression is useful in interpreting these parameters and in determining the values to assign to them. Note that α_0 is added to $\sum y_i$, the number of heads. This means that α_0 can be interpreted as "the number of heads obtained in the experiment on which the prior is based." If, for example, you had seen this coin tossed a large number of times and heads appeared frequently, you would set a relatively large value for α_0. Similarly, β_0 represents the number of tails in the "experiment" on which the prior is based. Setting $\alpha_0 = 1 = \beta_0$ yields the uniform distribution. This prior indicates that you are sure that both a head and tail can appear but otherwise have no strong opinion about the distribution of θ. Choosing $\alpha_0 = 0.5 = \beta_0$ yields a bimodal distribution with considerable probability around zero and one, indicating that you would not be surprised if the coin were two-headed or two-tailed.

It is easy to compute the mean of the posterior distribution from the properties of the beta distribution:

$$
\begin{aligned}
E(\theta|y) &= \frac{\alpha_1}{\alpha_1 + \beta_1} \\
&= \frac{\alpha_0 + \sum y_i}{\alpha_0 + \beta_0 + n} \\
&= \left(\frac{\alpha_0 + \beta_0}{\alpha_0 + \beta_0 + n} \right) \frac{\alpha_0}{\alpha_0 + \beta_0} + \left(\frac{n}{\alpha_0 + \beta_0 + n} \right) \bar{y},
\end{aligned}
\tag{2.5}
$$

where $\bar{y} = (1/n) \sum y_i$. The last line expresses $E(\theta|y)$ as a weighted average of the prior mean $\alpha_0/(\alpha_0 + \beta_0)$ and the maximum likelihood estimator (MLE) $\bar{y}$; that is, $\bar{y}$ is the value of θ that maximizes $p(y|\theta)$. This result shows how the prior distribution and the data contribute to determine the mean of the posterior distribution. It is a good illustration of the way Bayesian inference works: the posterior distribution summarizes all available information about θ, both from what was known before obtaining the current data and from the current data y.

As the sample size n becomes large, the weight on the prior mean approaches zero, and the weight on the MLE approaches one, implying that $E(\theta|y) \rightarrow \bar{y}$. This is an example of a rather general phenomenon: the prior distribution becomes less important in determining the posterior distribution as the sample size increases. We graph in Figure 2.2 the prior, likelihood, and posterior for the cases $n = 10, \sum y_i = 3, \alpha_0 = 2, \beta_0 = 2$ and $n = 50, \sum y_i = 15, \alpha_0 = 2, \beta_0 = 2$. (The likelihood has been normalized to integrate to one for easier comparison with the prior and posterior.) You can see how the larger sample size of the second example, reflected in the tighter likelihood function, causes the posterior to move further away from the prior and closer to the likelihood function than when $n = 10$.

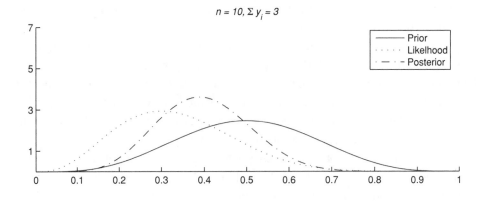

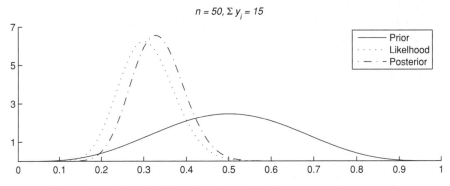

Figure 2.2. Prior, likelihood, and posterior for coin-tossing example.

Although the preceding discussion shows that the beta prior is a "natural" prior for Bernoulli data and that the choice of the two parameters in the beta prior can capture a wide variety of prior beliefs, it is important to note that it is not necessary to adopt a beta prior if no combination of parameters can approximate the prior you wish to specify. Beta priors, for example, do not easily accommodate bimodal distributions. We describe methods later in the book that can approximate the posterior distribution for any specified prior, even if the prior information does not lead to a posterior distribution of a standard form.

2.3 Summary

In this chapter, we first showed that subjective probabilities must satisfy the standard axioms of probability theory if you wish to avoid losing a bet regardless of the outcome. Having established that subjective probabilities must satisfy the usual axioms of probability theory and, therefore, the theorems of probability theory, we derived the fundamental result of Bayesian inference: the posterior distribution of a parameter is proportional to the likelihood function times the prior distribution.

2.4 Further Reading and References

Section 2.1.2 Excellent discussions of subjective probability may be found in Howson and Urbach (1993) and Hacking (2001).

2.5 Exercises

2.1 Prove the theorem $P(A \cup B) = P(A) + P(B) - P(AB)$ in two ways. First, write $A \cup B = AB^c \cup A^cB \cup AB$, and then use $A = AB^c \cup AB$ and $B = AB \cup A^cB$. Second, apply coherency to a betting scheme like those in Section 2.1.2, where the four possible outcomes are AB^c, A^cB, AB, and $(A \cup B)^c$, and the bets, prices, and stakes are (A, p_1, S_1), (B, p_2, S_2), (AB, p_3, S_3), and $(A \cup B, p_4, S_4)$, respectively.

2.2 The Poisson distribution has probability mass function

$$p(y_i|\theta) = \frac{\theta^{y_i} e^{-\theta}}{y_i!}, \quad \theta > 0, \; y_i = 0, 1, \ldots,$$

and let $y_1, \ldots, y_n$ be a random sample from this distribution.

(a) Show that the gamma distribution $G(\alpha, \beta)$ is a conjugate prior distribution for the Poisson distribution.

(b) Show that $\bar{y}$ is the MLE for θ.

(c) Write the mean of the posterior distribution as a weighted average of the mean of the prior distribution and the MLE.

(d) What happens to the weight on the prior mean as n becomes large?

2.3 The density function of the exponential distribution is

$$f(y_i|\theta) = \theta e^{-\theta y_i}, \quad \theta > 0, \; y_i > 0,$$

and let $y_1, \ldots, y_n$ be a random sample from this distribution.

(a) Show that the gamma distribution $G(\alpha, \beta)$ is a conjugate prior distribution for the exponential distribution.

(b) Show that $1/\bar{y}$ is the MLE for θ.

(c) Write the mean of the posterior distribution as a weighted average of the mean of the prior distribution and the MLE.

(d) What happens to the weight on the prior mean as n becomes large?

2.4 Consider the uniform distribution with density function $f(y_i|\theta) = 1/\theta$, $0 \leq y_i \leq \theta$, and θ unknown.

(a) Show that the Pareto distribution,

$$\pi(\theta) = \begin{cases} ak^a \theta^{-(a+1)}, & \theta \geq k, \; a > 0, \\ 0, & \text{otherwise}, \end{cases}$$

is a conjugate prior distribution for the uniform distribution.

(b) Show that $\hat{\theta} = \max(y_1, \ldots, y_n)$ is the MLE of θ, where the y_i are a random sample from $f(y_i|\theta)$.

(c) Find the posterior distribution of θ and its expected value.

Chapter 3

Posterior Distributions and Inference

The first section of this chapter discusses general properties of posterior distributions. It continues with an explanation of how a Bayesian statistician uses the posterior distribution to conduct statistical inference, which is concerned with learning about parameter values either in the form of point or interval estimates, making predictions, and comparing alternative models.

3.1 Properties of Posterior Distributions

In this section, we discuss general properties of posterior distributions, starting with the choice of the likelihood function. We continue by generalizing the concept to include models with more than one parameter and go on to discuss the revision of posterior distributions as more data become available, the role of the sample size, and the concept of identification.

3.1.1 The Likelihood Function

As we have seen, the posterior distribution is proportional to the product of the likelihood function and the prior distribution. The latter is somewhat controversial and is discussed in Chapter 4, but the choice of a likelihood function is also an important matter and requires discussion. A central issue is that the Bayesian must specify an explicit likelihood function to derive the posterior distribution. In some cases, the choice of a likelihood function appears straightforward. In the coin-tossing experiment of Section 2.2, for example, the choice of a Bernoulli distribution seems natural, but it does require the assumptions of independent trials and a constant probability. These assumptions might be considered prior information, but they are conventionally a part of the likelihood function rather than of the prior distribution.

In other cases, it may be more difficult to find a natural choice for the likelihood function. The normal linear regression model, discussed in detail later, is a good example. A special case is the simple model

$$y_i = \mu + u_i, \quad u_i \sim N(0, \sigma^2), \quad i = 1, \ldots, n.$$

In this model, there are n independent observations on a variable y, which is assumed to be normally distributed with mean μ and variance σ^2. E. T. Jaynes offers arguments for adopting the normal distribution when little is known about the distribution. He takes the position that it is a very weak assumption in the sense that it maximizes the uncertainty of the distribution of y_i, where uncertainty is measured by entropy. Others argue that the posterior distribution may be highly dependent on the choice of a likelihood function and are not persuaded by Jaynes's arguments. For example, a Student-t distribution with small degrees of freedom puts much more probability in the tail areas than does a normal distribution with the same mean and variance, and this feature may be reflected in the posterior distribution. Since for large degrees of freedom, there is little difference between the normal and t distributions, a possible way to proceed is to perform the analysis with several degrees of freedom and choose between them on the basis of posterior odds ratios (see Section 3.2.4). In addition, distributions more general than the normal and t may be specified; see Section 8.3 for further references.

Distributional assumptions also play a role in the frequentist approach to statistical inference. A commonly used estimator in the frequentist literature is the MLE, which requires a specific distribution. Accordingly, a frequentist statistician who employs that method must, like a Bayesian, specify a distribution. Of course, the latter is also required to specify a prior distribution. Other approaches used by frequentist econometricians, such as the generalized method of moments, do not require an explicit distribution. But, since the finite-sample properties of such methods are rarely known, their justification usually depends on a large-sample property such as consistency, which is invoked even with small samples. Although this type of analysis is more general than is specifying a particular distribution, the assumptions required to derive large-sample properties are often very technical and difficult to interpret. The limiting distribution may also be a poor approximation to the exact distribution. In contrast, the Bayesian approach is more transparent because a distributional assumption is explicitly made, and Bayesian analysis does not require large-sample approximations.

To summarize:

• The assumed form of the likelihood function is a part of the prior information and requires some justification, and it is possible to compare distributional assumptions with the aid of posterior odds ratios if there is no clear choice on a priori grounds.

- Several families of distributions can be specified and analyzed with the tools discussed in Parts II and III.

3.1.2 Vectors of Parameters

The single-parameter models we have studied thus far are now generalized to a model with d parameters contained in the vector $\theta = (\theta_1, \theta_2, \ldots, \theta_d)$. The previous definitions of likelihood, prior, and posterior distributions still apply, but they are now, respectively, the joint likelihood function, joint prior distribution, and joint posterior distribution of the multivariate random variable θ.

From the joint distributions, we may derive marginal and conditional distributions according to the usual rules of probability. Suppose, for example, we are primarily interested in θ_1. The *marginal* posterior distribution of θ_1 can be found by integrating out the remainder of the parameters from the joint posterior distribution:

$$\pi(\theta_1|y) = \int \pi(\theta_1, \ldots, \theta_d|y)\, d\theta_2 \ldots d\theta_d.$$

It is important to recognize that the marginal posterior distribution is different from the conditional posterior distribution. The latter is given by

$$\pi(\theta_1|\theta_2, \ldots, \theta_d, y) = \frac{\pi(\theta_1, \theta_2, \ldots, \theta_d|y)}{\pi(\theta_2, \ldots, \theta_d|y)},$$

where the denominator on the right-hand side is the marginal posterior distribution of $(\theta_2, \ldots, \theta_d)$ obtained by integrating θ_1 from the joint distribution. In most applications, the marginal distribution of a parameter is more useful than its conditional distribution because the marginal takes into account the uncertainty over the values of the remaining parameters, while the conditional sets them at particular values. To see this, write the marginal distribution as

$$\pi(\theta_1|y) = \int \pi(\theta_1|\theta_2, \ldots, \theta_d, y)\pi(\theta_2, \ldots, \theta_d|y)\, d\theta_2 \ldots d\theta_d.$$

In this form, we see that all values of $\theta_2, \ldots, \theta_d$ contribute to the determination of $\pi(\theta_1|y)$ in proportion to their probabilities computed from $\pi(\theta_2, \ldots, \theta_d|y)$. In other words, the marginal distribution $\pi(\theta_1|y)$ is an average of the conditional distributions $\pi(\theta_1|\theta_2, \ldots, \theta_d, y)$, where the conditioning values $(\theta_2, \ldots, \theta_d)$ are weighted by their posterior probabilities.

In some cases, it may be of interest to examine the marginal distribution of two parameters, say, θ_1 and θ_2. This may be found as above by integrating out the remaining parameters. The resulting distribution is a joint distribution because it involves two variables, and it is a marginal distribution because it is determined by integrating out the variables $\theta_3, \ldots, \theta_d$. It is thus a joint marginal posterior distribution, but it is called a marginal posterior distribution. While the marginal posterior distributions for any number of parameters can be defined, attention is usually focused on one- or two-dimensional distributions because these can be readily graphed and understood. Joint distributions in higher dimensions are usually difficult to summarize and comprehend.

Although it is easy to write down the definition of the marginal posterior distribution, performing the necessary integration to obtain it may be difficult, especially if the integral is not of a standard form. Parts II and III of this book are concerned with the methods of approximating such nonstandard integrals, but we now discuss an example in which the integral can be computed analytically.

Consider the multinomial distribution $Mn(\cdot)$, which generalizes the Bernoulli example discussed above. In this model, each trial, assumed independent of the other trials, results in one of d outcomes, labeled $1, 2, \ldots, d$, with probabilities $\theta_1, \theta_2, \ldots, \theta_d$, where $\sum \theta_i = 1$. When the experiment is repeated n times and outcome i arises y_i times, the likelihood function is

$$p(y_1, \ldots, y_d | \theta_1, \ldots, \theta_d) = \theta_1^{y_1} \theta_2^{y_2} \cdots \theta_d^{y_d}, \quad \sum y_i = n.$$

A simple example is the toss of a single die, for which $d = 6$. If the die is fair, $\theta_i = 1/6$ for each possible outcome. It is easy to see that the Bernoulli distribution discussed in Chapter 2 is the special case where $d = 2$ and $n = 1$.

The next step is to specify a prior distribution. To keep the calculations manageable, we specify a conjugate distribution that generalizes the beta distribution employed for the Bernoulli model. It is the Dirichlet distribution (see Section A.1.10):

$$\pi(\theta_1, \ldots, \theta_d) = \frac{\Gamma\left(\sum \alpha_i\right)}{\prod \Gamma(\alpha_i)} \theta_1^{\alpha_1-1} \theta_2^{\alpha_2-1} \cdots \theta_d^{\alpha_d-1}, \quad \alpha_i > 0, \quad \sum \theta_i = 1,$$

or $\theta \sim D(\alpha)$, where $\alpha = (\alpha_1, \ldots, \alpha_d)$. The α_i are chosen to represent prior beliefs about the likely values of the θ_i. As in the Bernoulli model of Chapter 2, each α_i can be interpreted as the number of times outcome i has appeared in previous experiments, and $\sum \alpha_i$ represents the total number of trials on which the prior is based. Setting $\alpha_i = \alpha$ for every i treats each outcome symmetrically and setting $\sum \alpha_i$ equal to a small value is equivalent to weak prior information.

Following our usual procedure, we find the posterior distribution given the data $y = (y_1, \ldots, y_d)$:

$$\pi(\theta|y) \propto \theta_1^{\alpha_1-1} \cdots \theta_d^{\alpha_d-1} \theta_1^{y_1} \cdots \theta_d^{y_d}$$
$$\propto \theta_1^{y_1+\alpha_1-1} \cdots \theta_d^{y_d+\alpha_d-1}.$$

Since this is $D(y + \alpha)$, where $y = (y_1, \ldots, y_d)$, we can see that the Dirichlet prior is a conjugate prior for the multinomial model.

We can now find the marginal distribution for any of the θ_i, for example, θ_1. From the result given in Section A.1.10,

$$\pi(\theta_1|y) \propto \text{Beta}\left(y_1 + \alpha_1, \sum_{i \neq 1}(y_i + \alpha_i)\right),$$

which is a beta distribution. In the die-throwing example, the probability of the 1 spot appearing when a single die is thrown is given by the beta distribution:

$$\theta_1 \sim \text{Beta}\left(y_1 + \alpha_1, \sum_{i=2}^{6}(y_i + \alpha_i)\right).$$

Note that this result is equivalent to considering the 1-spot as one outcome and the other die faces as a second outcome, transforming the multinomial model into a binomial model.

To summarize, when dealing with a model that contains more than one parameter, simply redefine the parameter as a vector. Then, all the definitions and concepts discussed in Section 2.1.2 apply to the vector of parameters. In addition, the marginal and conditional distributions of individual parameters or groups of parameters can be found by applying the usual rules of probability.

3.1.3 Bayesian Updating

This section explains a very attractive feature of Bayesian inference – the way in which posterior distributions are updated as new information becomes available. Let θ represent one parameter or a vector of parameters, and let y_1 represent the first set of data obtained in an experiment. As an example, you may think of y_1 as the number of heads found in tossing a coin n_1 times, where the probability of heads is θ. As usual,

$$\pi(\theta|y_1) \propto f(y_1|\theta)\pi(\theta).$$

Next, suppose that a new set of data y_2 is obtained, and we wish to compute the posterior distribution given the complete data set $\pi(\theta|y_1, y_2)$. By the usual rules of probability,

$$\begin{aligned}
\pi(\theta|y_1, y_2) &\propto f(y_1, y_2|\theta)\pi(\theta) \\
&= f(y_2|y_1, \theta)f(y_1|\theta)\pi(\theta) \\
&= f(y_2|y_1, \theta)\pi(\theta|y_1).
\end{aligned} \tag{3.1}$$

If the data sets are independent, $f(y_2|y_1, \theta)$ simplifies to $f(y_2|\theta)$.

Whether or not the data sets are independent, however, note that (3.1) has the form of a likelihood times a density for θ, but that the latter density is $\pi(\theta|y_1)$: the posterior distribution based on the initial set of data occupies the place where a prior distribution is expected. It is now easy to verify that, if more new data y_3 become available, $\pi(\theta|y_1, y_2, y_3)$ has $\pi(\theta|y_1, y_2)$ where you would expect to see $\pi(\theta)$. Thus, as new information is acquired, the posterior distribution becomes the prior for the next experiment. In this way, the Bayesian updates the prior distribution to reflect new information. It is important to emphasize that this updating is a consequence of probability theory and requires no new principles or ad hoc reasoning. Updating also justifies our interpretation of the prior distribution as being based on previous data, if such data are available, or on the equivalent of previous data in the researcher's view.

As a simple example of updating, consider data generated from the Bernoulli example. Assume a beta prior with parameters α_0 and β_0. Suppose the first experiment produces n_1 trials and set $s_1 = \sum y_{1i}$; let the second experiment produce n_2 trials and set $s_2 = \sum y_{2i}$. We can then compute the posterior based on the first experiment as

$$f(\theta|s_1) \propto \theta^{\alpha_0-1}(1-\theta)^{\beta_0-1}\theta^{s_1}(1-\theta)^{n_1-s_1},$$

or

$$\theta|s_1 \sim \text{Beta}(\alpha_0 + s_1, \beta_0 + (n_1 - s_1)).$$

If we take the latter as the prior for the second experiment, we find

$$f(\theta|s_1, s_2) \propto \theta^{\alpha_0+s_1}(1-\theta)^{\beta_0+(n_1-s_1)}\theta^{s_2}(1-\theta)^{n_2-s_2},$$

or

$$\theta|s_1, s_2 \sim \text{Beta}(\alpha_0 + (s_1 + s_2), \beta_0 + (n_1 + n_2) - (s_1 + s_2)).$$

The latter distribution is implied by a $\text{Beta}(\alpha_0, \beta_0)$ prior and obtaining $s_1 + s_2$ ones on $n_1 + n_2$ trials.

To summarize, when data are generated sequentially, the Bayesian paradigm shows that the posterior distribution for the parameter based on new evidence is proportional to the likelihood for the new data, given previous data and the parameter, times the posterior distribution for the parameter, given the earlier data. This is an intuitively reasonable way of allowing new information to influence beliefs about a parameter, and it appears as a consequence of standard probability theory.

3.1.4 Large Samples

Although the concepts of Bayesian inference hold true for any sample size, it is instructive to examine how the posterior distribution behaves in large samples.

This analysis offers important insights about the nature of the posterior distribution, particularly about the relative contributions of the prior distribution and likelihood function in determining the posterior distribution.

Consider the case of independent trials, where the likelihood function $L(\theta|y)$ is

$$
\begin{aligned}
L(\theta|y) &= \prod f(y_i|\theta) \\
&= \prod L(\theta|y_i);
\end{aligned}
$$

$L(\theta|y_i)$ is the likelihood contribution of y_i. Also define the log likelihood function $l(\theta|y)$ as

$$
\begin{aligned}
l(\theta|y) &= \log L(\theta|y) \\
&= \sum l(\theta|y_i) \\
&= n\bar{l}(\theta|y),
\end{aligned}
$$

where $l(\theta|y_i)$ is the log likelihood contribution of y_i and $\bar{l}(\theta|y) = (1/n)\sum l(\theta|y_i)$ is the mean log likelihood contribution.

The posterior distribution can be written as

$$
\begin{aligned}
\pi(\theta|y) &\propto \pi(\theta)L(\theta|y) \\
&\propto \pi(\theta)\exp[n\bar{l}(\theta|y)].
\end{aligned}
$$

We can now examine the effect of the sample size n on the posterior distribution, which is proportional to the product of the prior distribution and a term that involves an exponential raised to n times a number. For large n, the exponential term dominates $\pi(\theta)$, which does not depend on n. Accordingly, we can expect that the prior distribution will play a relatively smaller role than do the data, as reflected in the likelihood function, when the sample size is large. Conversely, the prior distribution has relatively greater weight when n is small.

As an example of this phenomenon, recall the coin-tossing example of Section 2.2. It was shown that

$$
E(\theta|y) = \left(\frac{\alpha+\beta}{\alpha+\beta+n}\right)\frac{\alpha}{\alpha+\beta} + \left(\frac{n}{\alpha+\beta+n}\right)\bar{y},
$$

which is a weighted average of the mean of the prior $\alpha/(\alpha+\beta)$ and the sample mean $\bar{y}$. For large n, the weight of the prior mean is small compared to that of the sample mean.

This idea can be taken one step further. If we denote the true value of θ by θ_0, it can be shown that

$$
\lim_{n\to\infty} \bar{l}(\theta|y) \to \bar{l}(\theta_0|y).
$$

Accordingly, for large n, the posterior distribution collapses to a distribution with all its probability at θ_0. This property is similar to the criterion of *consistency* in the frequentist literature and extends to the multiparameter case.

Finally, we can use these ideas to say something about the form of the posterior distribution for large n. To do this, take a second-order Taylor series approximation of $l(\theta|y)$ around $\hat{\theta}$, the MLE of θ:

$$l(\theta|y) \approx l(\hat{\theta}|y) - \frac{n}{2}(\theta - \hat{\theta})^2[-\bar{l}''(\hat{\theta}|y)]$$
$$= l(\hat{\theta}|y) - \frac{n}{2v}(\theta - \hat{\theta})^2,$$

where $\bar{l}''(\hat{\theta}|y) = (1/n)\sum_k l''(\hat{\theta}|y_k)$ and $v = [-\bar{l}''(\hat{\theta}|y)]^{-1}$. The term involving the first derivative $\bar{l}'(\hat{\theta}|y)$ vanishes because $l(\theta|y)$ is maximized at $\theta = \hat{\theta}$, and $\bar{l}''(\hat{\theta}|y) < 0$ for the same reason. The posterior distribution can therefore be written approximately as

$$\pi(\theta|y) \propto \pi(\theta)\exp\left[-\frac{n}{2v}(\theta - \hat{\theta})^2\right].$$

The second term is in the form of a normal distribution with mean $\hat{\theta}$ and variance v/n, and it dominates $\pi(\theta)$ because of the n in the exponential. If $\pi(\hat{\theta}) \neq 0$, $\pi(\theta|y)$ is approximately a normal distribution with mean $\hat{\theta}$ for large n.

The requirement that $\pi(\theta)$ does not vanish at $\hat{\theta}$ should be stressed. It is interpreted as a warning that the prior distribution should not be specified so as to rule out values of θ that are logically possible. Such values of θ may be strongly favored by the likelihood function, but would have zero posterior probability if $\pi(\hat{\theta}) = 0$.

In the multiparameter case, the second-order Taylor series is

$$l(\theta|y) \approx l(\hat{\theta}|y) - \frac{n}{2}(\theta - \hat{\theta})'[-\bar{l}''(\hat{\theta}|y)](\theta - \hat{\theta})$$
$$= l(\hat{\theta}|y) - \frac{n}{2}(\theta - \hat{\theta})'V^{-1}(\theta - \hat{\theta}), \tag{3.2}$$

where $\bar{l}''(\hat{\theta}|y) = (1/n)\sum_k\{\frac{\partial^2 l(\hat{\theta}|y_k)}{\partial\theta_i\partial\theta_j}\}$ is the mean of the matrix of second derivatives of the log likelihood evaluated at the MLE and $V = [-\bar{l}''(\hat{\theta}|y)]^{-1}$. For large n, we can therefore approximate $\pi(\theta|y)$ by a multivariate normal distribution with mean $\hat{\theta}$ and covariance matrix $(1/n)V$.

In summary, when n is large, (1) the prior distribution plays a relatively small role in determining the posterior distribution, (2) the posterior distribution converges to a degenerate distribution at the true value of the parameter, and (3) the posterior distribution is approximately normally distributed with mean $\hat{\theta}$.

3.1.5 Identification

In this section we discuss the idea of identification and the nature of the posterior distribution for unidentified parameters. Our starting point is the likelihood
function, which is also used by frequentist statisticians to discuss the concept. To
define identification, we suppose that there are two different sets of parameters θ
and ψ such that $f(y|\theta) = f(y|\psi)$ for all y. In that case, the two models are said to
be *observationally equivalent*. This means that the observed data could have been
generated by the model with parameter vector θ or by the model with parameter
vector ψ, and the data alone cannot determine which set of parameters generated
the data. The model or the parameters of the model are *not identified* or *unidentified*
when two or more models are observationally equivalent. The model is *identified*
(or the parameters are identified) if no model is observationally equivalent to the
model of interest.

A special case of nonidentifiability arises when $f(y|\theta_1, \theta_2) = f(y|\theta_1)$. In that
case, the parameters in θ_2 are not identified. A familiar example of this situation and
how to deal with it is the specification of a linear regression model with a dummy
(or indicator) variable. It is well known that a complete set of dummy variables
cannot be included in a model along with a constant, because the set of dummies
and the constant are perfectly correlated; this is a symptom of the nonidentifiability
of the constant and the coefficients of a complete set of dummies. The problem is
solved by dropping either one of the dummies or the constant.

The discussion of identification to this point has been based on the specification
of the likelihood function, what we might call "identification through the data,"
but the Bayesian approach also utilizes a prior distribution. Consider the likelihood
function $f(y|\theta_1, \theta_2) = f(y|\theta_1)$. It is clear that the data have no information about
θ_2 when θ_1 is given, but what can be said about the posterior distribution $\pi(\theta_2|y)$?
Although we might expect that it is equal to $\pi(\theta_2)$ since the data contain no
information about θ_2, consider the following calculation:

$$
\begin{aligned}
\pi(\theta_2|y) &= \int \pi(\theta_1, \theta_2|y)\, d\theta_1 \\
&= \left[\int f(y|\theta_1, \theta_2)\pi(\theta_1)\pi(\theta_2|\theta_1)\, d\theta_1 \right] \Big/ f(y) \\
&= \left[\int f(y|\theta_1)\pi(\theta_1)\pi(\theta_2|\theta_1)\, d\theta_1 \right] \Big/ f(y) \\
&= \int \pi(\theta_1|y)\pi(\theta_2|\theta_1)\, d\theta_1.
\end{aligned}
$$

If the prior distribution of θ_2 is independent of θ_1, that is, $\pi(\theta_2|\theta_1) = \pi(\theta_2)$, then
$\pi(\theta_2|y) = \pi(\theta_2)$, implying that knowledge of y does not modify beliefs about θ_2.

But if the two sets of parameters are not independent in the prior distribution, information about y modifies beliefs about θ_2 by modifying beliefs about θ_1.

This last result is the main point of our discussion of identification: since the data are only indirectly informative about unidentified parameters – any difference between their prior and posterior distributions is due to the nature of the prior distribution – inferences about such parameters may be less convincing than are inferences about identified parameters. A researcher should know whether the parameters included in a model are identified through the data or through the prior distribution when presenting and interpreting posterior distributions.

There are some situations when it is convenient to include unidentified parameters in a model. Examples of this practice are presented at several places later in the book, where the lack of identification will be noted.

3.2 Inference

We now show how the posterior distribution serves as the basis for Bayesian statistical inference.

3.2.1 Point Estimates

Suppose that the model contains a scalar parameter θ that we wish to estimate. The Bayesian approach to this problem uses the idea of a loss function $L(\hat{\theta}, \theta)$. This function specifies the loss incurred if the true value of the parameter is θ, but it is estimated as $\hat{\theta}$. Examples are the absolute value loss function $L_1(\hat{\theta}, \theta) = |\hat{\theta} - \theta|$, the quadratic loss function $L_2(\hat{\theta}, \theta) = (\hat{\theta} - \theta)^2$, and the bilinear loss function

$$L_3(\hat{\theta}, \theta) = \begin{cases} a|\hat{\theta} - \theta|, & \text{for } \theta > \hat{\theta}, \\ b|\hat{\theta} - \theta|, & \text{for } \theta \leq \hat{\theta}, \end{cases}$$

where $a, b > 0$. For these loss functions, loss is minimized if $\hat{\theta} = \theta$, and increases as the difference between $\hat{\theta}$ and θ increases. The *Bayes estimator* of θ is the value of θ that minimizes the expected value of the loss, where the expectation is taken over the posterior distribution of θ; that is, $\hat{\theta}$ is chosen to minimize

$$E[L(\hat{\theta}, \theta)] = \int L(\hat{\theta}, \theta)\pi(\theta|y)\,d\theta.$$

Under quadratic loss, we minimize

$$E[L(\hat{\theta}, \theta)] = \int (\hat{\theta} - \theta)^2\pi(\theta|y)\,d\theta.$$

This is easily done by differentiating the function with respect to $\hat{\theta}$ and setting the derivative equal to zero (it is assumed that the order of differentiation and integration can be interchanged), yielding

$$2 \int (\hat{\theta} - \theta)\pi(\theta|y)\,d\theta = 0,$$

or

$$\hat{\theta} = \int \theta \pi(\theta|y)\,d\theta.$$

From the last expression, we see that $\hat{\theta} = E(\theta|y)$: the optimal point estimator for θ under quadratic loss is the mean of the posterior distribution of θ. It is left for an exercise to derive the optimal estimators under the absolute value and bilinear loss functions. Another exercise considers a loss function that yields the mode of the posterior distribution as the optimal estimator.

It is enlightening to contrast the Bayesian approach to point estimation with that of a frequentist statistician. The frequentist stipulates one or more criteria that an estimator should satisfy and then attempts to determine whether a particular estimator satisfies those criteria. One such criterion is that of unbiasedness: an estimator $\hat{\theta}$, which is a function of the observed data, is unbiased for θ if $E(\hat{\theta}) = \theta$. For many models, it is impossible to determine whether an estimator is unbiased; in such cases, a large-sample property, such as consistency, is often substituted. For other models, there is more than one unbiased estimator, and a criterion such as efficiency is added to choose between them.

Although both frequentist and Bayesian approaches to point estimation involve an expected value, it is important to recognize that the expectations are taken over different probability distributions. The Bayesian calculation is taken over the posterior distribution of the parameter, which is conditioned on the observed data y. In contrast, the frequentist expectation to determine the expected value of an estimator is taken over the distribution of the estimator, which is conditioned on the unknown parameter θ.

The coin-tossing example illustrates this difference. Consider the estimator $\hat{\theta} = (1/n)\sum y_i = \bar{y}$. To determine whether this estimator is unbiased, we find the distribution of $\bar{y}$, given the assumed Bernoulli model, and compute its expected value *over the distribution of* $\bar{y}$:

$$E(\bar{y}) = \int \bar{y} f(\bar{y}|\theta)\,d\bar{y}.$$

This calculation considers every possible value of $\bar{y}$, which arises from every possible value of the data that might have been observed, not just the data that are actually observed. In contrast, Bayesian calculations are based on the posterior distribution, which is conditioned only on data that have been observed.

There is another very important difference between the approaches. In the frequentist approach, it is necessary to propose one or more estimators that are then tested to see whether they satisfy the specified criteria. There is no general method of finding candidates for estimators that are sure to satisfy such criteria. In contrast, the Bayesian approach is mechanical: given a loss function, the problem is to find the estimator that minimizes expected loss. Under quadratic loss, for example, it is necessary to find the mean of the posterior distribution. While the details of finding the mean may be difficult in some cases, the goal is clear. It is not necessary to devise an estimator for every type of model that might be encountered.

3.2.2 Interval Estimates

In addition to reporting a point estimate of a parameter θ, it is often useful to report an interval estimate of the form

$$P(\theta_L \leq \theta \leq \theta_U) = 0.95,$$

which tells us that $\theta_L \leq \theta \leq \theta_U$ with a probability of 0.95. Of course, 0.95 can be replaced by another value. Bayesians call such intervals *credibility intervals* (or Bayesian confidence intervals) to distinguish them from a quite different concept that appears in frequentist statistics, the confidence interval. For a Bayesian, values of θ_L and θ_U can be determined to obtain the desired probability from the posterior distribution. If more than one pair is possible, the pair that results in the shortest interval may be chosen; such a pair yields the *highest posterior density interval* (h.p.d.). This procedure is possible because probability statements can be made about the values of a parameter.

In contrast, frequentists define a *confidence interval*, which does not involve the probability distribution of a parameter. As in the case of point estimators, this approach makes use of unobserved data. Consider, for example, a confidence interval for the mean μ of a $N(\mu, 1)$ distribution based on n observations. The claim that $(\bar{x} - 1.96/\sqrt{n}, \bar{x} + 1.96/\sqrt{n})$ is a 95% confidence interval for the mean follows from the result that 95% of all possible sample means $\bar{x}$ lie in the interval $(\mu - 1.96/\sqrt{n}, \mu + 1.96/\sqrt{n})$. This calculation involves sample means that are not observed. The Bayesian approach, based on the posterior distribution, conditions on the observed data points and does not make use of data that are not observed.

3.2.3 Prediction

Another basic issue in statistical inference is the prediction of new data values. To fix ideas, consider the coin-tossing example. Suppose that the data $y = (y_1, \ldots, y_n)$ have been observed, and we wish to predict the outcome of the next toss, y_{n+1}. From the Bayesian viewpoint, we can compute $P(y_{n+1} = 1|y)$, the probability that the next toss results in a head, given the data previously observed; the probability of a tail is one minus this probability. We compute this probability by making use of the identity

$$P(y_{n+1} = 1|y) = \int f(y_{n+1} = 1, \theta|y)\, d\theta$$

$$= \int P(y_{n+1} = 1|\theta, y)\pi(\theta|y)\, d\theta$$

$$= \int P(y_{n+1} = 1|\theta)\pi(\theta|y)\, d\theta.$$

Notice carefully what we have done. Following the rules of probability, we write $P(y_{n+1} = 1|y)$ as an integral in which θ is first introduced into and then integrated out of the joint density $f(y_{n+1} = 1, \theta|y)$. In the second line, the joint distribution is written as the product of a distribution conditioned on θ and y, $P(y_{n+1} = 1|\theta, y)$, and a distribution of θ conditioned on the previous data y, $\pi(\theta|y)$. In the third line, we drop y from the conditioning set of $P(y_{n+1} = 1|\theta, y)$ because of the assumption of the Bernoulli model that the y_i are independent given θ. The expressions in the last line are the probability $P(y_{n+1} = 1|\theta)$ and the posterior distribution of θ. You can think of computing this integral as repeating the following calculation a large number of times: first draw a value of θ from its posterior distribution $\pi(\theta|y)$ and then compute $P(y_{n+1} = 1|\theta)$ using this value of θ. The average of these probabilities is $P(y_{n+1} = 1|y)$.

The general case has the same form. In predicting a new value of y, say y_f, whether θ is a scalar or a vector representing several parameters, we write

$$f(y_f|y) = \int f(y_f|\theta, y)\pi(\theta|y)\, d\theta,$$

where y is retained in the first expression under the integral to allow for the possibility that y_f is not independent of y. This situation arises in some models for time series.

Consider prediction in the coin-tossing example. The posterior distribution of θ is in the form of a beta distribution:

$$\pi(\theta|y) = \frac{\Gamma(\alpha_1 + \beta_1)}{\Gamma(\alpha_1)\Gamma(\beta_1)}\theta^{\alpha_1 - 1}(1 - \theta)^{\beta_1 - 1}.$$

Since $P(y_{n+1} = 1|\theta) = \theta$, we have

$$P(y_{n+1} = 1|y) = \frac{\Gamma(\alpha_0 + \beta_0 + n)}{\Gamma(\alpha_0 + \sum y_i)\Gamma(\beta_0 + n - \sum y_i)}$$
$$\times \int \theta\, \theta^{\alpha_0 + \sum y_i - 1}(1 - \theta)^{\beta_0 + n - \sum y_i - 1}\, d\theta$$

$$= \frac{\Gamma(\alpha_0 + \beta_0 + n)}{\Gamma(\alpha_0 + \sum y_i)\Gamma(\beta_0 + n - \sum y_i)}$$
$$\times \int \theta^{\alpha_0 + \sum y_i}(1 - \theta)^{\beta_0 + n - \sum y_i - 1}\, d\theta$$

$$= \frac{\Gamma(\alpha_0 + \beta_0 + n)}{\Gamma(\alpha_0 + \sum y_i)\Gamma(\beta_0 + n - \sum y_i)}$$
$$\times \frac{\Gamma(\alpha_0 + \sum y_i + 1)\Gamma(\beta_0 + n - \sum y_i)}{\Gamma(\alpha_0 + \beta_0 + n + 1)}$$

$$= \frac{\alpha_0 + \sum y_i}{\alpha_0 + \beta_0 + n},$$

where we have used $\Gamma(\alpha) = (\alpha - 1)\Gamma(\alpha - 1)$. Since we found in (2.5) that

$$E(\theta|y) = \frac{\alpha_0 + \sum y_i}{\alpha_0 + \beta_0 + n},$$

our estimate of $P(y_{n+1} = 1|y)$ is the mean of the posterior distribution of θ. This should not be surprising, because, for a Bernoulli variable,

$$E(y|\theta) = P(y = 1|\theta) = \theta.$$

3.2.4 Model Comparison

A fourth aspect of statistical inference is to determine which of the several competing models is better supported by our information. Suppose that we wish to compare two models: Model 1, M_1, consists of a prior probability $P(M_1) = p_1$ that M_1 is the true model, a set of parameters θ_1, a prior for those parameters $\pi_1(\theta_1)$, and a likelihood function $f_1(y|\theta_1)$. Model 2, M_2, consists of p_2, θ_2, $\pi_2(\theta_2)$, and $f_2(y|\theta_2)$. Two models may differ in their priors, their likelihoods, or their parameters. In linear regression, for example, two models might differ by which covariates are included, which corresponds to two different specifications of the parameter vector θ. This difference also implies different priors and different likelihood functions.

The Bayesian approach to this inferential problem is to compute $P(M_i|y)$, $i = 1, 2$, which is interpreted as "the probability that Model i is the correct model, given the data." If we have only two models, then $P(M_2|y) = 1 - P(M_1|y)$. To compute $P(M_1|y)$, use Bayes theorem and the approach taken in deriving the predictive distribution; that is, introduce the parameters and then integrate them out:

$$P(M_1|y) = \frac{P(M_1)f_1(y|M_1)}{f(y)}$$

$$= \frac{p_1 \int f_1(y, \theta_1|M_1)\, d\theta_1}{f(y)}$$

$$= \frac{p_1 \int f_1(y|\theta_1, M_1)\pi_1(\theta_1|M_1)\, d\theta_1}{f(y)},$$

where

$$f(y) = p_1 \int f_1(y|\theta_1, M_1)\pi_1(\theta_1|M_1)\, d\theta_1 + p_2 \int f_2(y|\theta_2, M_2)\pi_2(\theta_2|M_2)\, d\theta_2.$$

(3.3)

Each term of $f(y)$ is the integral of a likelihood function with respect to a prior distribution,

$$m_i(y) = \int f_i(y|\theta_i, M_i)\pi_i(\theta_i|M_i)\, d\theta_i.$$

(3.4)

It is called the *marginal likelihood* for model i and can be interpreted as the expected value of the likelihood function with respect to the prior distribution. From the definition of the posterior distribution in (2.2),

$$\pi(\theta|y) = \frac{f(y|\theta)\pi(\theta)}{f(y)}$$

$$= \frac{f(y|\theta)\pi(\theta)}{\int f(y|\theta)\pi(\theta)\, d\theta},$$

we see that the marginal likelihood is equal to the inverse of the normalizing constant of the posterior distribution. It is important to include the normalizing constants of $f(y|\theta)$ and $\pi(\theta)$ when computing the marginal likelihood.

In comparing two models, it is often instructive to compute the odds ratio in favor of Model 1 over Model 2, given the data,

$$R_{12} = \frac{P(M_1|y)}{P(M_2|y)}$$

$$= \left(\frac{p_1}{p_2}\right) \left(\frac{\int f_1(y|\theta_1, M_1)\pi_1(\theta|M_1)\, d\theta_1}{\int f_2(y|\theta_2, M_2)\pi_2(\theta|M_2)\, d\theta_2}\right)$$

$$= \left(\frac{p_1}{p_2}\right) \left(\frac{m_1(y)}{m_2(y)}\right).$$

The first term on the right-hand side is the prior odds ratio, the ratio of the prior probability of M_1 to the prior probability of M_2. The second term, the ratio of

Table 3.1. *Jeffreys Guidelines.*

$\log_{10}(R_{12}) > 2$	Decisive support for M_1
$3/2 < \log_{10}(R_{12}) < 2$	Very strong evidence for M_1
$1 < \log_{10}(R_{12}) < 3/2$	Strong evidence for M_1
$1/2 < \log_{10}(R_{12}) < 1$	Substantial evidence for M_1
$0 < \log_{10}(R_{12}) < 1/2$	Weak evidence for M_1

the marginal likelihoods of the two models, is called the *Bayes factor*. Note that $f(y)$ of (3.3) has dropped out of this expression because it has the same value for both $P(M_1|y)$ and $P(M_2|y)$. A large value of R_{12} is evidence that M_1 is better supported than is M_2 by the data and the prior information, and a small value is evidence that M_2 is better supported; values around 1 indicate that both models are supported equally well. Such pairwise comparisons can also be made when there are more than two models. It is convenient to present $\log_{10}(R_{12})$ rather than R_{12} because the ratio is often very large or very small, and the logarithm to base 10 is immediately interpreted as powers of 10. Table 3.1 presents guidelines for the interpretation of $\log_{10}(R_{12})$ suggested by Jeffreys (1961, p. 432). It should be clear that these values are arbitrary, as is the 5% level of significance often employed by frequentist statisticians.

If you are reluctant to specify the prior odds ratio, the burden falls on the Bayes factor to discriminate between models. If, for example, it is found that $\log_{10}(R_{12}) = 2$, a value of p_1/p_2 less than $1/100$ would be required to result in a posterior odds ratio in favor of M_2. This indicates that the results favor M_1 unless you think M_1 to be very improbable a priori compared to M_2.

Model choice can be implemented in terms of loss functions for making correct and incorrect choices, but, in practice, models are often informally compared by their Bayes factors or their posterior odds ratios. One possible outcome of such comparisons is that one or more models are effectively eliminated from consideration because other models have much greater support on the basis of these criteria. Another possibility is that several models that are not eliminated have pairwise Bayes factors or posterior odds ratios close to one (or zero on the log scale). In this case, it would be reasonable to conclude that two or more models are consistent with the data and prior information and that a choice between them must be delayed until further information becomes available.

When a prediction is to be made and more than one model is being considered, the technique of *model averaging* can be applied. If, for example, m models have been specified, a prediction may be formed as a weighted average of the predictions from each of the models under consideration:

$$f(y_f|y) = \sum_{i=1}^{m} p(M_i|y) f_i(y_f|y, M_i)$$

$$= \sum_{i=1}^{m} p(M_i|y) \int f_i(y_f|\theta_i, y, M_i) \pi_i(\theta_i|y, M_i) \, d\theta_i.$$

From this expression, you can see that models with small values of $p(M_i|y)$ contribute little to predictions.

The frequentist approach to model comparison makes use of hypothesis tests. In this approach, the null hypothesis H_0 is rejected in favor of the alternative hypothesis H_A if the value of a statistic computed from the data falls in the critical region. The critical region is usually specified to set the probability that H_0 is rejected when it is true at a small value, where the probability is computed over the distribution of the statistic. As mentioned before, this calculation depends on values of the statistic that were not observed.

An important advantage of the Bayesian approach to model comparison over the frequentist approaches is that the former can easily deal with nonnested hypotheses, especially with models that deal with different representations of the response variable. A common example is the choice between y and $\log(y)$ as the response variable. In general, suppose that under M_1, the likelihood function is $f_1(y|\theta_1)$, and under M_2, it is $f_2(z|\theta_2)$, where $z = g(y)$ and $g'(y) \neq 0$. Since y and $g(y)$ contain the same information, the posterior odds ratio should not depend on whether we compute

$$P(M_1|y)/P(M_2|y)$$

or

$$P(M_1|z)/P(M_2|z),$$

and it does not. Since, by the usual transformation of variables rule,

$$f(z_i|\theta) = f(y_i|\theta) \left| \frac{dy_i}{dz_i} \right|,$$

it is easy to see that the Bayes factor is independent of whether the response variable is y or $z = g(y)$ because the Jacobian term cancels. Note also that this result generalizes to multivariate y and z, where the absolute value of the derivative is replaced by the absolute value of the Jacobian of the transformation.

It is instructive to examine the effect of the sample size on the Bayes factor. Exponentiate (3.2) and substitute into (3.4) to obtain

$$m_i(y) \approx L_i(\hat{\theta}_i|y) \int \exp\left[-\frac{n}{2}(\theta_i - \hat{\theta}_i)' V_i^{-1}(\theta_i - \hat{\theta}_i)\right] \pi_i(\theta_i)\, d\theta_i$$

$$\approx L_i(\hat{\theta}_i|y)\pi_i(\hat{\theta}_i) \int \exp\left[-\frac{n}{2}(\theta_i - \hat{\theta}_i)' V_i^{-1}(\theta_i - \hat{\theta}_i)\right] d\theta_i,$$

where $\pi_i(\theta_i)$ is approximated by $\pi_i(\hat{\theta}_i)$ because the exponential term dominates the integral in the region around $\hat{\theta}_i$. The integration yields

$$m_i(y) \approx L_i(\hat{\theta}_i|y)\pi_i(\hat{\theta}_i)(2\pi)^{d_i/2}|n^{-1}V_i|^{1/2}$$

$$\approx L_i(\hat{\theta}_i|y)\pi_i(\hat{\theta}_i)(2\pi)^{d_i/2}n^{-d_i/2}|V_i|^{1/2},$$

where d_i is the dimension of θ_i; that is, the number of parameters in M_i. We can now approximate the logarithm of the Bayes factor for comparing models 1 and 2:

$$\log(B_{12}) \approx \left[\log\left(\frac{L_1(\hat{\theta}_1|y)}{L_2(\hat{\theta}_2|y)}\right) - \frac{d_1 - d_2}{2}\log(n)\right]$$

$$+ \left[\log\left(\frac{\pi_1(\hat{\theta}_1)}{\pi_2(\hat{\theta}_2)}\right) + \frac{1}{2}\log\left(\frac{|V_1|}{|V_2|}\right) + \frac{d_1 - d_2}{2}\log(2\pi)\right].$$

Since the second square-bracketed term does not depend on n, its importance may be neglected for large n. The first term in the first square bracket is the logarithm of the likelihood ratio. It will tend to become large if M_1 is the true model and small if M_2 is true. The second term shows that the log Bayes factor penalizes models with larger numbers of parameters, where the penalty is $\log(n)$ times the difference in the number of parameters divided by two.

We return to the coin-tossing example to illustrate the use of Bayes factors for model comparison. To specify two competing models, consider the following variation on our basic experiment. A coin is tossed m times by Michaela and then tossed m times by Lila. Suppose we believe it possible that the different ways in which the girls toss the coin result in different probabilities. Let θ_1 be the probability of a head when Michaela tosses the coin and $\theta_2 \neq \theta_1$ be the corresponding probability when Lila tosses it. We also consider a model in which there is no difference in the probabilities. Specifically, $\theta_1 = \theta_2 = \theta$ in M_1, and $\theta_1 \neq \theta_2$ in M_2. To simplify calculations, assume that $\pi_1(\theta_1) = \text{Beta}(1, 1) = \pi_2(\theta_2)$. Verify that this choice of a prior implies $\pi(\theta) = 1, 0 \leq \theta \leq 1$.

Let $\bar{y}_1$ be the proportion of heads when Michaela tosses the coin, $\bar{y}_2$ be Lila's proportion, and $\bar{y} = (\bar{y}_1 + \bar{y}_2)/2$ be the overall proportion. The marginal likelihood

Table 3.2. *Bayes Factors for Selected Possible Outcomes*

Michaela	Lila	$\log_{10}$(Bayes factor)	
Proportion heads	Proportion heads	$m = 10$	$m = 100$
0.1	0.9	-2.506	-30.775
0.2	0.8	-1.200	-15.793
0.3	0.7	-0.348	-6.316
0.4	0.6	0.138	-0.975
0.5	0.5	0.297	0.756

under M_1 is

$$\int \theta^{2m\bar{y}}(1-\theta)^{2m-2m\bar{y}} = \frac{\Gamma(2m\bar{y}+1)\Gamma(2m-2m\bar{y}+1)}{\Gamma(2m+2)}.$$

As an exercise, verify that the marginal likelihood under M_2 is

$$\frac{\Gamma(m\bar{y}_1+1)\Gamma(m-m\bar{y}_1+1)}{\Gamma(m+2)}\frac{\Gamma(m\bar{y}_2+1)\Gamma(m-m\bar{y}_2+1)}{\Gamma(m+2)}. \tag{3.5}$$

We list in Table 3.2 the $\log_{10}$(Bayes factors) for selected values of outcomes and for two different sample sizes, 10 and 100. Note that the Bayes factor in favor of M_1 increases as the proportion of heads for both girls approaches 0.5. You can see that M_1 is decisively rejected when there are large differences between Michaela's and Lila's results and that results are much sharper for the larger sample size.

3.3 Summary

We began by exploring the posterior distribution in more detail. In particular, we considered models with more than one parameter, updating posterior distributions as additional data become available, how the posterior distribution behaves as sample size increases, and the concept of identification. We then explained how posterior distributions can be used to find point and interval estimates, make predictions, and compare the credibility of alternative models.

3.4 Further Reading and References

Section 3.1.1 Jaynes's arguments may be found in Jaynes (2003, chap. 7). Zellner has proposed the Bayesian Method of Moments when there are difficulties in formulating a likelihood function. The method can be employed to compute postdata moments of parameters and future values of variables without a likelihood function, prior density, and use of Bayes theorem. See Zellner (1997) for further discussion and references.

Section 3.2 For critical discussions of hypothesis testing and comparisons with the Bayesian approach, see Howson and Urbach (1993, chaps. 8 and 9), Poirier (1995, chap. 7), Jaynes (2003, chaps. 16 and 17), and Christensen (2005).

Section 3.2.4 See Kadane and Lazar (2004) for a discussion of various methods of model comparison from Bayesian and frequentist viewpoints and Gelman, Carlin, Stern, and Rubin (2004, sec. 6.7) for critical comments about the use of Bayes factors and for alternative approaches. Our discussion of the effect of sample size and the dimension of θ on the Bayes factor follows O'Hagan (1994, pp. 194–195). O'Hagan also explains the relations among the Bayes factor, the Akaike information criterion, and the Schwartz criterion.

3.5 Exercises

3.1 Consider the following two sets of data obtained after tossing a die 100 and 1000 times, respectively:

n	1	2	3	4	5	6
100	19	12	17	18	20	14
1000	190	120	170	180	200	140

Suppose you are interested in θ_1, the probability of obtaining a one spot. Assume your prior for all the probabilities is a Dirichlet distribution, where each $\alpha_i = 2$. Compute the posterior distribution for θ_1 for each of the sample sizes in the table. Plot the resulting distribution and compare the results. Comment on the effect of having a larger sample.

3.2 Compute the predictive distribution for y_{n+1} if the y_i have independent Poisson distributions with parameter θ, given that the first n experiments yielded $y_1, y_2, \ldots, y_n$ events, respectively. Assume the prior distribution $G(\alpha, \beta)$.

3.3 Compute the predictive distribution for y_{n+1} if the y_i have independent normal distributions $N(\mu, 1)$, where the prior distribution for μ is $N(\mu_0, \sigma_0^2)$.

3.4 Explicitly verify the updating feature of the posterior distribution for the case where y has a Poisson distribution with parameter θ. Choose $G(\alpha, \beta)$ as the prior distribution, and consider observing a total of s_1 events in the first of two independent experiments and s_2 in the second.

3.5 Show that the median of the posterior distribution minimizes loss under the absolute value loss function.

3.6 The zero–one loss function is defined as

$$L_3(\hat{\theta}, \theta) = 1(|\hat{\theta} - \theta| > b),$$

where $1(A)$ is the indicator function that equals 1 if A is true and 0 otherwise. Verify that $\hat{\theta}$ goes to the mode of $\pi(\theta|y)$ as $b \to 0$.

3.7 Verify Equation (3.5).

3.8 Suppose the number of typographical errors per page has a Poisson distribution $P(\theta)$. Sam types the first m pages of a manuscript and makes e_1 errors in total, and Levi types the last m pages and makes e_2 errors. Let Sam's error rate be θ_1 and Levi's error rate be θ_2. To compare model $M_1 : \theta_1 = \theta_2 = \theta$ with model $M_2 : \theta_1 \neq \theta_2$, produce a table like Table 3.2 for $m = 100$ with 10 total errors and for $m = 200$ with 20 total errors and Sam's error proportions of 0.9, 0.8, 0.7, 0.6, and 0.5. Take $G(1, 1)$ as a prior for θ_1 and θ_2.

Chapter 4

Prior Distributions

THE NECESSITY OF specifying a prior distribution in Bayesian inference has been regarded by some as an advantage of the approach and by others a disadvantage. On the one hand, the prior distribution allows the researcher to include in a systematic way any information he or she has about the parameters being studied. On the other hand, the researcher's prior information may be very limited or difficult to quantify in the form of a probability distribution, and, as we have seen in Chapter 3, the prior distribution plays a large role in determining the posterior distribution for small samples.

This chapter puts forth, in general terms, some ideas on how to specify prior distributions. The topic is revisited in connection with specific models in Part III. The normal linear regression model, described next, is the primary example for the topics in this chapter.

4.1 Normal Linear Regression Model

The normal linear regression model is the workhorse of econometric, and more generally, statistical modeling. We consider it here because of its wide applicability and because it is a relatively easy model with which to illustrate the specification of hyperparameters.

Let y_i, $i = 1, \ldots, n$, be an observation on a variable that we wish to explain or predict, called the response or dependent variable, and let $x_i' = (x_{i1}, x_{i2}, \ldots, x_{iK})$ be a vector of K covariates that are believed to be related to y_i through the linear model

$$
\begin{aligned}
y_i &= \beta_1 x_{i1} + \beta_2 x_{i2} + \cdots + \beta_K x_{iK} + u_i \\
&= x_i'\beta + u_i,
\end{aligned}
$$

where $\beta = (\beta_1, \ldots, \beta_K)'$ is a vector of unknown regression coefficients and u_i is an unobserved random variable, called the disturbance or error term. We further assume that $u_i|x_i \sim N(0, \sigma^2)$, where σ^2 is unknown. Under these assumptions, $y_i|x_i, \beta, \sigma^2 \sim N(x_i'\beta, \sigma^2)$. The assumption $E(u_i|x_i) = 0$ implies that $E(u_i) = 0$ and $\text{Cov}(u_i, x_i) = 0$. Under the further assumption of joint normality of (u_i, x_i), the previous assumption implies that each x_{ik} is independent of u_i. Such covariates are said to be *exogenous*. We discuss in Chapter 11 how to proceed when the assumption of independence is untenable.

In writing the likelihood function, we invoke the additional assumption that the probability distributions of the covariates do not depend on any of the parameters in the equation for y_i. This assumption is relaxed when the covariates include lagged values of y_i, as in the time series models of Section 10.1 and the dynamic panel models of Section 10.4.

Vector–matrix notation can be utilized to write the model for all n observations in a compact fashion,

$$y = X\beta + u,$$

where $y = (y_1, \ldots, y_n)'$, X is the $n \times K$ matrix of covariates,

$$X = \begin{pmatrix} x_{11} & x_{12} & \cdots & x_{1K} \\ x_{21} & x_{22} & \cdots & x_{2K} \\ \vdots & \vdots & \vdots & \vdots \\ x_{n1} & x_{n2} & \cdots & x_{nK} \end{pmatrix},$$

and $u = (u_1, \ldots, u_n)'$.

Inference in this model finds point estimates for the unknown parameters β and σ^2, constructs interval estimates for the parameters, compares models that contain different sets of covariates, and predicts a value of y_i for a given set of covariate values.

The first covariate x_{i1} is often set equal to 1 for all observations, in which case β_1 is called the intercept. The other regression coefficients have the interpretation

$$\beta_k = \frac{\partial E(y_i|x_i)}{\partial x_{ik}},$$

if x_{ik} is a continuous variable. We may therefore think of β_k as the effect on the expected value of y_i of a small change in the value of the covariate x_{ik}. If x_{ik} is a dummy variable, β_k is the shift in the intercept associated with a change from $x_{ik} = 0$ to $x_{ik} = 1$. Prior distributions are placed on each of the β_k, which should be based on the researcher's knowledge of how $E(y_i|x_i)$ responds to a change in x_{ik}. The remainder of this chapter is devoted to methods for doing this, but we first derive the likelihood function for this model.

Given a sample of size n and assuming that the u_i are independent, we can write the probability density for the observed sample, which is also the likelihood function for the unknown parameters, as

$$f(y_1, \ldots, y_n | \beta, \sigma^2) = f(y_1 | \beta, \sigma^2) f(y_2 | \beta, \sigma^2) \cdots f(y_n | \beta, \sigma^2)$$

$$= \left(\frac{1}{2\pi\sigma^2} \right)^{n/2} \exp \left[-\frac{1}{2\sigma^2} \sum (y_i - x_i'\beta)^2 \right]$$

$$= \left(\frac{1}{2\pi\sigma^2} \right)^{n/2} \exp \left[-\frac{1}{2\sigma^2} (y - X\beta)'(y - X\beta) \right]$$

$$\propto \left(\frac{1}{\sigma^2} \right)^{n/2} \exp \left[-\frac{1}{2\sigma^2} (y - X\beta)'(y - X\beta) \right]. \qquad (4.1)$$

To derive this expression, we have used the normality of u_i and the transformation of random variables from u_i to y_i based on $y_i - x_i'\beta = u_i$, which has a Jacobian of one. In the last line, we absorbed the $(2\pi)^{-n/2}$ into a proportionality constant. This is done to focus attention on the important terms in the expression and is possible because it is a multiplicative term that does not contain the unknown parameters β and σ^2. Here and in the following, we follow the convention of usually not explicitly including the covariates X in the conditioning set of the posterior distribution.

4.2 Proper and Improper Priors

There have been many efforts to specify, in mechanical ways, prior distributions that reflect complete ignorance about parameter values. Many such specifications imply *improper* prior distributions, which are distributions that are not integrable; that is, their integral is infinite. In contrast, we assume that the researcher has sufficient knowledge to specify a *proper* prior, one that integrates to unity, even if it is highly dispersed.

As an example of an improper prior, consider data generated by a normal distribution with unknown mean μ. If there are no known restrictions on μ, a possible way to show prior ignorance about it is to assume a uniform distribution, $\pi(\mu) \propto c, c > 0, -\infty < \mu < \infty$. This prior is improper: its integral is unbounded, and it cannot be normalized to one.

Another example is the beta distribution prior discussed in connection with the coin-tossing example of Section 2.2. Setting $\alpha = 0$ or $\beta = 0$ results in an improper prior that has a mode at zero (if $\alpha = 0$) or one (if $\beta = 0$). As an exercise, you can verify that the *posterior* distribution for the Bernoulli parameter θ is proper if $0 < \sum y_i < n$, even if the *prior* is improper ($\alpha = 0$ or $\beta = 0$).

For the normal linear regression model, a uniform prior on β, that is, $\pi(\beta) \propto c$, $c > 0$, is improper, as is the Jeffreys prior on σ, $\pi(\sigma) \propto 1/\sigma$. The latter corresponds to a uniform prior on $\log(\sigma)$.

We assume that, in a particular application, either (1) finite, but possibly wide, bounds can be placed on μ or (2) the probability of extremely large or small values is sufficiently small that a proper distribution can be specified, even though the possible values are unbounded. In our view, a researcher should be able to provide enough information to specify a proper prior. In the regression model, for example, it is hard to believe that a researcher is so ignorant about a phenomenon that the probability of a regression coefficient falling in any interval of equal length from minus to plus infinity is equal. In addition, a number of methods to aid in the elicitation of prior probabilities from experts in the subject matter of the inquiry have been developed; see the references in Section 4.11.

The ability to specify proper prior distributions is crucial for the use of Bayes factors and posterior odds ratios for comparing models. Since an improper prior is not normalizable, $c\pi(\cdot)$, $c > 0$, is equivalent to the prior specified by $\pi(\cdot)$. But this means that a marginal likelihood based on an improper prior depends on the arbitrary value of c,

$$f(y|M) = \int f(y|\theta, M) c\pi(\theta|M) \, d\theta,$$

so that the marginal likelihood can be set to any desired positive number by choice of c. Note what this implies for the Bayes factor: if two models are being compared, both of which have improper priors, the Bayes factor can be written as

$$
\begin{aligned}
B_{12} &= \frac{\int f_1(y|\theta_1, M_1) c_1 \pi_1(\theta|M_1) \, d\theta_1}{\int f_2(y|\theta_2, M_2) c_2 \pi_2(\theta|M_2) \, d\theta_2} \\
&= \frac{c_1 \int f_1(y|\theta_1, M_1) \pi_1(\theta|M_1) \, d\theta_1}{c_2 \int f_2(y|\theta_2, M_2) \pi_2(\theta|M_2) \, d\theta_2}.
\end{aligned}
$$

Since c_1 and c_2 are arbitrary, the Bayes factor can take any value chosen by the researcher, and this is true even if only one of the prior distributions is improper. When the prior is proper, the value of the marginal likelihood is well defined. Accordingly, we assume proper priors.

4.3 Conjugate Priors

We now consider the conjugate priors that have been mentioned in Sections 2.2 and 3.1.2. A conjugate prior distribution for the parameters of the normal linear regression model is the one for which the posterior distribution $\pi(\beta, \sigma^2|y)$ is in the same family of distributions as the prior $\pi(\beta, \sigma^2)$. Two different distributions are in the same family when they have the same form and different parameters. For the model we are studying, where the likelihood function has the form of (4.1), a conjugate prior distribution, called the normal-inverse gamma conjugate prior, is given by

$$\pi(\beta, \sigma^2) = \pi(\beta|\sigma^2)\pi(\sigma^2)$$
$$= N_K(\beta|\beta_0, \sigma^2 B_0) \, \text{IG}(\sigma^2|\alpha_0/2, \delta_0/2), \tag{4.2}$$

where the hyperparameters α_0, δ_0, β_0, B_0 are assumed to be known. How to specify values for these parameters is discussed later; as of now, we concentrate on the mechanics of showing this is a conjugate prior and on some properties of the posterior distribution. In this formulation, it is important to note that the prior for β depends on σ^2. We present a prior that does not have this property in Section 4.9.

From the definition of the posterior distribution, we have

$$\pi(\beta, \sigma^2|y) = f(y|\beta, \sigma^2)\pi(\beta|\sigma^2)\pi(\sigma^2)$$

$$\propto \left(\frac{1}{\sigma^2}\right)^{n/2} \exp\left[-\frac{1}{2\sigma^2}(y - X\beta)'(y - X\beta)\right]$$

$$\times \left(\frac{1}{\sigma^2}\right)^{K/2} \exp\left[-\frac{1}{2\sigma^2}(\beta - \beta_0)'B_0^{-1}(\beta - \beta_0)\right] \tag{4.3}$$

$$\times \left(\frac{1}{\sigma^2}\right)^{\alpha_0/2+1} \exp\left[-\frac{\delta_0}{2\sigma^2}\right]$$

$$= \left(\frac{1}{\sigma^2}\right)^{(n+\alpha_0)/2+1} \left(\frac{1}{\sigma^2}\right)^{K/2}$$

$$\times \exp\left[-\frac{1}{2\sigma^2}\left\{(y - X\beta)'(y - X\beta) + (\beta - \beta_0)'B_0^{-1}(\beta - \beta_0) + \delta_0\right\}\right]. \tag{4.4}$$

By expanding the term in curly braces in (4.4) and completing the square in β (see Section A.1.12), you should verify that

$$\pi(\beta, \sigma^2|y) \propto \left(\frac{1}{\sigma^2}\right)^{K/2} \exp\left[-\frac{1}{2\sigma^2}(\beta - \bar{\beta})'B_1^{-1}(\beta - \bar{\beta})\right]$$

$$\times \left(\frac{1}{\sigma^2}\right)^{\alpha_1/2+1} \exp\left[-\frac{\delta_1}{2\sigma^2}\right], \tag{4.5}$$

where the updated parameters are

$$B_1 = (X'X + B_0^{-1})^{-1}$$
$$\bar{\beta} = B_1(X'y + B_0^{-1}\beta_0)$$
$$\alpha_1 = \alpha_0 + n$$
$$\delta_1 = \delta_0 + y'y + \beta_0'B_0^{-1}\beta_0 - \bar{\beta}'B_1^{-1}\bar{\beta}. \tag{4.6}$$

We recognize the product of the first two terms as proportional to the density of a K-dimensional normal distribution for β, $N_K(\bar{\beta}, \sigma^2 B_1)$, and the product of the second two terms as proportional to an inverted gamma distribution for σ^2, $\text{IG}(\alpha_1/2, \delta_1/2)$. This shows that the prior specified in (4.2) is a conjugate prior for the normal linear regression model.

The conjugate prior for this model allows us to find analytically the marginal posterior distributions of σ^2 and β. Indeed, this is the last model considered in the book where this is possible. First, it is easy to integrate out β since it appears only in the first term as a normally distributed variable. Doing so will leave us with only the third and fourth terms, from which we immediately have

$$\pi(\sigma^2|y) = \text{IG}(\alpha_1/2, \delta_1/2).$$

Since this is a known form for which the normalizing constant is known, we can find its moments, derive interval estimates, and plot it. Deriving the posterior distribution for β requires integration with respect to σ^2:

$$\pi(\beta|y) = \int \pi(\beta, \sigma^2|y)\, d\sigma^2$$

$$\propto \int \left(\frac{1}{\sigma^2}\right)^{(K+\alpha_1)/2+1} \exp\left[-\frac{Q}{2\sigma^2}\right] d\sigma^2,$$

where $Q = \delta_1 + (\beta - \bar{\beta})' B_1^{-1}(\beta - \bar{\beta})$. Since the integrand has the form of an inverted gamma function, integration yields the reciprocal of the constant of that function, $\Gamma([K + \alpha_1]/2)(Q/2)^{-(K+\alpha_1)/2}$, but only Q contains β. Accordingly, we have

$$\pi(\beta|y) \propto Q^{-(K+\alpha_1)/2}$$

$$\propto [\delta_1 + (\beta - \bar{\beta})' B_1^{-1}(\beta - \bar{\beta})]^{-(K+\alpha_1)/2}$$

$$\propto \left[1 + \frac{1}{\alpha_1}(\beta - \bar{\beta})'[(\delta_1/\alpha_1)B_1]^{-1}(\beta - \bar{\beta})\right]^{-(K+\alpha_1)/2}.$$

Finally, by comparing the last equation to that of the multivariate t distribution (see Section A.1.15), we find that

$$\pi(\beta|y) = t_K(\alpha_1, \bar{\beta}, (\delta_1/\alpha_1)B_1). \tag{4.7}$$

Because this distribution has been intensively studied, its marginal distributions and their moments are well known. Discussion of further properties of this model and its marginal likelihood is pursued in the exercises.

Before continuing, we note that many authors work with a different, but equivalent, parameterization of the model. Define the *precision* of a scalar random variable as the reciprocal of its variance: $h = 1/\sigma^2$. If it is decided to work with h rather than

σ^2, all of the results obtained previously are still valid if the prior distribution for h is $G(\alpha_0/2, \beta_0/2)$, rather than the inverse gamma distribution. In short, a gamma distribution for h is equivalent to an inverse gamma for $1/h = \sigma^2$. The concept of precision extends to covariance matrices in the case of multivariate random vectors. Thus, if Σ is the covariance matrix of the vector z, then Σ^{-1} is its precision matrix. In the linear regression model discussed earlier, the posterior variance of β is $[X'X + B_0^{-1}]^{-1}$, and its precision matrix is $X'X + B_0^{-1}$. Both precisions and variances are used in later chapters of this book.

4.4 Subject-Matter Considerations

Consider what is involved in specifying a prior distribution for the parameters of the normal linear regression model in the context of the conjugate family of priors discussed before. The regression parameters β_k are assumed to be normal with mean β_{k0} and variance $\sigma^2 B_{kk,0}$, where β_{k0} is the kth row of β_0 and $B_{kk,0}$ is the kkth element of B_0. To specify a prior, the researcher should utilize whatever information can be found from previous studies and theoretical subject-matter considerations to specify β_{k0} and express uncertainty about this value in the choice of the variance. Since information is not likely to be available about prior covariances, researchers will often take those to be zero and restrict attention to diagonal B_0. We continue by discussing typical applications to illustrate these ideas.

A common use of linear regression is to investigate the effects of prices and income on demand or supply for some product. For example, if x_{ik} is the price of bread and y_i is the quantity of bread purchased by household i, then β_k is the change in quantity demanded associated with a one-unit change in price. In this case, a reparameterization of the model is likely to facilitate the assignment of a prior. Thus, if we work with log(price) and log(quantity), β_k is the price elasticity; that is, the percentage change in quantity associated with a 1% change in price. This parameterization frees us from concern about units of measurement of y, currency units, and absolute price levels; moreover, such elasticities have been estimated in many studies for various types of data sets. Furthermore, the Gaussian assumption on the additive errors is consistent with both positive and negative values for the dependent variable log(price), but is inconsistent with price, which must be nonnegative, as the dependent variable.

If no information is available for a particular product, it is reasonable to start from the assumption that $\beta_{k0} = -1$, the borderline between elastic and inelastic demand. Given a mean, the properties of the normal distribution can be used. Thus, a researcher may be very sure that the elasticity is between -1.5 and -0.50. If "very sure" is interpreted as a probability of 0.99, then the properties of the normal distribution can be used to estimate the variance: the mean plus and minus three

standard deviations includes 99.73% of the area of a normal curve; this implies
for our example that three standard deviations equals 0.5, or the standard deviation
is 1/6. We therefore set $\sigma^2 B_{k0} = 1/36$. If, on the basis of previous studies or
other information, the researcher believes that the demand for bread is inelastic,
then setting $\beta_{k0} = -0.5$ with a variance of 1/36 will confine the prior distribution
of the coefficient to the interval $(-1, 0)$ with a probability of 0.99. Similarly, an
assumption about the income elasticity might start with a prior mean of 1.

For the prior distribution of the variance parameter σ^2, assumed to be inverted
gamma, we use (A.5) to specify (α_0, δ_0) from its moments. In our bread demand
example, on the basis of prior information, we might believe that the quantity
of bread consumed per week, controlling for household size and other variables,
does not exhibit great variation. If the quantity of bread purchased averages about
4 pounds per week ($\log(4) = 1.3863$), and few families are expected to consume
much more than 6 pounds per week ($\log(6) = 1.7918$), a standard deviation about
0.2, or a variance of 0.04, would seem reasonable. We take this as the mean of
the prior for σ^2. Finally, uncertainty over this value can be maximized by taking
the smallest value of the first parameter of the inverted gamma distribution that
leads to a finite variance: $\alpha_0/2 = 3$. From (A.4) and (A.5), we obtain $\alpha_0 = 6$ and
$\beta_0 = 0.16$. These calculations are rough – we have taken the mean of the logarithm
to be the logarithm of the mean – but, in many cases, it suffices to get orders of
magnitude right.

If y is in logarithm terms and x_d is a dummy variable, then $y_1/y_0 - 1 \approx \beta_d$, for
small β_d, where y_1 is the value of y when $x_d = 1$ and y_0 is the value when $x_d = 0$.

This example illustrates how knowledge of the subject matter can be used in a
family of conjugate prior distributions to specify hyperparameters for the prior. In
most research areas, there are likely to be previous studies that can be used to shed
light on likely values for the means and variances of the regression coefficients
and the variance. Since some element of subjectivity is inevitably involved, the
sensitivity of results to different prior specifications, as discussed later, should be
included in any empirical research.

As an empirical example, we consider the effect of union membership on wages.
The data are derived from Vella and Verbeek (1998), but we work with a highly
simplified version of their ambitious and sophisticated model. The data are taken
from the Youth sample of the National Longitudinal Survey and consist of 545
observations on young men. The response variable y is the logarithm of hourly
wages. The log transformation is made to allow us to think in terms of proportional,
rather than absolute, effects, and the transformed variable is consistent with the
assumption of additive Gaussian errors. The covariate of interest is a dummy
(indicator) variable for union membership. The remaining 31 covariates include
an intercept, indicator variables for race, marital status, rural area, section of the

United States, health, industry of employment, occupation, and variables measuring years of schooling and experience. Important specification issues taken up in the article are neglected here to present a simple example and to focus on the main point of this discussion.

We proceed to specify the prior parameters, beginning with the distribution of σ^2. To specify values for α_0 and δ_0, consider the variance of $y = \log(\text{wage})$ without any covariates. The average hourly wage in 1987 was \$9.10, and $\log(9.10) = 2.21$. The minimum wage in that year was \$3.35, and $\log(3.35) = 1.21$. If we assume that 90% of the work force earned more than the minimum wage, the difference between 2.21 and 1.21 should represent about 1.28 standard deviations, implying a standard deviation of about 0.78 and a variance of about 0.60. With 31 covariates other than the intercept, we expect the variance of u to be considerably smaller than the variance of y, say about 0.10. Accordingly, we assume $E(\sigma^2) = 0.10$. We take the smallest possible value for α, which is 3; this results in the largest possible variance, reflecting our uncertainty. Accordingly, from (A.4), we find $\delta = 2 \times 0.10 = 0.20$. These values for α and δ yield $\alpha_0 = 6$ and $\delta_0 = 0.40$.

We next turn to the prior distribution of the coefficient of the union indicator variable β_U. On the basis of many previous studies of this issue, we think that the mean, β_{U0}, should be about 0.10 and that it is very likely to be less than 0.20. If we interpret "very likely" as a 95% probability, a normal prior distribution implies a standard deviation of about 0.06 or a variance of 0.0036. For the conjugate prior we have adopted, the variance of β_{U0} is proportional to σ^2. Since the variance of β_U is $\sigma^2 B_{UU,0}$, where $B_{UU,0}$ is the value in B_0 corresponding to β_U, from our assumption that $E(\sigma^2) = 0.10$ we set $B_{UU,0} = 0.036$. For the remaining regression coefficients, we assume a mean of 0 and values in B_0 of 1. This assumption takes a neutral stance about the sign of the coefficient and allows each to have a fairly small impact.

This specification of the prior illustrates that choosing hyperparameter values in the context of a particular application can be done without appealing to devices that attempt to capture completely uninformative priors. In many, if not most, applications, there is relevant information. A specialist in labor economics should be able to assign more appropriate values than we have. We consider later the sensitivity of the results to the prior specification. Also, note that the conjugate prior assumption requires us to consider σ^2, which is the variance of u, when assigning a prior variance to the regression coefficients. The independent assignment of the two variances is considered in Section 4.9.

We can now compute the distribution of β_U with the result in (4.7) and the formula for the marginal distribution of a subset of multivariate t variates in (A.12). The posterior mean is 0.1347, and we plot the posterior distribution along with the prior in Figure 4.1. The posterior distribution is considerably tighter than the prior;

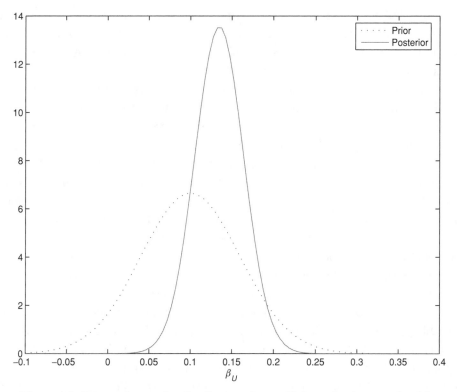

Figure 4.1. Prior and posterior distributions for coefficient of union membership.

the former indicates an almost certainly positive union effect, whereas the prior included negative values.

4.5 Exchangeability

Our discussion of prior distributions has focused on the use of subject-matter knowledge to specify parameters of distributions that are conjugate to the assumed form of the likelihood function. This approach is often computationally convenient and is widely applied in Part III. Another approach to specifying prior distributions takes advantage of a type of symmetry that appears in some models. That symmetry, called *exchangeability*, generalizes the property of statistical independence when applied to observable random variables, as we first explain. We then show how the idea may be applied in specifying a prior for unknown parameters.

The formal definition of exchangeability, a concept proposed by de Finetti, is in terms of the joint distribution of a set of random variables z_i: the random variables $z_1, z_2, \ldots, z_n$ are *finitely exchangeable* if $f(z_1, z, \ldots, z_n)$ is invariant to permutations in the indices $1, 2, \ldots, n$. (Exchangeability requires that this relationship hold for all *n*.) For example, if $n = 3$, the random variables z_1, z_2, and z_3 are exchangeable if

$$
\begin{aligned}
f(z_1, z_2, z_3) &= f(z_1, z_3, z_2) \\
&= f(z_2, z_1, z_3) \\
&= f(z_2, z_3, z_1) \\
&= f(z_3, z_1, z_2) \\
&= f(z_3, z_2, z_1).
\end{aligned}
$$

Exchangeability generalizes the concept of independence: identically distributed and mutually independent random variables are exchangeable, but exchangeability does not imply independence. de Finetti and others have shown the power and implications of this idea, but we use it in a more informal way.

Loosely speaking, a set of random variables is exchangeable if nothing other than the observations themselves distinguishes any of the z_is from any of the others. For example, if a coin is tossed three times and two heads appear, the possible outcomes are HHT, HTH, or THH. If the only information we have is that three tosses resulted in two heads, then exchangeability requires that we assign the same probability to each of these three outcomes.

As an example of exchangeability applied to prior distributions, consider the problem of *heteroskedasticity* in the linear regression model that arises when the assumption that Var(u_i) is the same for all i is untenable. Suppose that the linear regression model is

$$
f(y_i | \beta, \sigma^2, \lambda_i) = N(x_i'\beta, \lambda_i^{-1}\sigma^2), \tag{4.8}
$$

and we further specify

$$
\begin{aligned}
\beta &\sim N_K(\beta_0, B_0), \\
\sigma^2 &\sim \text{IG}(\alpha_0/2, \delta_0/2), \\
\lambda_i &\sim G(\nu/2, \nu/2).
\end{aligned} \tag{4.9}
$$

A gamma prior distribution is appropriate for λ_i because it is a precision parameter and therefore positive; the choice of parameters $(\nu/2, \nu/2)$ is explained later. This assumption about the distribution of λ_i embodies exchangeability: each i is associated with a particular λ_i, but the λ_i are drawn independently from the same gamma distribution. Knowing the value of i gives us no additional information about the value of λ_i. Although each observation has its own variance $\lambda_i^{-1}\sigma^2$, all we know about these variances is that they are drawn from the same distribution. This assumption about the variance can be contrasted with the assumption that $E(y_i) = x_i'\beta$, where the fact that each observation has its own covariate vector x_i

implies different expected values for each observation; that is, knowing the value of i gives us covariate values x_i that provide information about the mean level of y_i.

While the heteroskedastic regression model is an example of specifying an exchangeable prior, it is of interest in its own right as an extension of the linear model. You should verify that the prior family is not conjugate and that the posterior distribution is not of a standard form that permits analytic integration to obtain the marginal posterior distribution of β and σ^2. But the model has an interesting property that is exploited in Section 8.1.2. From our assumptions that $u_i|\lambda_i, \sigma^2 \sim N(0, \lambda_i^{-1}\sigma^2)$ and $\lambda_i \sim G(\nu/2, \nu/2)$, we can write

$$f(u_i, \lambda_i|\sigma^2) \propto \lambda_i^{1/2} \exp\left[-\frac{\lambda_i}{2\sigma^2}u_i^2\right] \lambda_i^{\nu/2-1} \exp\left[-\frac{\nu\lambda_i}{2}\right]$$

$$\propto \lambda_i^{(\nu+1)/2-1} \exp\left[-\frac{\lambda_i(u_i^2 + \nu\sigma^2)}{2\sigma^2}\right].$$

The marginal distribution $f(u_i|\sigma^2)$ is found by integrating (or marginalizing) over λ_i using the fact that $\lambda_i|u_i^2, \sigma^2$ has the distribution $G[(\nu + 1)/2, (u_i^2 + \nu\sigma^2)/2\sigma^2]$. Its normalizing constant is therefore proportional to $(u_i^2 + \nu\sigma^2)^{-(\nu+1)/2}$, from which we have

$$(u_i^2 + \nu\sigma^2)^{-(\nu+1)/2} \propto \left(1 + \frac{u_i^2}{\nu\sigma^2}\right)^{-(\nu+1)/2},$$

the kernel of the Student-t distribution $t(\nu, 0, \sigma^2)$. We conclude that the aforementioned assumption about the distribution of λ_i and the normality of $u_i|\lambda_i, \sigma^2$ is equivalent to assuming that the $u_i|\sigma^2$ have a t-distribution with ν degrees of freedom. We can say that the distribution of u_i is conditionally heteroskedastic because the variance of $u_i|\lambda_i, \sigma^2 = \lambda_i^{-1}\sigma^2$, but the distribution of $u_i|\sigma^2$ is homoskedastic.

4.6 Hierarchical Models

The models we have examined to this point contain two elements: a density function for the observed data conditioned on a vector of parameters and a prior distribution for the parameters, in turn conditioned on a vector of hyperparameters. In a *hierarchical* model, we add one or more additional levels, where the hyperparameters themselves are given a prior distribution depending on another set of hyperparameters; for example,

$$y \sim f(y|\theta), \tag{4.10}$$

$$\theta \sim \pi(\theta|\alpha_0), \tag{4.11}$$

$$\alpha_0 \sim \pi(\alpha_0|\alpha_{00}), \tag{4.12}$$

where α_{00} is specified. Other levels may be added, but this is rarely done. Before turning to an example, we make a few comments. First, α_0 is not identified from the data, because $f(y|\theta, \alpha_0) = f(y|\theta)$. Second, α_0 can be eliminated from the problem because

$$\pi(\theta|\alpha_{00}) = \int \pi(\theta|\alpha_0)\pi(\alpha_0|\alpha_{00}) \, d\alpha_0.$$

Accordingly, α_0 is neither identified nor necessary for analyzing the model; it is introduced to facilitate computations or modeling.

As an example, consider the heteroskedastic linear model of Section 4.5. The distribution of λ_i is given a gamma distribution depending on the parameter ν, which turns out to be the degrees of freedom parameter of a t-distribution. In that formulation, ν is chosen by the researcher. In a hierarchical version of the model, a prior distribution is placed on ν to reflect uncertainty over its value. Since $0 < \nu < \infty$, any distribution confined to positive values could serve. Examples are the gamma distribution, a distribution over a finite set of ν values, or the Poisson distribution truncated to $\nu > 0$, where parameters would be chosen to reflect prior views. It is helpful to recall that the t-distribution approaches the normal as ν increases, and the approximation is very close for the central part of the distribution when $\nu \approx 30$ or larger. We return to this model in Section 4.9.

4.7 Training Sample Priors

The device described in this section can be applied when the researcher has very little information on which to base a prior distribution, but has a large number of observations. The idea is to take advantage of the Bayesian updating discussed in Section 3.1.3. A portion of the sample is selected as the training sample. It is combined with a relatively uninformative prior to yield a first-stage posterior distribution. In turn, this the prior for the remainder of the sample. By a relatively uninformative prior, we mean a prior with a large variance and a mean of zero.

A limiting case of an uninformative prior is a flat, improper prior for the regression coefficients, $\pi(\beta) \propto c$, and a flat, improper prior on $\log(\sigma)$, $\pi(\sigma) \propto 1/\sigma$. These choices lead to $\pi(\beta|\sigma^2, y) = N_K(\beta|\hat{\beta}, \sigma^2(X'X)^{-1})$, where $\hat{\beta} = (X'X)^{-1}X'y$, the ordinary least squares estimator, and $\pi(\sigma^2|y) = \text{IG}(\sigma^2|(n-K)/2, S^2/2]$, where $S^2 = (y - X\hat{\beta})'(y - X\hat{\beta})$, the usual sum of squared residuals. Note that, in this case, the joint posterior distribution of (β, σ^2) is proper, despite the improper prior distribution.

Table 4.1. β_U as a Function of Hyperparameters
β_{U0} and $B_{UU,0}$.

	$B_{UU,0}$		
β_{U0}	0.010	0.036	0.050
0.050	0.095	0.123	0.128
0.100	0.122	0.135	0.137
0.200	0.174	0.158	0.155

4.8 Sensitivity and Robustness

Results should be checked for their sensitivity to the assumptions about prior distribution, especially when hyperparameters for those priors have been selected with considerable uncertainty. We illustrate a sensitivity check with the Vella–Verbeek union data discussed in Section 4.4. We focus on the prior mean of the union dummy coefficient β_{U0} and the term proportional to its variance $B_{UU,0}$. Table 4.1 displays the results.

The table shows some sensitivity around our benchmark result of 0.1347. When results seem rather sensitive to the prior mean, the researcher should attempt to justify the choice for this value by referring to the relevant literature. Another possibility of refining this choice might be to take a training sample approach. The Vella–Verbeek data set contains information on the same young men for 8 years. One possibility might be to take an earlier year as a training sample. Because they are the same people, however, the assumption of independence across samples would not be acceptable, and finding the distribution of the 1987 data, given a previous year's data, might be difficult. A rough compromise might involve taking the data for the earliest year as the training sample. While these data are not likely to be completely independent, the degree of independence may not be too great. There is sensitivity also to the value of $B_{UU,0}$, but this seems to be most serious when it is set to a small value of 0.01.

4.9 Conditionally Conjugate Priors

We now show the importance of assuming that the prior variance of β is proportional to σ^2. Suppose instead that we assume independent priors, which is more realistic in most cases. We continue to assume normal and inverse gamma distributions, but now

$$\pi(\beta, \sigma^2) = \pi(\beta)\pi(\sigma^2)$$

$$\propto \exp\left[-\frac{1}{2}(\beta - \beta_0)'B_0^{-1}(\beta - \beta_0)\right]\left(\frac{1}{2\sigma^2}\right)^{\alpha_0/2+1}\exp\left[-\frac{\delta_0}{2\sigma^2}\right].$$

To derive the posterior distribution, the prior is multiplied by the likelihood function of (4.1). In this distribution, the parameters β and σ^2 are so interwoven that we cannot separate them into the product of two marginal distributions or of a marginal and conditional distribution. The distribution is not a standard form, and its normalizing constant is not known. Accordingly, even for one of the most basic models in applied statistics, the apparent slight change in the prior distribution results in a model for which the desired marginal posterior distributions cannot be derived analytically.

But there is something interesting about this form: consider the conditional posterior distributions $\pi(\beta|\sigma^2, y)$ and $\pi(\sigma^2|\beta, y)$. To derive the former, we consider only the terms in the posterior that contain β. After some simplification, you should verify that

$$\pi(\beta|\sigma^2, y) \propto \exp\left[-\frac{1}{2}(\beta - \bar{\beta})' B_1^{-1}(\beta - \bar{\beta})\right],$$

where

$$B_1 = \left[\sigma^{-2}X'X + B_0^{-1}\right]^{-1},$$
$$\bar{\beta} = B_1\left[\sigma^{-2}X'y + B_0^{-1}\beta_0\right].$$

We see that the *conditional* posterior distribution $\pi(\beta|\sigma^2, y)$ is multivariate normal with mean $\bar{\beta}$ and covariance matrix B_1. When the conditional posterior distribution is in the same family as the prior, the prior is said to be *conditionally conjugate* or *semiconjugate*.

It is important to be aware of how we found the conditional distribution because the method is used frequently later in the book. We first wrote down the expression for the joint distribution of all parameters by the usual likelihood times prior formulation. We then picked out only the terms involving the parameters whose conditional distribution we wish to determine. All terms that do not involve these parameters are relegated to the proportionality constant. The remaining expression, which contains the parameters of interest, is proportional to the conditional distribution of those parameters.

The idea is now applied to $\pi(\sigma^2|\beta, y)$. To find this distribution, collect the terms in the joint posterior distribution that include σ^2 to obtain

$$\pi(\sigma^2|\beta, y) \propto \left(\frac{1}{\sigma^2}\right)^{\alpha_1/2+1} \exp\left[-\frac{\delta_1}{2\sigma^2}\right],$$

where $\alpha_1 = \alpha_0 + n$ and $\delta_1 = \delta_0 + (y - X\beta)'(y - X\beta)$. We now see that the conditional posterior distribution of $\sigma^2|\beta, y$ is $IG(\alpha_1/2, \delta_1/2)$, another example of a conditionally conjugate prior distribution.

As another example of conditionally conjugate priors, consider the heteroskedastic linear regression model specified in (4.8) and (4.9). We adopt a hierarchical approach to that model by taking ν as an additional parameter. You should verify that $\pi(\beta|\sigma^2, \lambda, y)$ is normal, $\pi(\sigma^2|\beta, \lambda, \nu, y)$ is inverted gamma, and $\pi(\lambda_i|\beta, \sigma^2, \nu, y_i)$ is gamma, where $\lambda = (\lambda_1, \ldots, \lambda_n)$. Note that, in each case, we have included in the conditioning set only those variables that actually appear in the conditional distributions, rather than including all variables. To complete the analysis, a prior for ν must be specified and an expression for its conditional distribution derived. For the prior, we assume that ν takes on J values, $\nu_1, \nu_2, \ldots, \nu_J$, with probabilities $p_{10}, p_{20}, \ldots, p_{J0}$, respectively. For example, the values of ν might be set to 5, 15, 30, and 50 to allow a range of possibilities. At 50, the t-distribution is very close to a normal distribution.

To derive the conditional posterior distribution of the probabilities, we write the joint posterior distribution of all parameters as

$$
\pi(\beta, \sigma^2, \lambda, \nu | y) \propto \pi(\beta)\pi(\sigma^2) \prod_i^n \left(\frac{\lambda_i}{\sigma^2}\right)^{1/2} \exp\left[-\frac{\lambda_i}{2\sigma^2}(y_i - x_i'\beta)^2\right]
$$

$$
\times \lambda_i^{\nu/2-1} \frac{1}{\Gamma(\nu/2, \nu/2)} \exp\left[-\frac{\nu\lambda_i}{2}\right] \sum_j^J p_{j0}1(\nu = \nu_j),
$$

(4.13)

where $1(A)$ is the indicator function that equals 1 if A is true and 0 otherwise. Note that only the last four terms involve ν, and these involve no parameters other than the λ_i. This reflects the fact that ν is not identified by the data, although it depends on y through the λ_i. We can therefore write

$$
\pi(\nu_j|\lambda) \propto p_{j0}\lambda_i^{\nu_j/2-1} \frac{1}{\Gamma(\nu_j/2, \nu_j/2)} \exp\left[-\frac{\nu_j \sum_i \lambda_i}{2}\right], \quad j = 1, \ldots, J. \quad (4.14)
$$

The requirement that $\sum_j \pi(\nu_j|\lambda) = 1$ is enforced by dividing the individual terms in (4.14) by their sum.

While we have no interest in conditional distributions per se, the conditional distributions derived in this chapter can be exploited to find the marginal posterior distributions of β and σ^2. How to do this is taken up in Part II and applied in Part III.

4.10 A Look Ahead

Methods of assigning prior distributions have been presented in this chapter along with the basics of the linear normal regression model. We have seen that the conjugate prior distribution leads to a standard form for the joint posterior distribution of β and σ^2, leading to analytic results for the marginal posteriors of β and σ^2.

In Exercise 4.3, you will find that the distributions of β and σ^2 can also be found analytically when the priors for β and σ^2 have the improper prior distributions specified there.

We have seen that when a conditionally conjugate prior is used, however, the resulting joint distribution does not have a standard form. The result is that the marginal distributions of β and σ^2 cannot be found analytically. This is a serious limitation because we are usually interested in the marginal posterior distribution of a few of the β_ks, and an inability to find these threatens the usefulness of the Bayesian approach. If we cannot find marginal distributions for the most commonly used model of econometrics and other fields, of what use is the approach?

There are several possible ways of dealing with this issue. One possibility is numerical integration, a traditional method of evaluating integrals that do not have analytic solutions. But this method is useful only in low-dimensional problems. The union example discussed in Section 4.4 contains 32 regression parameters and one variance parameter. Numerical integration would not allow us to find the marginal distribution of the union regression coefficient.

Another approach utilizes the ability of computers to generate pseudorandom numbers that are used to draw a sample from a distribution. A sample drawn this way is called a "simulated sample" or a "simulation." With a large sample from a distribution, it is possible to approximate the marginal distribution of the parameters and of any continuous function of the parameters, including their moments. Simulation is an alternative to integration that can be used in high-dimensional problems, and simulation can be applied to standard and nonstandard distributions. The insight that simulation can help us learn about marginal distributions greatly extends the reach of Bayesian inference, but to take advantage of this idea we must learn how to simulate samples from whatever joint distribution we encounter. New approaches to simulation have made this possible. Part II of the book explains general methods of simulating samples from both standard and nonstandard distributions.

4.11 Further Reading and References

Section 4.2 See Garthwaite et al. (2005) for a summary of methods for eliciting probability distributions. O'Hagan et al. (2006) is a book-length treatment of the elicitation of experts' probability judgments. It explains and evaluates numerous methods of elicitation and provides examples and many further references.

Section 4.5 See Bernardo and Smith (1994, chap. 4) and O'Hagan (1994, sec. 4.39–4.50, 6.36–6.38) for a detailed discussion of exchangeability, and Albert and Chib (1993b) and Geweke (1993) for further discussion of the heteroskedastic model.

4.12 Exercises

4.1 Show that (4.6) can be rewritten as

$$\delta_1 = \delta_0 + (y - X\hat{\beta})'(y - X\hat{\beta}) + (\beta_0 - \hat{\beta})'[(X'X)^{-1} + B_0]^{-1}(\beta_0 - \hat{\beta}),$$

where $\hat{\beta} = (X'X)^{-1}X'y$, the ordinary least squares estimator of β for the frequentist statistician in the normal linear regression model. (Hint: use (A.18).)

4.2 Let $y_i \sim N(\mu, 1)$ and take $\mu \sim N(\mu_0, \sigma_0^2)$ as the prior distribution, which becomes improper as $\sigma_0^2 \to \infty$. Derive $\pi(\mu|y)$, where y is a random sample of size n. Discuss how the posterior distribution behaves as $\sigma_0^2 \to \infty$.

4.3 This question refers to the expression for $\bar{\beta}$ in Section 4.3 and generalizes Exercise 4.2. Some authors suggest that weak prior information can be modeled as large prior variances for β. For example, suppose that B_0 is a matrix with large values on the main diagonal and zeros elsewhere, and consider what happens to $\bar{\beta}$ as the variances go to infinity. Interpret this result in terms of the weight assigned to the data and to the prior in determining the posterior distribution.

4.4 In Section 4.3, we showed that $\beta|y$ has a multivariate t-distribution. Equations (A.12)–(A.14) give the marginal distribution and its moments for a subset of the parameters. Choose a data set that includes at least two covariates and find a 95% interval estimate for β_2.

4.5 Since the posterior distribution of (β, σ^2) in Section 4.3 is of known form, it is possible to compute its marginal likelihood analytically. Start from the definition of the marginal likelihood:

$$\int f(y|\beta, \sigma^2)\pi(\beta, \sigma^2)\, d\beta\, d\sigma^2$$

$$= \int \left(\frac{1}{2\pi\sigma^2}\right)^{n/2} \exp\left[-\frac{1}{2\sigma^2}(y - X\beta)'(y - X\beta)\right] \left(\frac{1}{2\pi\sigma^2}\right)^{K/2}$$

$$\times \frac{1}{|B_0|^{1/2}} \exp\left[-\frac{1}{2\sigma^2}(\beta - \beta_0)'B_0^{-1}(\beta - \beta_0)\right]$$

$$\times \frac{(\delta_0/2)^{\alpha_0/2}}{\Gamma(\alpha_0/2)} \left(\frac{1}{\sigma^2}\right)^{\alpha_0/2+1} \exp\left[-\frac{\delta_0}{2\sigma^2}\right] d\beta\, d\sigma^2$$

$$= \left(\frac{1}{2\pi}\right)^{n/2} \frac{(\delta_0/2)^{\alpha_0/2}}{\Gamma(\alpha_0/2)} \frac{1}{|B_0|^{1/2}} \int \left\{ \left(\frac{1}{2\pi\sigma^2}\right)^{K/2} \right.$$

$$\times \left. \exp\left[-\frac{1}{2\sigma^2}(\beta - \bar{\beta})'B_1^{-1}(\beta - \bar{\beta})\right] d\beta \right\} \left\{ \left(\frac{1}{\sigma^2}\right)^{\alpha_1/2+1} \exp\left[-\frac{\delta_1}{2\sigma^2}\right] d\sigma^2 \right\},$$

where we have used (4.5). Now integrate the first pair of curly braces as a multivariate normal and the second as an inverted gamma to find this expression for the marginal likelihood:

$$\left(\frac{1}{\pi}\right)^{n/2} \frac{|B_1|^{1/2}}{|B_0|^{1/2}} \frac{\Gamma(\alpha_1/2)}{\Gamma(\alpha_0/2)} \frac{\delta_0^{\alpha_0/2}}{\delta_1^{\alpha_1/2}}.$$

4.6 Show that i.i.d. variables are exchangeable.

4.7 Suppose that an urn contains R red balls and B blue balls and that three balls are removed at random without replacement. Let B_i (respectively R_i) denote that a blue (respectively red) ball is removed at the ith draw, $i = 1, 2, 3$. Show that

$$P(R_1, B_2, B_3) = P(B_1, R_2, B_3) = P(B_1, B_2, R_3),$$

but that $P(R_1) \neq P(R_1|B_2)$. Conclude that this distribution is finitely exchangeable and that the draws are not independent.

Part II
Simulation

Chapter 5

Classical Simulation

AS WE MENTIONED at the end of the previous chapter, simulation has greatly expanded the scope of Bayesian inference. In this chapter, we review methods for generating *independent* samples from probability distributions. The methods discussed here form the basis for the newer methods discussed in Chapter 7 that are capable of dealing with a greater variety of distributions but do not generate independent samples.

All major statistics packages contain routines for generating random variables from such standard distributions as those summarized in the appendix. The examples presented here are intended to illustrate methods of generating samples. We do not claim that the algorithms are the best that can be designed, and we do not study the methods in great detail. Our goal for the chapter is to present the standard techniques of simulation and explain the kinds of questions that simulated samples can help answer.

Many of the applications discussed later can be regarded as attempts to approximate a quantity such as $E[g(X)]$ where $X \sim f(X)$, but the necessary integral, $\int g(x)f(x)\,dx$, cannot be computed analytically. This problem includes the computation of expected values (where $g(X) = X$) and other moments, as well as $P(c_1 \leq X \leq c_2)$, for which we set $g(X) = 1(c_1 \leq X \leq c_2)$.

5.1 Probability Integral Transformation Method

The most basic method of generating samples takes advantage of the ability of computers to generate values that can be regarded as drawn independently from a uniform distribution on $(0,1)$, $U(0, 1)$. For this discussion, we adopt the convention that a capital letter such as Z represents a random variable and the corresponding small letter z represents a particular value of that random variable.

Suppose we wish to draw a sample of values from a random variable that has d.f. $F(\cdot)$, assumed to be nondecreasing. Consider the distribution of Z, which is obtained by drawing U from $U(0, 1)$ and setting $Z = F^{-1}(U)$, which implies $U = F(Z)$:

$$P(Z \leq z) = P(F(Z) \leq F(z))$$
$$= P(U \leq F(z))$$
$$= F(z),$$

where the first line relies on the fact that the d.f. is nondecreasing and the last line uses the property of the uniform distribution that $P(U \leq u) = u$. (If $F(\cdot)$ is constant over one or more intervals of Z, it is evaluated at the smallest value of each such interval.) We conclude that the random variable Z computed in this fashion can be regarded as a draw from the d.f. $F(\cdot)$. This method, the *probability integral transformation* (PIT) method, takes its name from the fact that $U = F(Z)$ is called the probability integral transformation. It is also called the *inverse d.f.* method. Note that a multivariate random variable cannot be simulated by this method, because its d.f. is not one-to-one and therefore not invertible.

In algorithmic form, we have the following.

Algorithm 5.1: Probability integral transform method

5.1 Draw u from $U(0, 1)$.
5.2 Return $y = F^{-1}(u)$ as a draw from $f(y)$.

Implementing this method requires that the d.f. be known completely (i.e., its normalizing constant is known as well as its kernel) and that $F^{-1}(\cdot)$ can be readily computed. Because accurate approximations to the inverse function have been computed for standard distributions and are available in many computer program, the latter requirement can be met even if the inverse function cannot be computed analytically.

As our first example, suppose we desire to sample from $U(a, b)$, a generalization of the uniform distribution. Since

$$f(z) = \begin{cases} \frac{1}{b-a}, & \text{if } a \leq z \leq b, \\ 0, & \text{otherwise,} \end{cases}$$

we find $F(z) = (z - a)/(b - a)1(a \leq z \leq b)$. If $U \sim U(0, 1)$, then $U = (Z - a)/(b - a)$, and $Z = a + (b - a)U$ is a draw from $U(a, b)$.

As another example, suppose we wish to draw a sample from a random variable with density function

$$y \sim f(y) = \begin{cases} \frac{3}{8}y^2, & \text{if } 0 \leq y \leq 2, \\ 0, & \text{otherwise.} \end{cases}$$

We first find the d.f. for $0 \leq y \leq 2$ by computing

$$F(y) = \frac{3}{8} \int_0^y t^2 \, dt = \frac{1}{8} y^3.$$

The next step is to draw a value U from $U(0, 1)$ and set $U = (1/8)Y^3$. We then solve to find $Y = 2U^{1/3}$, which is a draw from $f(Y)$.

An important application of this method is to the problem of sampling from a truncated distribution. Suppose that X has d.f. $F(X)$ and that we wish to generate values of X restricted to $c_1 \leq X \leq c_2$. The distribution of the truncated values is $[F(X) - F(c_1)]/[F(c_2) - F(c_1)]$ for $c_1 \leq X \leq c_2$. Following our usual procedure, we generate $U \sim U(0, 1)$ and set

$$U = \frac{F(X) - F(c_1)}{F(c_2) - F(c_1)},$$

which implies that

$$X = F^{-1}(F(c_1) + U[F(c_2) - F(c_1)]) \tag{5.1}$$

is a drawing from the truncated distribution. This method is routinely used to sample from univariate truncated normal or Student-t densities because accurate approximations to the inverse d.f.s are available and included in statistics packages.

5.2 Method of Composition

The method of composition uses the relationship

$$f(x) = \int g(x|y)h(y) \, dy,$$

where f, g, and h are densities. The method is useful when we know how to sample y from $h(y)$ and x from $g(x|y)$. By drawing a y from $h(y)$ and then an x from $g(x|y)$, the value of x is a drawing from $f(x)$.

We have seen an example of this idea in Section 4.5 in connection with the heteroskedastic linear regression model. It was shown that if $u_i|\lambda_i \sim N(0, \lambda_i^{-1}\sigma^2)$, $\lambda_i \sim G(\nu/2, \nu/2)$, and

$$f(u_i|\sigma^2) = \int g(u_i|\lambda_i, \sigma^2)h(\lambda_i) \, d\lambda_i,$$

where $g(u_i|\lambda_i, \sigma^2)$ is the density function of $N(u_i|0, \lambda_i^{-1}\sigma^2)$ and $h(\lambda_i)$ is the density function of $G(\lambda_i|\nu/2, \nu/2)$, then $f(u_i|\sigma^2)$ is the density function of $t(\nu, 0, \sigma^2)$. This result shows that we can simulate draws from a t-distribution with ν degrees of freedom if we know how to simulate draws from a gamma distribution and from a normal distribution: draw a value of λ_i from the gamma distribution and then draw a value of u_i from the normal distribution conditional on the value of λ_i. This result generalizes to simulation from t-distributions with nonzero means.

The method of composition can be thought of as a *mixture* distribution, where the density of interest can be written as the marginal distribution of a joint distribution,

$$f(x) = \int g(x, y) \, dy.$$

In this form, $g(\cdot, \cdot)$ is not explicitly written as the product of a conditional and a marginal density. The mixture distribution idea can be used when it is convenient to sample a joint distribution. The expression implies that the values of x are a sample from its marginal distribution when a sample (x, y) is generated from their joint distribution.

It is sometimes possible to write a p.d.f. in the form of a *finite mixture distribution*,

$$f(x) = \sum_i^k P_i f_i(x),$$

where $\sum P_i = 1$ and each $f_i(x)$ is a p.d.f. If it is known how to sample from each of the $f_i(\cdot)$, a sample from $f(\cdot)$ can be obtained by choosing i with probability P_i and then generating a value from f_i. See Exercise 5.3 for an example.

5.3 Accept–Reject Algorithm

The accept–reject (AR) algorithm can be used to simulate values from a density function $f(\cdot)$ if it is possible to simulate values from a density $g(\cdot)$ and if a number c can be found such that $f(Y) \le cg(Y)$, $c \ge 1$, for all Y in the support of $f(\cdot)$. The density $f(Y)$ to be sampled is called the *target* density, the distribution $g(y)$ that is simulated is called the *majorizing*, *instrumental*, or *proposal* density, and $cg(\cdot)$ is called the *majorizing function* or *dominating density*. The target density must be dominated over the entire support of Y, which is often difficult to achieve in the multivariate case.

The AR algorithm proceeds as follows.

Algorithm 5.2: Accept–reject method

5.1 Generate a value y from $g(\cdot)$.
5.2 Draw a value u from $U(0, 1)$.
5.3 Return y as a draw from $f(\cdot)$ if $u \le f(y)/cg(y)$. If not, reject it and return to step 1.
(The effect of this step is to accept y with probability $f(y)/cg(y)$.)

The procedure is continued until the desired number of draws is obtained.

Here is a proof to show the method works. Consider the distribution of the accepted values of y, $h[y|u \leq f(y)/cg(y)]$. By Bayes theorem and the property of the uniform distribution that $P(u \leq t) = t, 0 \leq t \leq 1$, we have

$$
\begin{aligned}
h[y|u \leq f(y)/cg(y)] &= \frac{P[u \leq f(y)/cg(y)|y]g(y)}{\int P[u \leq f(y)/cg(y)|y]g(y)\,dy} \\
&= \frac{[f(y)/cg(y)]g(y)}{(1/c)\int f(y)\,dy} \\
&= f(y).
\end{aligned}
$$

We have shown that the distribution of the accepted values has the distribution of the random variable from which we wish to sample. Note that

$$
\int P(u \leq f(y)/cg(y)|y)g(y)\,dy = 1/c
$$

is the probability that a generated value of y is accepted. This implies that we should choose c as small as possible to maximize the probability of acceptance because rejected values use computer time without adding to the sample.

Before proceeding with examples, we point out an interesting feature of the AR algorithm that is useful when the normalizing constant of $f(\cdot)$ is unknown; that is, $f(\cdot) = kr(\cdot)$ and $r(\cdot)$ is known but k is not. Let c be chosen so that $r(y) \leq cg(y)$. You can verify that if a value of y generated from $g(y)$ is accepted with probability $r(y)/cg(y)$, the accepted values of y are a sample from $f(y)$. This method can therefore be used even if the normalizing constant of the target distribution is unknown; in this case, it is no longer required that $c \geq 1$.

As our first example, consider the problem of sampling from Beta$(3, 3)$ with $U(0, 1)$ as the proposal density. The maximum of the target density occurs at $y = 1/2$, where the density function equals 1.8750. Accordingly, we set $c = 1.8750$, and the probability of accepting a draw is $1/c = 0.5333$. You can see from Figure 5.1 why this proposal density is not a particularly good choice. It generates values uniformly along the horizontal axis, but the target density is far from uniform. Since values near zero and one are oversampled by the proposal density, they are accepted with low probability to compensate for the oversampling. The figure shows that a value of 0.15 generated by the proposal is accepted with probability $0.4877/1.875 = 0.2601$.

The algorithm to implement this procedure may be summarized as follows.

Algorithm 5.3: Beta distribution

5.1 Draw u_1 and u_2 from $U(0, 1)$.
5.2 If

$$
u_2 \leq \frac{\text{Beta}(3, 3)^{-1}u_1^2(1 - u_1)^2}{1.8750},
$$

return $y = u_1$ as a draw from the target distribution. Otherwise reject it and return to 1.

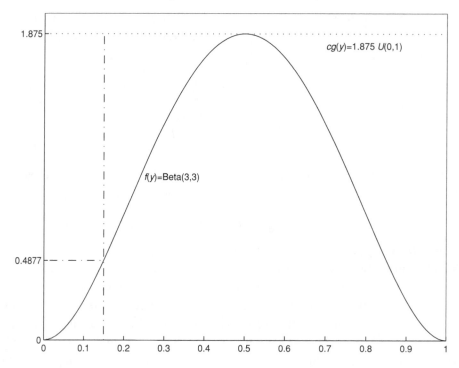

Figure 5.1. Target and proposal density to sample from Beta(3, 3).

As a second example, let the target density be $N(0, 1)$ and the proposal density be the Laplace distribution, $g(y) = (1/2) e^{-|y|}$. Since both of these are symmetric about zero, we first sample from the exponential distribution, e^{-y}, $y > 0$, and accept or reject the value with the AR algorithm. If the proposal is accepted, it is assigned a positive value with probability one half and a negative value with probability one half. This algorithm can be used for general normal distributions: if $Y \sim N(0, 1)$, then $X = \mu + \sigma Y \sim N(\mu, \sigma^2)$. To determine c verify that the maximum of $(\sqrt{2\pi})^{-1} e^{-y^2/2}/e^{-y}$ occurs at $y = 1$, implying that $c = \sqrt{e/2\pi}$ and that the probability of acceptance is $1/c = 0.6577$. Figure 5.2 displays the target and proposal densities. In algorithmic form, we have the following.

Algorithm 5.4: Normal distribution

5.1 Generate u_1, u_2, and u_3 from $U(0, 1)$.

5.2 Sample from the exponential distribution $g(x) = e^{-x}$ by the method of Section 5.1: from $g(x) = e^{-x}$, verify that $G(x) = 1 - e^{-x}$. Accordingly, write $u_1 = 1 - e^{-x}$ or $x = -\log(1 - u_1)$, which is equivalent to $x = -\log(u_1)$ since u_1 and $1 - u_1$ have the same distribution.

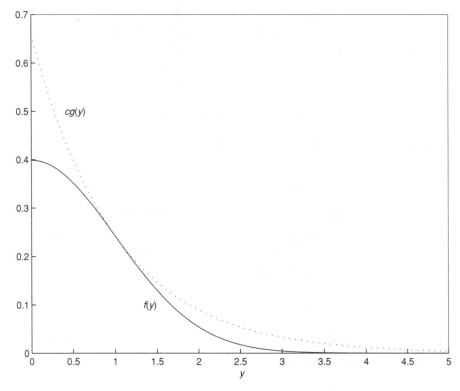

Figure 5.2. Target and proposal density to sample from $N(0, 1)$.

5.3 If

$$u_2 \leq \frac{1}{\sqrt{2\pi}} e^{-x^2/2} \bigg/ ce^{-x}$$

$$= \frac{1}{\sqrt{2\pi}} e^{-x^2/2} \bigg/ \sqrt{\frac{e}{2\pi}} e^{-x} \qquad (5.2)$$

$$= e^{x-x^2/2-1/2},$$

return $y = x$ if $u_3 \leq 1/2$ and $y = -x$ if $u_3 > 1/2$. If (5.2) is not satisfied, reject x and return to step 1.

The AR method may appear to be similar to the Metropolis–Hastings (MH) algorithm, discussed in the next chapter, because both involve a rejection step, but there are important differences. First, the MH method is more general than the AR method, in the sense that it can be employed to sample from a greater variety of distributions. Second, the MH method generates correlated, rather than independent, samples. Independent samples are, in general, preferred to positively correlated samples because they have a smaller variance and therefore provide more information from a given sample size. Although negatively correlated samples have an even smaller variance than do independent samples, the MH method tends to produce positively correlated samples. Moreover, there are no known methods that are sure to generate independent or negatively correlated samples.

5.4 Importance Sampling

Suppose that $X \sim f(X)$ and we wish to estimate

$$E[g(X)] = \int g(x)f(x)\,dx,$$

but the integral is not computable analytically and the method of composition is not available, because we cannot sample from $f(x)$. The *importance sampling* method, a type of *Monte Carlo integration*, works as follows. Let $h(X)$ be a distribution from which we know how to simulate and consider the integral

$$E[g(X)] = \int \frac{g(x)f(x)}{h(x)}h(x)\,dx.$$

This integral can be approximated by drawing a sample of G values from $h(X)$, with values $X^{(g)}$, and computing

$$E[g(X)] \approx \frac{1}{G}\sum g(X^{(g)})\frac{f(X^{(g)})}{h(X^{(g)})}.$$

This expression can be regarded as a weighted average of the $g(X^{(g)})$, where the *importance weights* are $f(X^{(g)})/h(X^{(g)})$.

The main issue in implementation of importance sampling is the choice of $h(\cdot)$. To find a suitable distribution we examine the variance of the estimate. Since $\mathrm{Var}(\hat{g}) = E(\hat{g}^2) - E(\hat{g})^2$ and the latter converges to $E[g(X)]^2$, we may concentrate on

$$E(\hat{g}^2) = \int g(x)^2 \left(\frac{f(x)}{h(x)}\right)^2 h(x)\,dx.$$

This integral is large when $f(x)/h(x)$ is large, a situation that tends to occur when the tail values of $h(\cdot)$ are very small compared to the tail values of $f(\cdot)$. Since the normal distribution tends to zero very quickly, it is often not a good choice for $h(\cdot)$. In general, $\mathrm{Var}(\hat{g})$ is small when $f(\cdot)/h(\cdot)$ does not vary greatly.

As an example of importance sampling, we approximate $E[(1 + x^2)^{-1}]$, where $x \sim \exp(1)$, truncated to $[0, 1]$; that is, we approximate the integral

$$\frac{1}{1 - e^{-1}}\int_0^1 \frac{1}{1 + x^2}e^{-x}\,dx.$$

We choose as an importance function Beta(2, 3) because it is defined on [0, 1] and because, for this choice of parameters, the match between the beta function and the target density is good over part of the [0, 1] interval. By applying the following algorithm and setting $G = 10,000$, we obtained an estimate of 0.8268 and an approximate standard error of 0.0030. An approximation by numerical integration yields 0.8302.

Algorithm 5.5: Truncated exponential

5.1 Generate a sample of G values, $X^{(1)}, \ldots, X^{(G)}$ from Beta(2, 3).
5.2 Calculate

$$\frac{1}{G} \sum_{1}^{G} \left(\frac{1}{1 + (X^{(g)})^2} \right) \left(\frac{e^{-X^{(g)}}}{1 - e^{-1}} \right) \left(\frac{B(2, 3)}{X^{(g)}(1 - (X^{(g)})^2)} \right).$$

As a second example, we approximate $P(a_1 < X_1 \le b_1, a_2 < X_2 \le b_2)$, where $(X_1, X_2) \sim N_2(\mu, \Sigma)$, $\mu = (\mu_1, \mu_2)'$, and $\Sigma = \{\sigma_{ij}\}$. The desired integral is

$$P(a_1 < X_1 \le b_1, a_2 < X_2 \le b_2) = \int_{a_1}^{b_1} \int_{a_2}^{b_2} f(x_1, x_2) \, dx_1 \, dx_2,$$

where $f(x_1, x_2)$ is the density function of the bivariate normal distribution. The first step is to rewrite the joint density in marginal-conditional form, $f(x_1) f(x_2|x_1)$ using the results (see Section A.9) that $x_1 \sim N(\mu_1, \sigma_{11})$ and that $x_2|x_1 \sim N(\mu'_2, \sigma'_{22})$, where

$$\mu'_2 = \mu_2 + (\sigma_{12}/\sigma_{11})(x_1 - \mu_1),$$
$$\sigma'_{22} = \sigma_{22} - \sigma_{12}^2/\sigma_{11}.$$

Now let

$$y_1 = (x_1 - \mu_1)/\sqrt{\sigma_{11}}, \qquad y_2 = (x_2 - \mu'_2)/\sqrt{\sigma'_{22}},$$
$$a'_1 = (a_1 - \mu_1)/\sqrt{\sigma_{11}}, \qquad a'_2 = (a_2 - \mu'_2)/\sqrt{\sigma'_{22}},$$
$$b'_1 = (b_1 - \mu_1)/\sqrt{\sigma_{11}}, \qquad b'_2 = (b_2 - \mu'_2)/\sqrt{\sigma'_{22}}.$$

With this transformation, y_1 and $y_2|y_1$ have standard normal distributions, enabling us to write

$$P(a_1 < x_1 \le b_1, a_2 < x_2 \le b_2) = \int_{a'_1}^{b'_1} \int_{a'_2}^{b'_2} \phi(y_1) \phi(y_2|y_1) \, dy_1 \, dy_2$$
$$= \int_{a'_1}^{b'_1} \phi(y_1) \int_{a'_2}^{b'_2} \phi(y_2|y_1) \, dy_2 \, dy_1$$
$$= \int_{a'_1}^{b'_1} \phi(y_1) [\Phi(b'_2|y_1) - \Phi(a'_2|y_1)] \, dy_1.$$

The algorithm is now implemented by choosing the standard normal distribution truncated to (a'_1, b'_1) as the importance distribution; that is, draw $Y_1^{(g)}$ from the truncated standard normal using (5.1). With this choice for the importance function, we have

$$P(a_1 < X_1 \le b_1, a_2 < X_2 \le b_2)$$

$$\approx \frac{1}{G} \sum \left[\Phi\left(b'_2 | Y_1^{(g)}\right) - \Phi\left(a'_2 | Y_1^{(g)}\right) \right] \left[\Phi\left(b'_1\right) - \Phi\left(a'_1\right) \right]. \qquad (5.3)$$

5.5 Multivariate Simulation

We have seen an example of simulating from a multivariate distribution in the previous section. In general, as might be expected, sampling from multivariate distributions is more difficult than is sampling from univariate distributions.

The multivariate distribution most studied is the multivariate normal $N_p(\mu, \Sigma)$. Independent samples generated from the univariate normal can be transformed into samples from the multivariate normal. To draw a sample from $N_p(\mu, \Sigma)$, first draw p values from $N(0, 1)$ and place them in a $p \times 1$ vector Z, so that $Z \sim N_p(0, I_p)$. Next, write $\Sigma = C'C$, where C is a $p \times p$ upper-triangular Cholesky matrix. (The Cholesky matrix for a given Σ is computed in many statistical packages, although some provide a lower-triangular version.) Finally, compute $X = \mu + C'Z$. You can now verify that $X \sim N_p(\mu, \Sigma)$.

Although algorithms to simulate from all the multivariate distributions discussed in the appendix are available in the major statistical packages, designing an algorithm to generate independent samples from a nonstandard distribution can be extremely challenging. The AR and importance sampling methods can be used in principle, but their implementation may be difficult: the AR requires finding a dominating density over the whole support, and importance sampling requires finding a distribution with sufficiently heavy tails.

5.6 Using Simulated Output

A sample of size G generated from $f(Y)$, where the individual values are denoted by $Y^{(g)}$, $g = 1, \ldots, G$, can be used to investigate properties of the distribution in many ways. For example, we can graph the histogram or a kernel-smoothed version of the histogram to see the shape of the distribution; we can approximate the distribution of any continuous function of the sample, including moments; and we can approximate the quantiles of a distribution.

As an example, suppose we are interested in the distribution of $Z = XY$, where $X \sim \text{Beta}(3, 3)$ and $Y \sim \text{Beta}(5, 3)$, independently. A search turned up no analytic solution to the distribution of Z, so we proceed by generating samples from X and

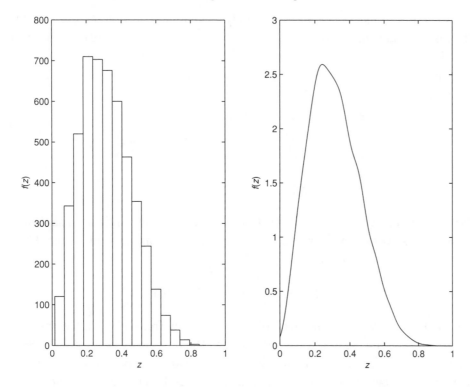

Figure 5.3. Simulation results for $Z = XY$, where $X \sim \text{Beta}(3, 3)$ and $Y \sim \text{Beta}(5, 3)$.

Y, $X^{(g)}$ and $Y^{(g)}$, respectively, and then computing $Z^{(g)} = X^{(g)}Y^{(g)}$. The resulting $Z^{(g)}$s are a sample from the target distribution. Figure 5.3 displays results for a sample of $G = 5{,}000$. The left panel is a histogram of the results, and the right panel is a kernel-smoothed histogram. The sample mean, $\bar{Z} = G^{-1}\sum Z^{(g)}$, an estimate of $E(Z)$, is 0.3146. The sample variance,

$$\frac{1}{G - 1}\sum(Z^{(g)} - \bar{Z})^2,$$

is an estimate of $\text{Var}(Z)$; it is 0.0215 in our simulation.

The *numerical standard error* (n.s.e.) is an estimate of the variation that can be expected in computing the mean of some function of the observations $Z = h(Y)$ over different simulations of the same length. It is defined as $\sqrt{\text{Var}(Z)/G}$ and equals 0.0021 for this simulation. Note that the n.s.e. can be controlled by varying the simulation sample size G.

By finding the $5{,}000 \times 0.025$th ordered value and the $5{,}000 \times 0.975$th ordered value of the sample, we can approximate an interval in which Z lies with probability 0.95. In our example, this interval is $(0.0719, 0.6279)$.

A major use of simulated data is to study the marginal distribution of a variable. This is especially important for Bayesian inference. Suppose that the target distribution is the posterior distribution $\pi(\theta|y)$ of a vector of parameters $\theta = (\theta_1, \ldots, \theta_d)$ and that we have generated a sample of size G from that distribution, arrayed as follows:

$$
\begin{array}{cccc}
\theta_1^{(1)} & \theta_2^{(1)} & \cdots & \theta_d^{(1)} \\
\theta_1^{(2)} & \theta_2^{(1)} & \cdots & \theta_d^{(2)} \\
\vdots & \vdots & \vdots & \vdots \\
\theta_1^{(G)} & \theta_2^{(G)} & \cdots & \theta_d^{(G)}.
\end{array}
$$

Each row is a draw from the joint posterior distribution, but what can be said about the columns? Let us focus on the first column as an example. From the definition of the marginal distribution,

$$
\pi(\theta_1|y) = \int \pi(\theta|y)\, d\theta_2 \cdots d\theta_d ,
$$

we see that the values in the first column are a draw from $\pi(\theta_1|y)$, the values in the second column are draws from $\pi(\theta_2|y)$, and so on. This is a remarkable result: drawing a sample from the joint distribution provides samples from each of the marginal distributions without computing any integrals. This result extends to the methods presented in the next chapter with the difference that the samples from each of the marginal distributions are not independent, because the draws from the joint distribution are not independent.

5.7 Further Reading and References

Section 5 The increasing importance of learning about simulation is highlighted by noting that the only new chapter in the third edition of a widely used statistics text, DeGroot and Schervish (2002), is about simulation. Useful references are Rubinstein (1981), Devroye (1986), Ripley (1987), Robert and Casella (2004), and Gentle (2003). The Devroye book is freely available at cgm.cs.mcgill.ca/~luc/rnbookindex.html.

Section 5.2 See Robert and Casella (2004, p. 45) for the mixture distribution idea.

Section 5.3 The example in which a normal is approximated by a Laplace is based on an exercise in DeGroot and Schervish (2002, p. 726, ex. 6).

Section 5.4 Importance sampling is discussed in several of the books cited before. An important reference to the subject in the econometrics literature is Geweke (1989). The truncated exponential algorithm is based on an example in DeGroot and Schervish (2002, pp. 728–729), where different importance functions are used. The GHK algorithm, which generalizes the bivariate normal example, is named for J. Geweke, V. Hajivassiliou, and M. Keane. It is described in Greene (2003, pp. 932–933) and in Train (2003, sec. 5.6.3)

5.8 Exercises

5.1 Use the probability integral transformation method to simulate from the distribution

$$f(x) = \begin{cases} \frac{2}{a^2}x, & \text{if } 0 \le x \le a, \\ 0, & \text{otherwise}, \end{cases}$$

where $a > 0$. Set a value for a, simulate various sample sizes, and compare results to the true distribution.

5.2 Use the probability integral transformation method to simulate 500 values from the logistic distribution,

$$f(x) = \frac{e^{-x}}{(1 + e^{-x})^2}, \qquad -\infty < x < \infty.$$

Compare your simulated values to the true distribution. Explore how the simulation improves with larger sample sizes. Generalize your result to the general form of the distribution,

$$f(x) = \frac{\exp[-(x - \alpha)/\beta]}{\beta(1 + \exp[-(x - \alpha)/\beta])^2}, \qquad -\infty < x < \infty, \quad \alpha, \beta > 0.$$

5.3 Generate samples from the distribution

$$f(x) = \frac{2}{3} e^{-2x} + 2 e^{-3x}$$

using the finite mixture approach. Hint: Note that the p.d.f. can be written as

$$f(x) = \frac{1}{3}(2 e^{-2x}) + \frac{2}{3}(3 e^{-3x}).$$

5.4 Draw 500 observations from Beta(3, 3) using algorithm 5.3. Compute the mean and variance of the sample and compare them to the true values.

5.5 Draw 500 observations from $N(2, 4)$ using Algorithm 5.4. Compute the mean and variance of the sample and compare them to the true values. Overlay a histogram of the sample values on a graph of the true distribution and discuss how well the sample approximates the true distribution.

5.6 Verify Equation (5.3).

5.7 Use importance sampling to compute $P(0.2 < x_1 \le 2, -1 < x_2 \le 5)$, where $(x_1, x_2) \sim N_2(\mu, \Sigma)$, $\mu = (1, -0.5)'$, and

$$\Sigma = \begin{pmatrix} 2 & 1 \\ 1 & 3 \end{pmatrix}.$$

Chapter 6

Basics of Markov Chains

WE HAVE SEEN in the previous chapter that there exist methods to generate independent observations from the standard probability distributions, including those described in the appendix. But we still have the problem of what to do when faced with a nonstandard distribution such as the posterior distribution of parameters of the conditionally conjugate linear regression model. Although the methods described before can, in principle, deal with nonstandard distributions, doing so presents major practical difficulties. In particular, they are not easy to implement in the multivariate case, and finding a suitable importance function for the importance sampling algorithm or a majorizing density for the AR algorithm may require a very large investment of time whenever a new nonstandard distribution is encountered.

These considerations impeded the progress of Bayesian statistics until the development of Markov chain Monte Carlo (MCMC) simulation, a method that became known and available to statisticians in the early 1990s. MCMC methods have proved to be extremely effective and have greatly increased the scope of Bayesian methods. Although a disadvantage of this family of methods is that it does not provide independent samples, it has the great advantage of flexibility: it can be implemented for a great variety of distributions without having to undertake an intensive analysis of the special features of the distribution. We note, however, that an analysis of the distribution may shed light on the best algorithm to use when more than one is available.

Since these methods rely on Markov chains, a type of stochastic process, this chapter presents some basic concepts of the theory, and the next chapter utilizes these concepts to explain MCMC methods.

6.1 Finite State Spaces

Consider a stochastic process indexed by t, X_t, that takes values in the finite set $S = \{1, 2, \ldots, s\}$. The index t is interpreted as time or iterate. For any pair of integers $i, j \in S$, p_{ij} is defined as the probability that $X_{t+1} = j$ given that $X_t = i$, that is,

$$p_{ij} = P(X_{t+1} = j | X_t = i), \qquad i, j \in S. \tag{6.1}$$

The p_{ij} are *transition probabilities*. The assumption that the probability distribution at time $t + 1$ depends only on the state of the system at t is called the Markov property, and the resulting stochastic process is a Markov process. A Markov process is more general than is an independent process, but does not include all stochastic processes. We further assume, implicit in the notation, that the p_{ij} do not depend on t. This type of stochastic process is called a *homogeneous* Markov chain. These simple definitions and assumptions generate a powerful and elegant mathematical theory.

Since the p_{ij} are probabilities, we have $p_{ij} \geq 0$, and since the process remains in S,

$$\sum_{j=1}^{s} p_{ij} = 1.$$

It is convenient to define the $s \times s$ *transition matrix* $P = \{p_{ij}\}$. The ith row of P, $(p_{i1}, \ldots, p_{is})$, specifies the distribution of the process at $t + 1$, given that it is in state i at t.

For example, the transition matrix,

$$P = \begin{pmatrix} 0.750 & 0.250 \\ 0.125 & 0.875 \end{pmatrix}, \tag{6.2}$$

specifies that the process remains in state 1 with probability 0.750 and moves to state 2 with probability 0.250 if it starts in state 1. And, if it starts in state 2, it moves to state 1 with probability 0.125 and remains in state 2 with probability 0.875.

Now consider the distribution of the state at $t + 2$, given that it is in i at t. This distribution is denoted by $p_{ij}^{(2)}$ and can be computed as follows: to go from state i to state j in two steps, the process goes from i at t to any other state k at time $t + 1$ and then from k to j at $t + 2$. This transition occurs with probability

$$p_{ij}^{(2)} = \sum_{k} p_{ik} p_{kj}. \tag{6.3}$$

You can verify that the matrix of the $p_{ij}^{(2)}$ is given by $PP \equiv P^2$. Having done so, you can show by induction that the values of $p_{ij}^{(n)}$ are the ijth entries in the matrix P^n, where n is any integer. It is convenient to define $p_{ij}^{(0)}$ as 1 if $i = j$ and 0 otherwise. We will be mostly concerned with what happens to $p_{ij}^{(n)}$ as n becomes large. Before doing so, we present an example and a few definitions.

A simple example is that of completely random motion or independence: let all rows of P be identical, that is, $p_{ij} = p_j$ for all i. In this case, the probability of moving from state i to state j depends only on j. An independent coin tossing experiment is an example. Let heads be state 1 and tails be state 2. Let $p_1 = 2/3$ and $p_2 = 1/3$. Verify that each row of the transition matrix is the same.

If $p_{ij}^{(n)} > 0$ for some $n \geq 1$, we say j *is accessible from* i and write $i \to j$. If $i \to j$ and $j \to i$, we say i and j *communicate*, and write $i \leftrightarrow j$. It can be shown that the communication relationship between states defines an equivalence relationship; that is, $i \leftrightarrow i$ (reflexivity); $i \leftrightarrow j \iff j \leftrightarrow i$ (symmetry); and $i \leftrightarrow j$ and $j \leftrightarrow k \Rightarrow i \leftrightarrow k$ (transitivity).

This equivalence relationship places the states into equivalence classes within which the states communicate. A very important idea in the theory can now be defined: a Markov process is *irreducible* if there is just one equivalence class. What this means is that starting from state i, the process can reach any other state with positive probability. Suppose, for example, P takes the form

$$P_R = \begin{pmatrix} P_1 & 0 \\ 0 & P_2 \end{pmatrix}, \tag{6.4}$$

where P_1 and P_2 are $m \times m$. Then it should be easy to see that if the process starts in any of the first m states, it will never leave them. And, of course, if it starts in one of the states $m + 1, \ldots, 2m$, it will never leave them either. The process P_R is not irreducible, and the state at which the process begins has a very large effect on its subsequent path.

Another important property of a chain is periodicity. Consider a transition matrix of the form

$$P_P = \begin{pmatrix} 0 & P_1 \\ P_2 & 0 \end{pmatrix}, \tag{6.5}$$

where P_1 and P_2 are $m \times m$. If at $t = 1$, the process is in one of the first m states, it must go to one of the second m at $t = 2$, whereupon it must return to the first m states at $t = 3$, and so on. Positive probabilities of returning to a state in either of the two subsets exist only at even values of n. This is described by saying the period is of the chain is 2. If the period is 1 for all states, the chain is said to be *aperiodic*. More formally, if $i \to i$, then the *period of i* is the greatest common divisor of the integers in the set $A = \{n \geq 1 : p_{ii}^{(n)} > 0\}$. In words, if d_i is the period of i, then $p_{ii}^{(n)} = 0$ whenever n is not a multiple of d_i, and d_i is the largest integer with this property. Note that a chain is aperiodic if $p_{ii}^{(n)} > 0$ for all i and for sufficiently large n.

MCMC methods are based on the next definition. The probability distribution $\pi = (\pi_1, \ldots, \pi_s)'$ is an *invariant* distribution for P if $\pi' = \pi'P$, or

$$\pi_j = \sum_i \pi_i p_{ij}, \quad j = 1, \ldots, s. \tag{6.6}$$

The right-hand side of this equation is the probability that the process is in state j at any t marginalized over the states at $t - 1$; it can be interpreted as the probability of starting the process at state i with probability π_i and then moving to state j with probability p_{ij}. The fact that the resulting value is π_j is what makes π an invariant distribution: if the states are chosen according to π, the probability is π_j that the system is in state j at any time. Note that π' is a characteristic vector of P with a characteristic root equal to 1.

For an example of an invariant distribution, consider the transition matrix of Equation (6.2). From $\pi'P = \pi'$, we have

$$(\pi_1, \pi_2) \begin{pmatrix} 0.750 & 0.250 \\ 0.125 & 0.875 \end{pmatrix} = (\pi_1, \pi_2),$$

or

$$0.750\pi_1 + 0.125\pi_2 = \pi_1,$$

and, since $\pi_2 = 1 - \pi_1$,

$$\pi_1 = 0.750\pi_1 + 0.125(1 - \pi_1),$$

which implies $\pi = (1/3, 2/3)$. This example is generalized in Exercise 6.2.

An important topic in Markov chain theory is the existence and uniqueness of invariant distributions. We can see immediately that irreducibility is a necessary condition for P to have a unique invariant distribution: in P_R mentioned earlier, let π_1 satisfy $\pi_1'P_1 = \pi_1'$ and π_2 satisfy $\pi_2'P_2 = \pi_2'$. Then it is easy to verify that $\pi = (w\pi_1, (1 - w)\pi_2)$, $0 \leq w \leq 1$, is an invariant distribution for P, which shows that the invariant distribution is not unique.

A special case of an irreducible and aperiodic Markov chain is one in which all $p_{ij} > 0$. For these, we have the following theorem.

Theorem 6.1 *Suppose S is finite and $p_{ij} > 0$ for all i, j. Then there exists a unique probability distribution π_j, $j \in S$, such that $\sum_i \pi_i p_{ij} = \pi_j$ for all $j \in S$. Moreover,*

$$|p_{ij}^{(n)} - \pi_j| \leq r^n, \tag{6.7}$$

where $0 < r < 1$, for all i, j and $n \geq 1$.

A proof may be found in Bhattacharya and Waymire (1990, p. 126).

The theorem tells us that, in a finite state space with all probabilities positive, not only is there a unique invariant distribution, but also that $p_{ij}^{(n)}$ converges at a geometric rate (r^n) to π_j. What is interesting about the latter result is that for large enough n, the initial state i plays almost no role. Another way of putting it is to note that the result implies that P^n converges quickly to a matrix whose rows are all π'. Recall that this is the property of an independent process. We illustrate this property of P^n with the transition matrix of (6.2) by computing

$$P^{10} = \begin{pmatrix} 0.339 & 0.661 \\ 0.330 & 0.670 \end{pmatrix},$$

and

$$P^{20} = \begin{pmatrix} 0.333 & 0.667 \\ 0.333 & 0.667 \end{pmatrix},$$

from which we see that P^n has already reached its invariant distribution to three decimal places when $n = 20$.

This theorem, in more general forms, is the basis for MCMC methods. It tells us that if a Markov chain satisfies certain conditions, the probability distribution of its nth iterate is, for large n, very close to its invariant distribution; that is, if drawings are made from the nth, $(n + 1)$st, ... iterate of the process, for large n the probability distribution of the drawings is the invariant distribution. This fact has an important implication for simulation: if we can find a Markov process for which the invariant distribution is the target distribution, we can simulate draws from the process to generate values from the target distribution.

As an example, we may simulate values from the transition matrix of (6.2) by arbitrarily choosing the starting state (1 or 2) and then choosing subsequent states according to the probabilities of the transition matrix. After generating a large number of draws in this fashion, the proportion of the time the process is in state 1 is an estimate of π_1; see Exercise 6.3.

The restriction $p_{ij} > 0$ for all i, j is unnecessarily restrictive. The theorem can be generalized to the following theorem.

Theorem 6.2 *Let P be irreducible and aperiodic over a finite state space. Then there is a unique probability distribution π such that $\sum_i \pi_i p_{ij} = \pi_j$ for all $j \in S$ and*

$$|p_{ij}^{(n)} - \pi_j| \le r^{n/\nu},$$

for all i, $j \in S$, where $0 < r < 1$, for some positive integer ν.

A proof may be found in Bhattacharya and Waymire (1990, p. 128). The proof involves making estimates of the difference between successive values of $|p_{ij}^{(n)} - \pi_j|$ and showing these go to zero with n.

Rather than prove the theorem, let us see what happens when the assumptions are violated. First consider the reducible transition matrix P_R. We have already noted that it does not have a unique invariant distribution. Since

$$P_R^n = \begin{pmatrix} P_1^n & 0 \\ 0 & P_2^n \end{pmatrix},$$

its nth iterate does not have the same probability distribution in each of its rows and does not converge to anything useful for MCMC purposes. Next consider the irreducible but periodic matrix P_P: we have

$$P_P^2 = \begin{pmatrix} P_1 P_2 & 0 \\ 0 & P_2 P_1 \end{pmatrix},$$

and

$$P_P^3 = \begin{pmatrix} 0 & P_1 P_2 P_1 \\ P_2 P_1 P_2 & 0 \end{pmatrix}.$$

Since this alternating pattern continues for every iterate, P_P^n does not converge to a matrix with identical rows. Thus, irreducibility and aperiodicity are necessary conditions for the theorem.

Although Theorem 6.2 states that irreducibility and aperiodicity are sufficient to yield a result that justifies the MCMC method for finite state spaces, we need to consider more general state spaces because most applications involve continuous distributions. Before turning to these and the additional complications they bring, we briefly examine Markov chains with a countable number of states.

6.2 Countable State Spaces

An example of a countable state space is the simple random walk. In this process, $S = \{0, \pm 1, \pm 2, \ldots\}$, and the transition probabilities are

$$p_{ij} = \begin{cases} p, & \text{if } j = i + 1, \\ q, & \text{if } j = i - 1, \\ 0, & \text{otherwise}, \end{cases}$$

where $0 < p < 1$ and $q = 1 - p$. The possible states are all positive and negative integers, a countable space.

Irreducibility and aperiodicity no longer imply the existence of a unique invariant distribution when S is countable but not finite. Another concept, *recurrence*, must

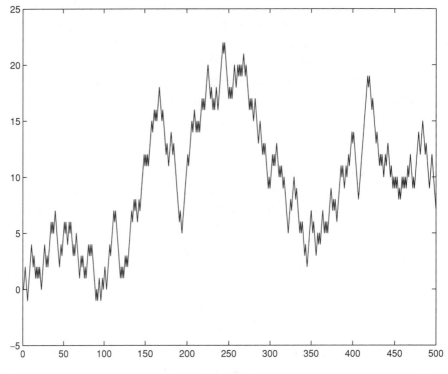

Figure 6.1. Random walk, $p = q = 0.5$.

be introduced. To see the problem, consider the Markov chain defined by the following transition probabilities:

$$p_{ij} = \begin{cases} p, & \text{if } j = i + 1, \\ r, & \text{if } j = i, \\ q, & \text{if } j = i - 1. \end{cases}$$

This process is called a random walk. Starting from i, it moves to $i + 1$ with probability p, to $i - 1$ with probability q, and stays at i with probability r, where $p + q + r = 1$ and $p, q, r \geq 0$. If all three probabilities are positive, it should be verified that the process is irreducible and aperiodic. Figure 6.1 illustrates the first 500 values generated from a random walk with $p = q = 0.5$. Note that the process drifts with no clear pattern.

Suppose now that p and q are positive and $p > q$. Figure 6.2 illustrates the case $p = 0.55, q = 0.45$. You can see how the process trends upward. It can be shown that the process drifts off to $+\infty$ in the sense that $p_{ij}^{(n)} \to 0$ for all i, j. This means that, starting from i, the probability that any finite value of j will be reached goes to zero, which implies that this process has no invariant probability distribution.

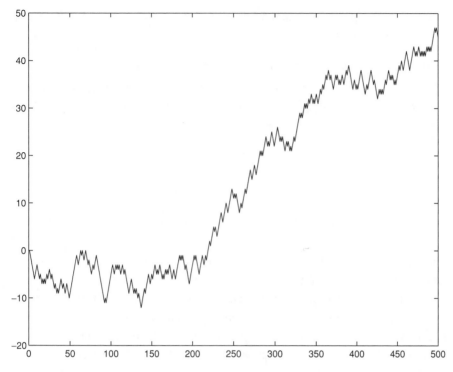

Figure 6.2. Random walk, $p = 0.55, q = 0.45$.

To salvage a counterpart of Theorems 6.1 and 6.2, the concept of *recurrence* is needed.

Let $P_j(A)$ denote the probability that event A occurs, given that the process starts at j. Then state j is called recurrent if

$$P_j(X_n = j \text{ i.o.}) = 1,$$

where i.o. means "infinitely often." In words, the definition states that the process returns to state j an infinite number of times with probability 1. If a state is not recurrent, it is *transient*. In the random walk with $p > q$, none of the states are recurrent. Because the process drifts off to infinity with probability 1, the probability of an infinite number of returns to any state is not one. It can be proved that if a process is irreducible, all states are either transient or recurrent. In the random walk example, all states are recurrent if $p = q$.

Recurrence is not strong enough to imply a unique invariant distribution. To specify a stronger condition, let $\tau_j^{(1)}$ be the time it takes for the process to make its first return to state j:

$$\tau_j^{(1)} = \min\{n > 0 : X_n = j\}.$$

A state j is called *positive recurrent* if $E\tau_j^{(1)} < \infty$. Otherwise, it is *null recurrent*. We can now state a theorem.

Theorem 6.3 *Assume that the process is irreducible. Then*

6.1 *If all states are recurrent, they are either all positive recurrent or all null recurrent.*

6.2 *There exists an invariant distribution if and only if all states are positive recurrent. In that case, the invariant distribution π is unique and is given by*

$$\pi_j = (E_j\tau_j^{(1)})^{-1}.$$

6.3 *In case the states are positive recurrent, for any initial distribution, if $E_\pi |f(X_1)| < \infty$,*

$$\lim_{n\to\infty} \frac{1}{n} \sum_{m=1}^{n} f(X_m) = E_\pi f(X_1).$$

For a proof, see Bhattacharya and Waymire (1990, p. 145).

This theorem has many implications for MCMC methods and generalizes readily to continuous state spaces. Under the conditions stated in the theorem, we know that there is a unique invariant distribution and that averages of functions evaluated at sample values converge to their expected values under the invariant distribution. Since a possible function is the indicator function $1(X_n = i)$, which has expected value π_i, this value can be estimated from sample data. A central limit theorem may also be proved in this setup; see Bhattacharya and Waymire (1990, p. 149).

Convergence of P^n to a matrix whose rows are the invariant distribution requires aperiodicity.

Theorem 6.4 *If P is an aperiodic recurrent chain, $\lim_{n\to\infty} P^n$ exists. If P is an aperiodic positive-recurrent chain, then $\lim_{n\to\infty} P^n = A$, where A is a matrix whose rows are the invariant distribution.*

For a proof, see Kemeny et al. (1976, p. 153).

Markov chain theory, as presented here and in most textbooks, starts with the transition probabilities P and determines conditions under which the rows of P^n converge to an invariant distribution. In contrast, MCMC theory starts with an invariant distribution and finds a P that converges to it. Since the existence of an invariant distribution is not in doubt, we can quote another theorem that covers this case.

Theorem 6.5 *Suppose P is π-irreducible and that π is an invariant distribution for P. Then P is positive recurrent and π is the unique invariant distribution of P. If P is also aperiodic, then for π-almost all x,*

$$\|P^n(x, \cdot) - \pi\| \to 0.$$

In this theorem, which also applies to the continuous case, π-irreducible means that for some n, $P^n(x, A) > 0$ for any set A such that $\pi(A) > 0$. The implication for our discussion is that recurrence need not be assumed explicitly if it is known that an invariant distribution exists. The distribution mentioned in the theorem must be a proper (normalizable) distribution. Generalizations to some nonnormalizable distributions are given in Meyn and Tweedie (1993).

6.3 Continuous State Spaces

Now suppose that the states of a Markov process take values in R. The counterpart of the transition probabilities is the *transition kernel* or *transition density* $p(x, y)$. The notation $p(x, y)$ is used because the kernel is the continuous counterpart of p_{ij}, but it is more instructive to interpret it as the conditional density $p(y|x)$. The Markov property is captured by assuming that the joint density, conditional on the initial value $X_0 = x_0$, is given by

$$f_{(X_1,\ldots,X_n|X_0=x_0)}(x_1, \ldots, x_n) = p(x_0, x_1)p(x_1, x_2)\cdots p(x_{n-1}, x_n).$$

Given that the process is currently at state x, the probability that it moves to a point in $A \subseteq R$ is given by

$$P(x, A) = \int_A p(x, y)\,dy. \tag{6.8}$$

The nth step ahead transition is computed analogously to Equation (6.3),

$$P^{(n)}(x, A) = \int_R P(x, dy)P^{(n-1)}(y, A).$$

An invariant density $\pi(y)$ for the transition kernel $p(x, y)$ is a density that satisfies

$$\pi(y) = \int_R \pi(x)p(x, y)\,dx. \tag{6.9}$$

As an example of an invariant density, consider the autoregressive process of order 1,

$$y_t = \theta y_{t-1} + u_t,$$

where $|\theta| < 1$ and $u_t \sim N(0, \sigma^2)$. This process is taken up in more detail and generality in Section 10.1, where it is shown that $E(y_t) = 0$ and $\mathrm{Var}(y_t) = \sigma^2/(1 - \theta^2)$.

We now verify that the invariant distribution is Gaussian with those parameters:

$$\pi(y_t) = \int \pi(y_{t-1}) f(y_{t-1}, y_t) \, dy_{t-1}$$

$$\propto \int \exp\left[-\frac{1-\theta^2}{2\sigma^2} y_{t-1}^2\right] \exp\left[-\frac{1}{2\sigma^2}(y_t - \theta y_{t-1})^2\right] dy_{t-1}$$

$$\propto \int \exp\left[-\frac{1}{2\sigma^2}[(1-\theta^2)y_{t-1}^2 + y_t^2 - 2\theta y_{t-1} y_t + \theta^2 y_{t-1}^2]\right] dy_{t-1}$$

$$\propto \int \exp\left[-\frac{1}{2\sigma^2}[(y_{t-1} - \theta y_t)^2 + (1-\theta^2)y_t^2]\right] dy_{t-1}$$

$$\propto \exp\left[-\frac{1-\theta^2}{2\sigma^2} y_t^2\right],$$

the last expression is that of a $N(0, \sigma^2/(1-\theta^2))$ distribution as was to be shown.

For processes in continuous state spaces, the definitions of irreducibility and aperiodicity are as before, with $p(x, y)$ in place of p_{ij}. To define recurrence for continuous state spaces, let $P_x(A)$ denote the probability of event A given that the process started at x. Then, a π-irreducible chain with invariant distribution π is recurrent if for each B with $\pi(B) > 0$,

$$P_x(X_n \in B \text{ i.o.}) > 0, \quad \text{for all } x,$$

$$P_x(X_n \in B \text{ i.o.}) = 1, \quad \text{for } \pi\text{-almost all } x.$$

The chain is *Harris recurrent* if $P_x(X_n \in B \text{ i.o.}) = 1$ for all x.

The following theorems use the total variation distance between two measures, defined as follows. The total variation norm of a bounded, signed measure λ is $\|\lambda\| = \sup_A \lambda(A) - \inf_A \lambda(A)$, and the *total variation distance* between two such measures λ_1 and λ_2 is $\|\lambda_1 - \lambda_2\|$. Tierney (1994, p. 10) states the following theorems.

Theorem 6.6 *Suppose that P is π-irreducible and that π is an invariant distribution for P. Then P is positive recurrent and π is the unique invariant distribution of P. If P is also aperiodic, then for π-almost all x,*

$$\|P^n(x, \cdot) - \pi\| \to 0,$$

with $\|\cdot\|$ denoting the total variation distance. If P is Harris recurrent, then the convergence occurs for all x.

Theorem 6.7 *If $\|P^n(x, \cdot) - \pi\| \to 0$ for all x, the chain is π-irreducible, aperiodic, positive recurrent, and has invariant distribution π.*

These theorems form the basis of MCMC methods. In practice, the researcher attempts to construct an irreducible, aperiodic, and positive recurrent transition kernel for which the invariant distribution is the target distribution. Several sets of sufficient conditions appear in the literature to guarantee this, some of which are quoted in Chapter 7.

We conclude by noting that all of the aforementioned results generalize immediately to the case in which the random variables X_n are vectors. Thus, in the finite and countable cases, the states over which the X_n are defined may be vector valued. In the continuous case, the X_n can be vectors in d-dimensional space, so that $X_n \in R^d$ under a suitably defined norm.

6.4 Further Reading and References

Chapter 6 Most introductions to Markov chain theory – an excellent one is Norris (1997) – do a thorough job on finite and countable state spaces but provide little on continuous state spaces. Bhattacharya and Waymire (1990) has some material on both, and Billingsley (1986) is an excellent source for the discrete and countable case; we also referred to Kemeny, Snell, and Knapp (1976). Meyn and Tweedie (1993) cover the continuous case.

6.5 Exercises

6.1 Consider the transition matrix P,

$$
P = \begin{pmatrix}
\frac{1}{3} & \frac{2}{3} & 0 & 0 & 0 & 0 \\
0 & 0 & 1 & 0 & 0 & 0 \\
\frac{1}{4} & 0 & 0 & \frac{1}{4} & \frac{1}{2} & 0 \\
0 & 0 & 0 & \frac{1}{8} & \frac{7}{8} & 0 \\
0 & 0 & 0 & 0 & 0 & 1 \\
0 & 0 & 0 & 0 & 1 & 0
\end{pmatrix},
$$

and let $i = 1, \ldots, 6$.
   (a) Find the states accessible from state i.
   (b) Find the states with which state i communicates.
   (c) Identify the equivalence classes of this process.
   (d) Is this process irreducible?
   (e) Compute P^{100} and P^{101} (use a computer!), and explain the probabilities that you find.
6.2 Let

$$
P = \begin{pmatrix}
1 - \alpha & \alpha \\
\beta & 1 - \beta
\end{pmatrix}. \tag{6.10}
$$

   (a) Find the invariant distribution if $0 < \alpha, \beta < 1$. Is the process aperiodic? Is it irreducible? What is $\lim P^n$ in this case?

(b) Suppose $\alpha = \beta = 0$. Is there a unique invariant distribution? Is the process aperiodic? Is it irreducible? What is $\lim P^n$?

(c) Suppose $\alpha = \beta = 1$. Is there a unique invariant distribution? Is the process aperiodic? Is it irreducible? What is $\lim P^n$?

6.3 Consider the transition matrix of (6.2).

(a) Compute and interpret P^2.

(b) Write a program to generate states $\{1, 2\}$ of the chain using the probabilities from the matrix. For example, $P(s_t = 1 | s_{t-1} = 1) = 3/4$. Allow the process to run for a number of iterations, called the burn-in period, and then keep track of the generated states. Compute the fraction of the iterations in which the chain is in state 1, and compare your result to the invariant distribution. Experiment with the number of burn-in and total iteration values to see how well the approximation works.

6.4 Write a computer program to generate 500 state values from the random walk with parameters $p = 0.3, q = 0.3, r = 0.4$. Vary the values of p, q, and r to see how the process behaves.

6.5 We can examine the speed of convergence to an invariant distribution with some matrix algebra. Let P have a unique invariant distribution π, which implies that π' is a characteristic vector with a characteristic root of unity. Let the rows of V contain the characteristic vectors of P,

$$V = \begin{pmatrix} v_1' \\ v_2' \\ \vdots \\ v_s' \end{pmatrix},$$

and set $\Lambda = \text{diagonal}(\lambda_1, \ldots, \lambda_s)$, assumed to be distinct.

(a) Verify that $VP = \Lambda V$.

(b) Verify that $P^t = V^{-1} \Lambda^t V$ and that the jth row of P^t, $p_j^{(t)'} = \sum_k v^{jk} \lambda_k^t v_k'$, where v^{jk} is the jkth element of V^{-1}.

(c) Show that $p_j^{(t)'} \to \pi'$ and that, by setting $v_1' = \pi'$, we have $|\lambda_k| < 1, k = 2, \ldots, s$. Conclude that we can write $p_j^{(t)'} = \pi' + \sum_{k=2} v^{jk} \lambda_k^t v_k'$ and that the speed of convergence is governed by the characteristic root with the second largest absolute value.

(d) Apply the result of the previous question to examine the speed of convergence of Equation (6.10): verify that $\lambda_2 = 1 - \alpha - \beta$. Show that the rate of convergence is maximized when $\alpha + \beta = 1$. What does P equal in that case and why does convergence take place so quickly? Discuss values of α and β that lead to slow convergence.

6.6 (Norris, 1997, Example 1.3.3) Suppose you enter a casino with $\$i$ and win \$1 with probability p and lose \$1 with probability $q = 1 - p$ on each play of the game. The transition probabilities are $p_{i,i+1} = p$, $p_{i,i-1} = q$. We compute $h_i = P(\text{hit } 0 | W = i)$, where W is your wealth; this is the probability that you lose all your money. (It is assumed that the casino cannot go broke.)

(a) Argue that $h_0 = 1$ and $h_i = ph_{i+1} + qh_{i-1}$.

(b) Show that, if $p \neq q$, h_i satisfies the recurrence relation $h_i = A + B(q/p)^i$.

(c) If $p < q$, which is the usual case, argue that $B = 0$ and $A = 1$. (Remember that $h_i \leq 1$. Why?)

(d) If $p = q$, show that $h_i = A + Bi$, and argue that $h_i = 1$.

6.7 Let

$$P = \begin{pmatrix} 0 & 0.4 & 0.6 \\ 0.3 & 0 & 0.7 \\ 0.8 & 0.2 & 0 \end{pmatrix}.$$

Do the zeros on the main diagonal imply periodicity? Explain.

6.8 (Bhattacharya and Waymire, 1990, p. 216) Show that

$$\pi(y) = 2(1 - y), \quad 0 \leq y \leq 1$$

is an invariant density for the transition kernel

$$p(x, y) = \begin{cases} e^{1-x}, & \text{if } y < x, \\ e^{1-x} - e^{y-x}, & \text{if } y > x. \end{cases}$$

Chapter 7

Simulation by MCMC Methods

THE BASIS OF an MCMC algorithm is the construction of a transition kernel (see Section 6.3), $p(x, y)$, that has an invariant density equal to the target density. Given such a kernel, the process can be started at x_0 to yield a draw x_1 from $p(x_0, x_1)$, x_2 from $p(x_1, x_2), \dots$, and x_G from $p(x_{G-1}, x_G)$, where G is the desired number of simulations. After a transient period, the distribution of the x_g is approximately equal to the target distribution. The question is how to find a kernel that has the target as its invariant distribution. It is remarkable that there is a general principle for finding such kernels, the Metropolis–Hastings (MH) algorithm. We first discuss a special case – the Gibbs algorithm or Gibbs sampler – and then explain a more general version of the MH algorithm.

It is important to distinguish between the number of simulated values G and the number of observations n in the sample of data that is being analyzed. The former may be made very large – the only restriction comes from computer time and capacity, but the number of observations is fixed at the time the data are collected. Larger values of G lead to more accurate approximations. MCMC algorithms provide an approximation to the *exact* posterior distribution of a parameter; that is, they approximate the posterior distribution of the parameters, taking the number of observations to be fixed at n. In contrast, frequentist procedures that invoke such criteria as consistency are concerned with the effects of letting n become large.

A brief comment on notation: when discussing simulation techniques in this chapter, we follow the literature in denoting random variables by such symbols as x, which usually denotes the current value of the chain, and y, which usually denotes the next value, and the target distribution by $f(\cdot)$. For applications to Bayesian inference, the random variables of interest are parameters θ and the target is the posterior distribution $\pi(\theta|y)$, where y represents the data. We utilize the latter notation in Part III.

7.1 Gibbs Algorithm

7.1.1 Basic Algorithm

The Gibbs algorithm is a special case of the MH algorithm that can be used when it is possible to sample from each conditional distribution. For example, suppose we wish to sample from a nonstandard joint distribution $f(x_1, x_2)$, where the variables appear in two blocks, both of which may be vectors. Further suppose that the two conditional distributions $f(x_1|x_2)$ and $f(x_2|x_1)$ are distributions for which simulation algorithms are known. Then consider the following algorithm.

Algorithm 7.1: Gibbs algorithm with two blocks

7.1 Choose a starting value $x_2^{(0)}$.
7.2 At the first iteration, draw

$$x_1^{(1)} \text{ from } f(x_1|x_2^{(0)}),$$
$$x_2^{(1)} \text{ from } f(x_2|x_1^{(1)}).$$

7.3 At the gth iteration, draw

$$x_1^{(g)} \text{ from } f(x_1|x_2^{(g-1)}),$$
$$x_2^{(g)} \text{ from } f(x_2|x_1^{(g)}),$$

until the desired number of iterations is obtained. (The roles of x_1 and x_2 may be interchanged.)

Because the starting value is not drawn from the invariant distribution, some portion of the initial sample must be discarded; this portion is the *transient* or *burn-in* sample. The burn-in sample size B is usually set at several hundred to several thousand, and checks can be made to see whether the choice matters; in most cases, there are no theorems that indicate what B should be. For $g > B$, the distribution of the draws is approximately the target distribution. We denote by G the sample size after discarding the first B observations. Convergence diagnostics are discussed in Section 7.3.

We now show that the invariant distribution of the Gibbs kernel is the target distribution. To simplify the notation, let $x = (x_1, x_2)$ be the values of the random variables at the beginning of one iteration of the algorithm and $y = (y_1, y_2)$ be the values at the end of the iteration. The Gibbs kernel is

$$p(x, y) = f(y_1|x_2)f(y_2|y_1),$$

from which we can compute

$$
\int p(x, y) f(x)\, dx = \int f(y_1|x_2) f(y_2|y_1) f(x_1, x_2)\, dx_1\, dx_2
$$

$$
= f(y_2|y_1) \int f(y_1|x_2) f(x_2)\, dx_2
$$

$$
= f(y_2|y_1) f(y_1)
$$

$$
= f(y),
$$

which proves that $f(\cdot)$ is the invariant distribution for the Gibbs kernel $p(x, y)$.

Proof that the invariant distribution of the Gibbs kernel is the target distribution is a necessary, but not sufficient condition for the kernel to converge to the target. Such conditions are very technical and difficult to verify for particular cases, but some general results are available. For example, Tierney (1994, p. 1712) states that most Gibbs samplers satisfy the conditions of the following theorem.

Theorem 7.1 *Suppose P is π-irreducible and has π as its invariant distribution. If $P(x, \cdot)$ is absolutely continuous with respect to π for all x, then P is Harris recurrent.*

Extending Gibbs sampling to d blocks of variables is possible when all of the conditional densities $f(x_i|x_{-i})$ are distributions from which random draws can be generated, where x_{-i} are all the variables in the joint distribution other than x_i. The algorithm proceeds as follows (the ordering of the x_i is arbitrary).

Algorithm 7.2: Gibbs algorithm with d blocks

7.1 Choose $x_2^{(0)}, \ldots, x_d^{(0)}$.

7.2 Draw

$$
x_1^{(1)} \text{ from } f(x_1|x_2^{(0)}, \ldots, x_d^{(0)})
$$

$$
x_2^{(1)} \text{ from } f(x_2|x_1^{(1)}, x_3^{(0)}, \ldots, x_d^{(0)})
$$

$$
\vdots
$$

$$
x_d^{(1)} \text{ from } f(x_d|x_1^{(1)}, \ldots, x_{d-1}^{(1)}).
$$

7.3 At the gth iteration, draw

$$
x_1^{(g)} \text{ from } f(x_1|x_2^{(g-1)}, \ldots, x_d^{(g-1)})
$$

$$
x_2^{(g)} \text{ from } f(x_2|x_1^{(g)}, x_3^{(g-1)}, \ldots, x_d^{(g-1)})
$$

$$
\vdots
$$

$$
x_d^{(g)} \text{ from } f(x_d|x_1^{(g)}, \ldots, x_{d-1}^{(g)}).
$$

Since many applications of Gibbs sampling are presented in Part III, we offer only two examples here.

Let $y_i \sim N(\mu, h^{-1})$, $i = 1, \ldots, n$, be independently distributed, where the distribution has been parameterized in terms of the precision. We assume the conditionally conjugate priors $\mu \sim N(\mu_0, h_0^{-1})$ and $h \sim G(\alpha_0/2, \delta_0/2)$. Verify that this model is a special case of the normal linear regression model. From this specification, we have

$$\pi(\mu, h|y) \propto h^{n/2} \exp\left[-\frac{h}{2}\sum(y_i - \mu)^2\right] \exp\left[-\frac{h_0}{2}(\mu - \mu_0)^2\right]$$
$$\times h^{\alpha_0/2-1} \exp\left[-\frac{\delta_0 h}{2}\right].$$

From here, it is easy to derive the conditional posterior distribution of h,

$$\pi(h|\mu, y) \propto h^{(\alpha_0+n)/2-1} \exp\left[-h\frac{\delta_0 + \sum(y_i - \mu)^2}{2}\right]. \tag{7.1}$$

Equation (7.1) is recognized as the density function of $G[(\alpha_0 + n)/2, (\delta_0 + \sum(y_i - \mu)^2)/2]$, which is available for sampling in all statistical packages.

We complete the square in μ to obtain

$$\pi(\mu|h, y) \propto \exp\left[-\frac{h_0 + hn}{2}\left(\mu - \frac{h_0\mu_0 + hn\bar{y}}{h_0 + hn}\right)^2\right], \tag{7.2}$$

which should be recognized as $N[(h_0\mu_0 + hn\bar{y})/(h_0 + hn), (h_0 + hn)^{-1}]$ and is available for sampling in all statistical packages. In algorithmic form,

Algorithm 7.3: Mean and precision for normal model

7.1 Choose a starting value for $\mu = \mu^{(0)}$.
7.2 Sample $h^{(1)}$ from $G(\alpha_1/2, \delta_1/2)$, where $\alpha_1 = \alpha_0 + n$ and $\delta_1 = \delta_0 + \sum(y_i - \mu^{(0)})^2$.
7.3 At the gth iteration, draw

$$\mu^{(g)} \text{ from } N[(h_0\mu_0 + h^{(g-1)}n\bar{y})/(h_0 + h^{(g-1)}n), (h_0 + h^{(g-1)}n)^{-1}],$$
$$h^{(g)} \text{ from } G\left[\alpha_1/2, \left(\delta_0 + \sum(y_i - \mu^{(g)})^2\right)/2\right].$$

If desired, the sampling can begin with $h^{(0)}$ and the algorithm modified accordingly.

As a second example, we consider a more general version of the Poisson model with changing parameters that is described in Exercise 3.8. We assume that

$$p(y_i) = \begin{cases} \dfrac{e^{-\theta_1}\theta_1^{y_i}}{y_i!}, & \text{for } i = 1, \ldots, k, \\ \dfrac{e^{-\theta_2}\theta_2^{y_i}}{y_i!}, & \text{for } i = k+1, \ldots, n, \end{cases} \tag{7.3}$$

where $y_i = 0, 1, \ldots$, and the switch point k is unknown. The specification is completed by assigning the conditionally conjugate priors,

$$\theta_1 \sim G(\alpha_{10}, \beta_{10}), \qquad \theta_2 \sim G(\alpha_{20}, \beta_{20}), \qquad \pi(k = j) = 1/n, \quad j = 1, \ldots, n. \quad (7.4)$$

We have assigned gamma distributions to θ_1 and θ_2 because they are positive and the discrete uniform distribution to k over the values $1, \ldots, n$, which includes the possibility that no change occurs; that is, $k = n$. The details of the algorithm are taken up in Exercise 7.3, and references may be found in Section 7.4.

Although the Gibbs sampler usually works well in practice, there are some situations in which it does not. If there is a high correlation between one or more of the random variables in different blocks, the algorithm may not "mix well." This means that the sampler fails to traverse the full support of the sample space, generating iterations from only a limited portion. For a large enough number of iterations, it will traverse the space, but it may fail for the number of iterations generated in practice.

As an example, consider the problem of sampling $X = (X_1, X_2)$ from the bivariate normal distribution $N_2(0, \Sigma)$, where

$$\Sigma = \begin{pmatrix} 1 & \rho \\ \rho & 1 \end{pmatrix}.$$

We emphasize that most statistical packages allow efficient and independent sampling from the bivariate normal distribution, and the method we examine is not used in practice. We employ the Gibbs sampler with X_1 and X_2 as our two blocks. You should verify that $f(X_1|x_2) \sim N(\rho x_2, 1 - \rho^2)$ and $f(X_2|x_1) \sim N(\rho x_1, 1 - \rho^2)$. This algorithm performs badly if $\rho \approx 1$, which implies that the conditional variance of both variables $(1 - \rho^2)$ is close to zero. Accordingly, in each iteration, the sampler generates values that are very close to the value of the previous iteration, which implies that the initial value $x_1^{(0)}$ or $x_2^{(0)}$ can play a large role in the generated sample. Since the marginal distribution is known to be $X_1 \sim N(0, 1)$, we can compare the results of a Gibbs sampler, where $G = 5,000$ and $N = 500$, to the true distribution. With $\rho = 0.999$ we find that $\bar{x}_1 = 1.084$ when $x_2^{(0)} = 1$ and $\bar{x}_1 = -0.623$ when $x_2^{(0)} = -2$. Note that the mean is greatly affected by the starting value of the algorithm. In contrast, when $\rho = 0.5$, the starting value of -2 has little effect, yielding a mean of 0.0587. We discuss in Section 7.3 some methods for detecting poor mixing.

7.1.2 Calculation of Marginal Likelihood

We next consider the problem of computing the marginal likelihood when working with a nonstandard distribution. In Section 3.2.4, we point out that the marginal likelihood is the inverse of the normalizing constant of the posterior distribution. The normalizing constant is unknown when working with nonstandard distributions, but it is not needed for the implementation of the Gibbs and MH algorithms. It is, however, needed for computing Bayes factors. Several methods have been proposed, and we describe Chib's widely used approach to estimating the marginal likelihood when a sample is generated from a Gibbs algorithm.

The *Chib method* begins with the identity

$$\pi(\theta^*|y) = \frac{f(y|\theta^*)\pi(\theta^*)}{f(y)},$$

where θ^* is a particular value of θ and $f(y)$ is the marginal likelihood. For numerical accuracy, θ^* is usually chosen to be the mean of the sample values. The identity can be written as

$$f(y) = \frac{f(y|\theta^*)\pi(\theta^*)}{\pi(\theta^*|y)},$$

and the Chib method computes the right-hand side from the output of a Gibbs sampler. The terms in the numerator of the right-hand side are readily computed; they are the likelihood function and prior distribution, respectively, evaluated at θ^*. The main problem is to compute $\pi(\theta^*|y)$, for which the normalizing constant is not known.

Consider the simple case where the Gibbs algorithm is run in two blocks, denoted by θ_1 and θ_2. We may write

$$\pi(\theta_1^*, \theta_2^*|y) = \pi(\theta_1^*|\theta_2^*, y)\pi(\theta_2^*|y).$$

The first term on the right can be evaluated immediately because the conditional distributions are known when running the Gibbs sampler. To compute the second, Chib employs the identity

$$\pi(\theta_2^*|y) = \int \pi(\theta_1, \theta_2^*|y)\, d\theta_1$$

$$= \int \pi(\theta_2^*|\theta_1, y)\pi(\theta_1|y)\, d\theta_1,$$

which can be approximated by

$$\hat{\pi}(\theta_2^*|y) = \frac{1}{G}\sum \pi(\theta_2^*|\theta_1^{(g)}, y),$$

where the values of $\theta_1^{(g)}$ are taken from the Gibbs output.

When there are three or more blocks, the computation requires additional simulations. Taking the three-block case as an example, we start with the identity

$$f(y) = \frac{f(y|\theta_1^*, \theta_2^*, \theta_3^*)\pi(\theta_1^*, \theta_2^*, \theta_3^*)}{\pi(\theta_1^*, \theta_2^*, \theta_3^*|y)}.$$

The numerator is readily available, and we write the denominator as

$$\pi(\theta_1^*, \theta_2^*, \theta_3^*|y) = \pi(\theta_1^*|y)\pi(\theta_2^*|\theta_1^*, y)\pi(\theta_3^*|\theta_1^*, \theta_2^*, y).$$

The Gibbs output can be used to approximate the first term as

$$\hat{\pi}(\theta_1^*|y) = \frac{1}{G}\sum \pi(\theta_1^*|\theta_2^{(g)}, \theta_3^{(g)}, y).$$

For the second term, we use

$$\pi(\theta_2^*|\theta_1^*, y) = \int \pi(\theta_2^*|\theta_1^*, \theta_3, y)\pi(\theta_3|\theta_1^*, y)\, d\theta_3.$$

Then

$$\hat{\pi}(\theta_2^*|\theta_1^*, y) = \frac{1}{G}\sum \pi(\theta_2^*|\theta_1^*, \theta_3^{(g)}, y),$$

where the $\theta_3^{(g)}$ are generated from a "reduced run," in which $\theta_2^{(g)}$ and $\theta_3^{(g)}$ are sampled from $\pi(\theta_2|\theta_1^*, \theta_3, y)$ and $\pi(\theta_3|\theta_1^*, \theta_2, y)$, respectively, and θ_1 is fixed at θ_1^*. Computations for the reduced run can use the same code as the original run, but θ_1 is held constant at θ_1^*. Finally, the value of $\pi(\theta_3^*|\theta_1^*, \theta_2^*, y)$ is available directly from the conditional distribution.

Since many of the models discussed in Part III use only the Gibbs algorithm, readers interested in applications may proceed to Section 7.3 and then to Part III, returning to Section 7.2 when the MH algorithm is encountered.

7.2 Metropolis–Hastings Algorithm

7.2.1 Basic Algorithm

The MH algorithm is more general than the Gibbs sampler because it does not require that the full set of conditional distributions be available for sampling. Although it can be used in blocks, we first explain it in the one-block case. To generate a sample from $f(X)$, where X may be a scalar or vector random variable, the first step is to find a kernel $p(X, Y)$ that has $f(\cdot)$ as its invariant distribution. Since the Gibbs sampler is of no use when one or more of the conditionals are not available for sampling, a different approach to finding a kernel is necessary. To that end, we introduce the idea of a *reversible* kernel, defined as a kernel $q(\cdot, \cdot)$ for which

$$f(x)q(x, y) = f(y)q(y, x).$$

If q is reversible,

$$P(y \in A) = \int_A \int_{R^d} f(x)q(x, y) \, dx \, dy$$

$$= \int_A \int_{R^d} f(y)q(y, x) \, dx \, dy$$

$$= \int_A f(y) \, dy.$$

This shows that $f(\cdot)$ is the invariant distribution for the kernel $q(\cdot, \cdot)$ because the probability that y is contained in A is computed from $f(\cdot)$.

The fact that a reversible kernel has this property can help in finding a kernel that has the desired target distribution. Chib and Greenberg (1995b) show how this can be done when starting with a nonreversible proposal density. We now follow their derivation of the algorithm. The trick is to make an irreversible kernel reversible. If a kernel is not reversible, for some pair (x, y) we have

$$f(x)q(x, y) > f(y)q(y, x).$$

The MH algorithm deals with this situation by multiplying both sides by a function $\alpha(\cdot, \cdot)$ that turns the irreversible kernel $q(\cdot, \cdot)$ into the reversible kernel $p(x, y) = \alpha(x, y)q(x, y)$:

$$f(x)\alpha(x, y)q(x, y) = f(y)\alpha(y, x)q(y, x). \tag{7.5}$$

The expression $\alpha(x, y)q(x, y)$ is interpreted as follows: if the present state of the process is x, generate a value y from the kernel $q(x, y)$ and make the move to y with probability $\alpha(x, y)$. If the move to y is rejected, the process remains at x. We call $q(x, y)$ the proposal density because of its analogous role in the AR algorithm, but the MH algorithm is very different from the latter. In the AR case, the algorithm continues to generate values until a candidate is accepted. In contrast, in the MH algorithm, the procedure returns the current state of the process as the next state when a candidate is rejected and continues to the next iteration; this implies that values may be repeated in a simulation run. Note that this transition kernel combines a continuous kernel $q(x, y)$ and a probability mass function $\alpha(x, y)$.

How to define $\alpha(x, y)$ is the next question. Suppose that

$$f(x)q(x, y) > f(y)q(y, x).$$

Roughly speaking, this means that the kernel goes from x to y with greater probability than it goes from y to x. Accordingly, if the process is at y and the kernel proposes a move to x, that move should be made with high probability. This can be done by setting $\alpha(y, x) = 1$. But then, $\alpha(x, y)$ is determined because, from (7.5),

$$f(x)q(x, y)\alpha(x, y) = f(y)q(y, x)$$

implies

$$\alpha(x, y) = \begin{cases} \min\left\{ \dfrac{f(y)q(y, x)}{f(x)q(x, y)}, 1 \right\}, & \text{if } f(x)q(x, y) \neq 0, \\ 0, & \text{otherwise.} \end{cases} \qquad (7.6)$$

The condition that $f(x)q(x, y) \neq 0$ is usually satisfied in practice because the starting value is always chosen in the support of the distribution and the kernel usually generates values in the support of the distribution. In some cases, however, it is convenient to generate values outside the support. As an example, draws from an untruncated proposal distribution are sometimes used to generate values from a truncated distribution because it is difficult to specify an appropriate truncated proposal density.

It is important to recognize that, in computing $\alpha(\cdot, \cdot)$, an unknown constant in the target distribution is not needed, because it cancels out via the fraction $f(y)/f(x)$.

To summarize in algorithmic form:

Algorithm 7.4: MH algorithm

7.1 Given x, generate Y from $q(x, y)$.
7.2 Generate U from $U(0, 1)$. If

$$U \leq \alpha(x, Y) = \min\left\{ \frac{f(Y)q(Y, x)}{f(x)q(x, Y)}, 1 \right\},$$

return Y. Otherwise, return x and go to 1.

Although we have shown that the MH kernel has the desired target distribution, this is only a necessary condition for convergence to the target. For Metropolis kernels, Tierney (1994, p. 1713) provides the following theorem.

Theorem 7.2 *Suppose P is a π-irreducible Metropolis kernel. Then P is Harris recurrent.*

The next implementation issue is how to choose the proposal density $q(\cdot, \cdot)$. In many cases, there are several possible choices, and which is best is often a matter of judgment. Several considerations enter into this decision. On the one hand, the kernel should generate proposals that have a reasonably good probability of acceptance; if not, the same value will be returned often, and the algorithm will mix poorly. On the other hand, there may be a high acceptance rate if the kernel generates only proposals that are close to the current point, but the sampling may then be confined to a small part of the support, again leading to poor mixing.

Two straightforward, but not necessarily good, kernels are the random-walk kernel and the independence kernel. For the former, the proposal y is generated from the current value x by the addition of a random variable or vector u, $y = x + u$, where the distribution of u is specified. If that distribution is symmetric around zero, that is, $h(u) = h(-u)$, the kernel has the property that $q(x, y) = q(y, x)$, which implies that $\alpha(x, y) = f(y)/f(x)$. Accordingly, with a random-walk kernel, a move from x to y is made for certain if $f(y) > f(x)$. A move from a higher density point to a lower density point is not ruled out, but the probability of such a move $f(x)/f(y)$ is less than one.

The independence kernel has the property $q(x, y) = q(y)$; that is, the proposal density is independent of the current state of the chain. For this type of kernel

$$\alpha(x, y) = \frac{f(y)/q(y)}{f(x)/q(x)},$$

and our comments about the probability of a move are similar to those about the random-walk chain if $f(\cdot)$ is replaced by $f(\cdot)/q(\cdot)$.

As a simple example of an independence chain, we generate data from a Beta(3, 4) distribution with $U(0, 1)$ as the proposal density. In algorithm form, we have the following.

Algorithm 7.5: MH for Beta(3, 4) with $U(0, 1)$ proposal

7.1 Set $x^{(0)}$ equal to a number between zero and one.
7.2 At the gth iteration, generate U_1 and U_2 from $U(0, 1)$.
7.3 If

$$U_1 \leq \alpha(x^{(g-1)}, U_2) = \frac{U_2^2(1 - U_2)^3}{(x^{(g-1)})^2(1 - x^{(g-1)})^3},$$

  set $x^{(g)} = U_2$. Otherwise set $x^{(g)} = x^{(g-1)}$.
7.4 Go to 2 and continue until the desired number of iterations is obtained.

Figure 7.1 displays results for 5,000 iterations after discarding the first 500; it indicates a good fit between the generated values, plotted as a histogram, and the true distribution, plotted as a solid line. The acceptance probability is 0.57, meaning that 57% of the proposals were accepted. The mean of the sample values is 0.4296, compared to the theoretical mean of $3/7 = 0.4286$.

We recommend a "tailored" kernel: construct a kernel that approximates the target distribution. This may be done by choosing a fat-tailed distribution, such as the multivariate t with small ν, whose mean and scale matrix are chosen to coincide with the mode and negative inverse of the second-derivative matrix at the mode, respectively. An example of a tailored kernel may be found in Section 9.2. If there is just one parameter block, the tailored kernel is an independence kernel. If there

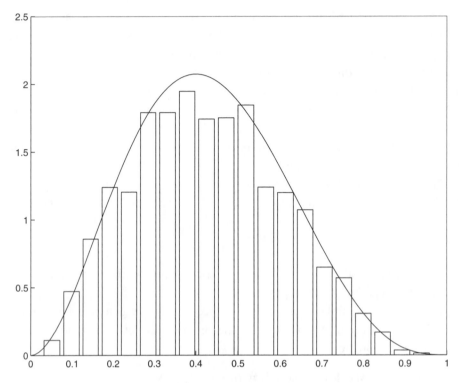

Figure 7.1. Simulation results for MH sampling of Beta(3, 4) with $U(0, 1)$ proposal.

is more than one block, the tailored kernel for the block being updated may depend on the current values of parameters in the other blocks.

Implementation of the MH algorithm is often facilitated by blocking, as in the Gibbs sampler. Blocking allows sampling for a few variables at a time, which may make it easier to find suitable proposal densities. Thus, if the target density $f(X_1, X_2)$ has two blocks, we can use the MH algorithm to generate from each block.

Algorithm 7.6: MH algorithm with two blocks

7.1 Let the state be (x_1, x_2) at the gth iteration and (y_1, y_2) at the $g + 1$st iteration. Draw

$$Z_1 \text{ from } q_1(x_1, Z_1|x_2) \text{ and } U_1 \text{ from } U(0, 1).$$

7.2 If

$$U_1 \leq \alpha(x_1, Z_1|x_2) = \frac{f(Z_1, x_2)q_1(Z_1, x_1|x_2)}{f(x_1, x_2)q_1(x_1, Z_1|x_2)},$$

return $y_1 = Z_1$. Otherwise return $y_1 = x_1$.

7.3 Draw

$$Z_2 \text{ from } q_2(x_2, Z_2|y_1) \text{ and } U_2 \text{ from } U(0, 1).$$

7.4 If

$$U_2 \leq \alpha(x_2, Z_2|y_1) = \frac{f(y_1, Z_2)q_2(Z_2, x_2|y_1)}{f(y_1, x_2)q_2(x_2, Z_2|y_1)},$$

return $y_2 = Z_2$. Otherwise return $y_2 = x_2$.

In this algorithm, the kernel $q_1(x_1, Y_1|x_2)$ is analogous to $q(x, Y)$; it generates a value Y_1 conditional on the current value x_1 in the same block and the current value x_2 in the other block. If "tailored" proposal densities are used, new densities are specified for $q_1(x_1, Z_1|x_2)$ and $q_2(x_2, Z_2|y_1)$ for each value of x_2 and y_1, respectively. This algorithm can be extended to an arbitrary number of blocks.

Having introduced blocks of parameters, we can show that the Gibbs sampler is a special case of the MH algorithm. Consider $\alpha(\cdot, \cdot)$ when the kernel for moving from the current value x_1 to the proposal value Y_1 is the conditional distribution $f(x_1|x_2)$, which is assumed to be available for sampling. Then

$$\alpha(x_1, Y_1|x_2) = \frac{f(Y_1, x_2)f(x_1|x_2)}{f(x_1, x_2)f(Y_1|x_2)},$$

but, since $f(Y_1|x_2) = f(Y_1, x_2)/f(x_2)$ and $f(x_1|x_2) = f(x_1, x_2)/f(x_2)$, it follows that $\alpha(x_1, Y_1|x_2) = 1$, showing that the Gibbs algorithm is an MH algorithm where the proposal is always accepted.

When implementing the MH algorithm to blocks of parameters, Gibbs sampling may be employed in any blocks for which the conditional distributions are available for sampling. In the remaining blocks, the MH algorithm may be employed in the usual way, that is, by finding suitable proposal densities and accepting with probability $\alpha(x, y)$. At each iteration, the algorithm works through the blocks, either moving to a new value or retaining the current value of the variables in the block. Examples of such algorithms appear in Part III.

7.2.2 Calculation of Marginal Likelihood

Chib and Jeliazkov (2001) have developed a modification of the Chib method for computing the marginal likelihood from MH output. We explain it for the one-block case; extensions may be found in their article. The method again starts with the identity

$$f(y) = \frac{\pi(y|\theta^*)\pi(\theta^*)}{\pi(\theta^*|y)},$$

where computing the denominator on the right-hand side is the biggest problem. From (7.5),

$$\alpha(\theta, \theta^*|y)q(\theta, \theta^*|y)\pi(\theta|y) = \alpha(\theta^*, \theta|y)q(\theta^*, \theta|y)\pi(\theta^*|y),$$

from which we find

$$\pi(\theta^*|y) = \frac{\int \alpha(\theta, \theta^*|y)q(\theta, \theta^*|y)\pi(\theta|y)\,d\theta}{\int \alpha(\theta^*, \theta|y)q(\theta^*, \theta|y)\,d\theta}.$$

The numerator of this expression can be estimated directly from the MH output $\theta^{(g)}$ as

$$\frac{1}{G}\sum_g \alpha(\theta^{(g)}, \theta^*|y)q(\theta^{(g)}, \theta^*|y),$$

and the denominator can be estimated by drawing $\theta^{(j)}$ from $q(\theta^*, \theta|y)$, $j = 1, \ldots, J$; that is, generate J values from the proposal density, all of which are conditioned on θ^*, and then compute

$$\frac{1}{J}\sum_j \alpha(\theta^*, \theta^{(j)}|y).$$

It is important for this computation that $\alpha(\theta^{(g)}, \theta^*|y)$ be computed from (7.6) as the minimum of 1 and the fraction in the curly braces.

7.3 Numerical Standard Errors and Convergence

The n.s.e. is defined in Section 5.6 as $\sqrt{\mathrm{Var}(Z)/G}$. For independent samples, the variance can be estimated as

$$\widehat{\mathrm{Var}}(Z) = \frac{1}{G-1}\sum(z^{(g)} - \bar{z})^2.$$

When the sample is not independent, as in the case of MCMC output, this expression is not valid. For nonindependent samples, the expectation of the sum of squared deviations from the mean includes covariance terms that must be taken into account, which the aforementioned expression fails to do. Several methods have been proposed to do this; we present the "batch means" method and refer to others in Section 7.4.

The logic behind the batch means method applied to MCMC output is that the autocorrelations of high-enough order tend to zero. By examining the empirical autocorrelations, we can determine a lag at which the autocorrelation is small enough that it can be neglected; a cutoff value of 0.05 is often adopted. Let j_0 be a lag length such that the absolute value of the autocorrelation at lag j_0 is less than 0.05. Then divide the sample of G observations into $G/j_0 = N$ groups or batches, adjusting j_0 or G if necessary to get an integer value for N. Compute the mean of the simulated output in batch b, $b = 1, \ldots, N$, and then estimate the variance by

$$\widehat{\text{Var}}(\bar{Z}_b) = \frac{1}{N-1} \sum_{b=1}^{N} (\bar{Z}_b - \bar{Z})^2,$$

where $\bar{Z}_b$ is the mean of batch b and $\bar{Z}$ is the overall mean. The n.s.e. is then computed as $\sqrt{\widehat{\text{Var}}(\bar{Z}_b)/N}$.

Since positive autocorrelation leads to a larger variance than would be obtained with independent samples, several measures have been proposed to compare the variances as an indication of the cost of being forced to work with correlated samples. One is the *relative numerical efficiency* (r.n.e.), defined as

$$\text{r.n.e.} = \sqrt{\frac{\sum_g (Z^{(g)} - \bar{Z})^2}{G} \bigg/ \frac{\widehat{\text{Var}}(\bar{Z}_b)}{N}}.$$

Small values indicate substantial autocorrelation in the chain. The *inefficiency factor* or *autocorrelation time* is defined as the reciprocal of the r.n.e. Large values of the inefficiency factor indicate the cost of working with correlated samples.

Knowing when an MCMC chain has converged is, at this writing, as much an art as a science. Although there are a few indicators of nonconvergence, there are no widely applicable theorems to compute the length of the burn-in period. Several indicators have been proposed, many of which are concerned with attempting to measure the amount of mixing that is taking place as the sampler runs. The justification is that a well-mixing sampler is likely to provide a good approximation to the target distribution. Although this justification may not work in all cases, in practice it seems adequate. A measure of the degree of mixing is the autocorrelation function, which is the estimated autocorrelation of the series at various lags. If the algorithm is mixing well, we would expect that the autocorrelation would drop off to zero within a few lags; in contrast, a poorly mixing algorithm may have substantial correlation at very large lags.

As an example, consider the bivariate normal sampling problem of Section 7.1. Figure 7.3 presents autocorrelations. As we saw previously, there is extremely poor mixing when $\rho = 0.999$. The autocorrelations for these cases show this clearly: they are over 0.900 even at lag 20. In contrast, the absolute values of the autocorrelations for the $\rho = 0.50$ case are less than 0.05 at lag 3.

7.4 Further Reading and References

Chapter 7 Robert and Casella (2004) presents the material covered in this chapter at a reasonable level. An advanced book, used as the source for much of the

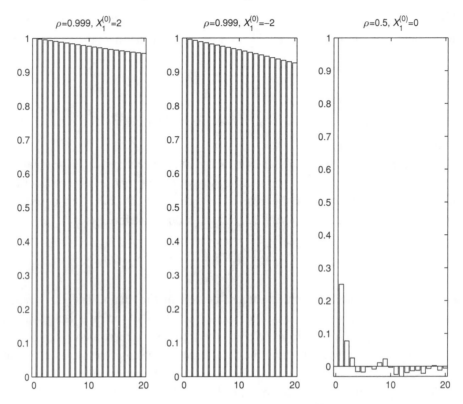

Figure 7.2. Autocorrelations of $X^{(g)}$.

research in this area, is Nummelin (1984). It is heavy going, and the pertinent material is scattered throughout the book. An excellent book that covers much of the same material is Meyn and Tweedie (1993). It takes up many applications of the theory and is somewhat difficult, but well worth the effort for those who wish to go more deeply into these topics. Two summary articles for MCMC methods in econometrics are Chib (2001) and Geweke and Keane (2001); the former's approach is closer to the one taken in this book.

Section 7.1 The Poisson model with an unknown switch point is analyzed from the Bayesian viewpoint in Carlin et al. (1992a); they consider prior distributions more general than those we have specified and take up more complex versions of the model, including multiple switch points and the hidden Markov switch point model. An alternative approach to computations for the latter is presented in Chib (1998).

If there are at least two blocks of parameters, say (θ_1, θ_2), and we are interested in estimating the marginal density function of one of the blocks, say $\pi(\theta_2|y)$, it is sometimes preferable to compute it by averaging $\pi(\theta_2|\theta_1, y)$, which is known when a Gibbs algorithm is employed, over the realizations of θ_1 than to kernel-smooth the realizations of θ_2. A good discussion of this idea, called *Rao–Blackwellizing*, can be found in Lancaster (2004, sec. 4.4.5–4.4.6).

Chib (1995) shows how to compute the marginal likelihood from the Gibbs output.

Section 7.2 The MH algorithm first appears in Metropolis et al. (1953), but in a nonstatistical application. Hastings (1970) applies the method to statistical problems, and Gelfand and Smith (1990) show its power for Bayesian inference. An expository article about the MH algorithm is Chib and Greenberg (1995b), and Chib and Jeliazkov (2001) contains the modification of Chib's method for MH chains and applications of the method to multiple blocks. Hitchcock (2003) presents a brief history of the MH algorithm. Tierney (1994) is an important contribution to the theory of MH algorithms. Tailored proposal densities are proposed and explained in Chib and Greenberg (1994).

An interesting MH algorithm, called ARMH, uses an AR step to generate candidates for an MH algorithm. It is described in Tierney (1994, p. 1707) and Chib and Greenberg (1995b, sec. 6.1). A method for computing the marginal likelihood for data generated by the ARMH algorithm is presented in Chib and Jeliazkov (2005).

Section 7.3 The numerical standard error is proposed in Geweke (1989), and the inefficiency factor is used by Chib (2001). Details about estimating the autocovariance function may be found in Geyer (1992), Ripley (1987, chap. 6), and Priestley (1981, chaps. 5–7). The latter is particularly strong on window estimation and spectral methods. Ripley discusses the batch means method.

Robert and Casella (2004, chap. 12) is a clear and thorough discussion of convergence issues, and it contains many further references. Programs to compute convergence diagnostics for MCMC simulations are contained in coda at its Web site, http://www-fis.iarc.fr/coda/.

7.5 Exercises

7.1 Verify (7.1) and (7.2).

7.2 Download the data in "Birth weight I," from the StatLabs Web site, www.stat.berkeley.edu/users/statlabs/labs.html. Specify a prior distribution for the average birth weight and the variance of birth weights, and then implement Algorithm 7.3 to generate a sample from the joint distribution. Compute the n.s.e. for your output. (It would be good practice to program this algorithm yourself; otherwise the calculations can be done in BACC or one of the other packages discussed in Appendix B.)

7.3 Construct a Gibbs algorithm to analyze the Poisson model with unknown switch point. Given the specification in Equations (7.3) and (7.4), show that

$$\pi(\theta_1, \theta_2, k | y) \propto \theta_1^{\alpha_{10}-1} e^{-\beta_{10}\theta_1} \theta_2^{\alpha_{20}-1} e^{-\beta_{20}\theta_2} \prod_{i=1}^{k} e^{-\theta_1} \theta_1^{y_i} \prod_{i=k+1}^{n} e^{-\theta_2} \theta_2^{y_i},$$

and verify that

$$\theta_1 | y, k \sim G\left(\alpha_{10} + \sum_{1}^{k} y_i, \beta_{10} + k\right),$$

$$\theta_2 | k, y \sim G\left(\alpha_{20} + \sum_{k+1}^{n} y_i, \beta_{20} + n - k\right),$$

$$\pi(k | y, \theta_1, \theta_2) = \frac{e^{k(\theta_2 - \theta_1)}(\theta_1/\theta_2)^{\sum_1^k y_i}}{\sum_{k=1}^{n} e^{k(\theta_2 - \theta_1)}(\theta_1/\theta_2)^{\sum_1^k y_i}}, \quad k = 1, \dots, n.$$

Apply your algorithm to the mining disaster data analyzed by Carlin et al. (1992a); the data may be found in the article. Your analysis should generate marginal posterior distributions for θ_1, θ_2, $p(k)$, and the marginal likelihood computed by the method of Chib (1995). For simplicity, set $\alpha_{10} = \alpha_{20} = 0.5$ and $\beta_{10} = \beta_{20} = 1.0$. (Curiously, although these data have been analyzed from the Bayesian viewpoint in several papers, none of them present historical material that might shed light on when changes in parameters took place. For example, changes in government regulation, technology, or the location of mines might be expected to affect the probability of a disaster. A more general version of the model permits multiple switch points if necessary.)

7.4 Derive $\alpha(x, y)$ for Algorithm 7.5.

7.5 Construct a random walk MH sampler to generate a sample of 10,000 from the Laplace distribution, $f(x) = (1/2) e^{-|x|}$, $-\infty < x < \infty$. Use $u \sim N(0, \sigma^2)$ to generate proposals $y = x^{(g-1)} + u$. Compare the mean, variances, and autocorrelations of the generated series for various values of σ^2.

7.6 Estimate the mean of a Beta(3.7, 4.8) distribution with (1) an AR algorithm and a Beta(4, 5) proposal density (you will need to determine the value of c needed in Algorithm 5.2); (2) an MH algorithm with a Beta(4, 5) proposal density. After the break-in sample, graph the values of the mean against the iteration number to monitor convergence. Compare your answers to the true value.

7.7 Consider the model

$$y_i = \beta x_i + u_i, \quad u_i \sim N(0, 1), \quad i = 1, \dots, n,$$

with the gamma prior distribution $\beta \sim G(2, 1)$, $\beta > 0$. Verify the posterior distribution

$$\pi(\beta | y) \propto \beta \exp[-\beta] \exp\left[-\frac{1}{2} \sum_{i=1}^{n}(y_i - \beta x_i)^2\right] 1(\beta > 0).$$

Note that this distribution does not have a standard form. Construct an MH algorithm to sample from this distribution with an independence kernel, where the kernel is a

Student-*t* distribution truncated to the region $(0, \infty)$, with five degrees of freedom, mean equal to the value of β that maximizes the posterior distribution $(\hat{\beta})$, and scale factor equal to the negative inverse of the second derivative of the log posterior distribution evaluated at $\hat{\beta}$. Verify that

$$\hat{\beta} = \frac{\left(\sum x_i y_i - 1\right) + \sqrt{\left(\sum x_i y_i - 1\right)^2 + 4 \sum x_i^2}}{2 \sum x_i^2}$$

and that the scale factor is $(1/\hat{\beta}^2 + \sum x_i^2)^{-1}$. Generate a data set by choosing $n = 50$, x_i from $N(0, 1)$, and a value of β from its prior distribution. Write a program to implement your algorithm and see how well β is determined. You may try larger values of n to explore the effect of sample size, and, depending on the acceptance rate, you may wish to change the scale factor.

7.8 Generalize Exercise 7.7 to allow for an unknown variance, $u_i \sim N(0, \sigma^2)$, with prior distribution $\sigma^2 \sim IG(5/2, 3/2)$. Verify that $\sigma^2 | y, \beta$ has an inverse gamma distribution, but that the distribution of $\beta | y, \sigma^2$ is not standard. Devise a two-block algorithm in which $\sigma^2 | y, \beta$ is generated in a Gibbs step and β is generated by a tailored kernel where $\hat{\beta}$ depends on σ^2, so that the mean and scale factor of the truncated Student-*t* distribution must be recomputed at each step. Choose a value of σ^2 from its prior distribution, and generate and analyze a data set as in Exercise 7.7.

Part III

Applications

Chapter 8

Linear Regression and Extensions

THE FIRST PART of this chapter concludes the discussion of the normal linear regression model with the conditionally conjugate prior presented in Sections 4.1 and 4.9. This is a model for continuous, unrestricted data. The second part of the chapter takes up several models in which y is restricted, but the linear regression framework can be used by the device of introducing latent data.

8.1 Continuous Dependent Variables

This section presents an MCMC algorithm for the linear regression model with Gaussian errors and continues with a discussion of the model with Student-t errors.

8.1.1 Normally Distributed Errors

In the model of Section 4.9, the observed data $y = (y_1, \ldots, y_n)'$ have the distribution

$$y \sim N_n(X\beta, \sigma^2 I_n),$$

with prior distributions

$$\beta \sim N_K(\beta_0, B_0) \quad \text{and} \quad \sigma^2 \sim \text{IG}(\alpha_0/2, \delta_0/2). \tag{8.1}$$

As a consequence of these assumptions, we find that

$$\beta | \sigma^2, y \sim N_K(\bar{\beta}, B_1), \tag{8.2}$$

where

$$B_1 = \left[\sigma^{-2} X'X + B_0^{-1} \right]^{-1},$$
$$\bar{\beta} = B_1 \left[\sigma^{-2} X'y + B_0^{-1} \beta_0 \right],$$

111

and that

$$\sigma^2 | \beta, y \sim \mathrm{IG}(\alpha_1/2, \delta_1/2), \tag{8.3}$$

where

$$\alpha_1 = \alpha_0 + n,$$
$$\delta_1 = \delta_0 + (y - X\beta)'(y - X\beta).$$

Since both conditional posterior distributions are standard, the Gibbs sampler may be applied to find the posterior distribution of (β, σ^2). The elements of β are sampled in one block, which is desirable because of the possibility of high correlations between them, and experience has shown that β and σ^2 tend to be relatively uncorrelated. In algorithmic form,

Algorithm 8.1: Gibbs algorithm for normal linear regression model

8.1 Choose a starting value $\sigma^{2(0)}$.

8.2 At the gth iteration, draw

$$\beta^{(g)} \sim N_K\left(\bar{\beta}^{(g)}, B_1^{(g)}\right)$$
$$\sigma^{2(g)} \sim \mathrm{IG}\left(\alpha_1/2, \delta^{(g)}/2\right),$$

where

$$B_1^{(g)} = \left[\sigma^{-2(g-1)} X'X + B_0^{-1}\right]^{-1},$$
$$\bar{\beta}^{(g)} = B_1^{(g)} \left[\sigma^{-2(g-1)} X'y + B_0^{-1}\beta_0\right],$$
$$\delta^{(g)} = \delta_0 + \left(y - X\beta^{(g)}\right)'\left(y - X\beta^{(g)}\right).$$

8.3 Go to 2 until $g = B + G$, where B is the burn-in sample and G is the desired sample size.

The values of $\beta^{(g)}$ and $\sigma^{2(g)}$, $g = B + 1, \ldots, B + G$, produced by the algorithm are an approximation to the posterior distribution of β and σ^2, respectively. The kth row of $\beta^{(g)}$ is a drawing from the marginal posterior density of β_k. The drawings may be graphed as histograms or smoothed histograms to provide a picture of the marginal density, and their moments and quantiles may be computed to estimate the corresponding distribution values.

As an example we return to the Vella–Verbeek data discussed in Section 4.4. For the reasons discussed there, we set $\alpha_0 = 6$, $\delta_0 = 0.40$, $\beta_{U0} = 0.10$, $\beta_{k0} = 0$ for the coefficients of variables other than the union membership indicator, $B_{UU,0} = 0.0036$, and $B_{kk,0} = 1$ for the variances of the β_k other than the union membership indicator. We employed the BACC "nlm" procedure (see Appendix B) to generate 1000 burn-in observations and a sample of 10,000.

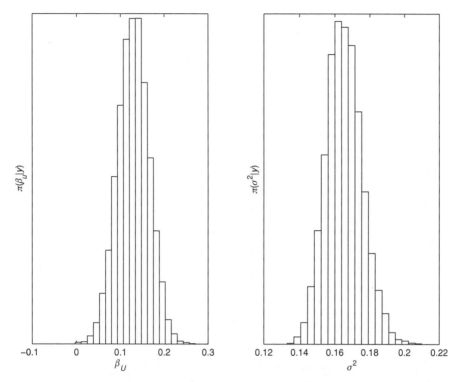

Figure 8.1. Posterior distributions of β_U and σ^2, Gaussian errors.

The results for β_U and σ^2 are graphed in Figure 8.1. The mean and standard deviation of β_U are 0.129 and 0.036, respectively, and the mean and standard deviation of σ^2 are 0.165 and 0.010. A 95% credibility interval for β_U is $(0.059, 0.198)$; this interval reinforces the impression from the graph that β_U is very likely to be positive, but not larger than 2. The n.s.e. for β_U, computed by the batch means method (100 batches of 100 observations), is 3.666×10^{-4}. This is close to the value reported by BACC, which uses a different method. Figure 8.2 presents the autocorrelations of the sample values of β_U and σ^2 as convergence diagnostics. Note that the autocorrelations for both drop off very quickly, an indication that convergence has taken place. From an r.n.e. of 0.931 and an inefficiency factor of 1.074, we see that the penalty for working with a nonindependent sample is small because of the low autocorrelations.

BACC reports a $\log_{10}$ marginal likelihood of -152.78. To illustrate the use of the Bayes factor, we specify a model in which β_U is set to zero; that is, a model in which being a union member has no effect on log(wages). The $\log_{10}$ marginal likelihood for this model is -158.17 with an n.s.e. of 0.030. The $\log_{10}$ Bayes factor in favor of the original model is 5.390, which is strong evidence that union membership is important in determining wages.

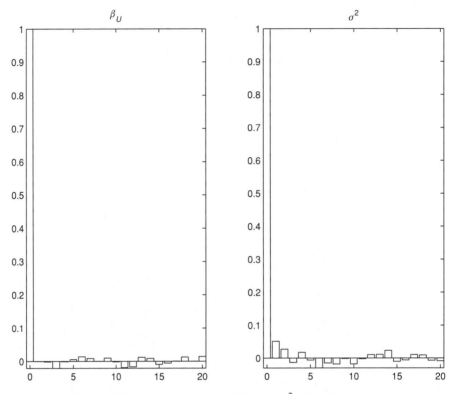

Figure 8.2. Autocorrelations of β_U and σ^2, Gaussian errors.

8.1.2 Student-t Distributed Errors

As explained in Section 4.5, we can modify the assumption made about the error term to obtain conditionally heteroskedastic errors, a model equivalent to assuming that the errors are marginally distributed as Student-t with a specified number of degrees of freedom. For this model, we assume

$$f(y_i|\beta, \sigma^2, \lambda_i) = N\left(x_i'\beta, \lambda_i^{-1}\sigma^2\right), \quad \lambda_i \sim G(\nu/2, \nu/2), \quad \nu \text{ known.} \quad (8.4)$$

Prior distributions for β and σ^2 are those of Equation (8.1). In contrast to Equation (4.13), we are here assuming that ν is known.

With this specification we develop a Gibbs algorithm to generate a sample from the joint distribution $(\beta, \sigma^2, \lambda)$, where $\lambda = (\lambda_1, \dots, \lambda_n)$. We include the λ_i in the sampler to make it possible to simulate β and σ^2 from standard distributions. After the sample is generated, we marginalize over the λ_i by reporting only the posterior distributions of β and σ^2. In Exercise 8.2 you are asked to verify that the direct way of specifying this model does not permit the use of the Gibbs algorithm and that a Student-t prior for β does not yield conditional distributions that permit a Gibbs algorithm.

As usual, we start with the product of the likelihood and prior distribution,

$$\pi(\beta, \sigma^2, \lambda | y) \propto \pi(\beta)\pi(\sigma^2) \left[\prod_{i}^{n} \lambda_i^{\nu/2-1} \exp\left[-\frac{\nu\lambda_i}{2}\right] \left(\frac{\lambda_i}{\sigma^2}\right)^{1/2} \right]$$

$$\times \exp\left[-\sum_{i} \frac{\lambda_i}{2\sigma^2}(y_i - x_i'\beta)^2\right].$$

To develop the algorithm, first verify that

$$\sum_{i} \frac{\lambda_i}{2\sigma^2}(y_i - x_i'\beta)^2 = \frac{1}{2\sigma^2}(y - X\beta)'\Lambda(y - X\beta),$$

where $\Lambda = \text{diagonal}(\lambda_i)$. It follows that

$$\beta | y, \lambda, \sigma^2 \sim N_K(\bar{\beta}, B_1),$$
$$\sigma^2 | y, \beta, \lambda \sim \text{IG}(\alpha_1/2, \delta_1/2),$$
$$\lambda_i | y, \beta, \sigma^2 \sim G(\nu_1/2, \nu_{2i}/2), \quad i = 1, \ldots, n,$$

where

$$B_1 = \left(\sigma^{-2}X'\Lambda X + B_0^{-1}\right)^{-1},$$
$$\bar{\beta} = B_1\left(\sigma^{-2}X'\Lambda y + B_0^{-1}\beta_0\right),$$
$$\alpha_1 = \alpha_0 + n,$$
$$\delta_1 = \delta_0 + (y - X\beta)'\Lambda(y - X\beta),$$
$$\nu_1 = \nu + 1,$$
$$\nu_{2i} = \nu + \sigma^{-2}(y_i - x_i'\beta)^2.$$

This algorithm was run on the Vella–Verbeek data with $\nu = 5$, a specification that allows for much heavier tails in the likelihood than those of the Gaussian distribution. Results are graphed in Figure 8.3. The mean of β_U is 0.128, with a standard deviation of 0.033, and a 95% credibility interval is $(0.062, 0.192)$; these are close to those obtained for the Gaussian errors. The n.s.e. (batch means method) is 3.730×10^{-4} yielding an r.n.e. of 0.785 and an inefficiency factor of 1.274. Figure 8.4 shows that the autocorrelations drop off rather quickly, but the autocorrelation at lag 1 is considerably larger than for the Gaussian model. The larger n.s.e. obtained in this case arises because the sampling for λ_i introduces additional correlation. The posterior distribution of σ^2 has a mean of 0.105 and a standard deviation of 0.008.

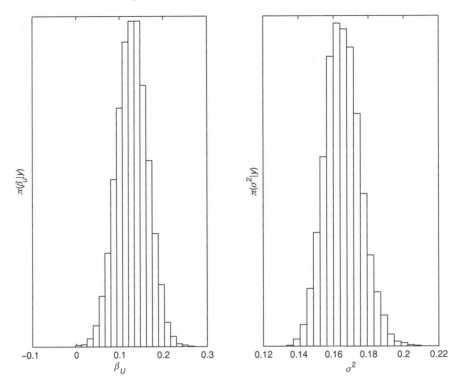

Figure 8.3. Posterior distributions of β_U and σ^2, Student-t errors.

The Chib method for computing the marginal likelihood for this problem is based on the identity

$$f(y) = \frac{\prod f(y_i|\beta^*, \sigma^{2*})\pi(\beta^*)\pi(\sigma^{2*})}{\pi(\beta^*, \sigma^{2*}|y)},$$

where $f(y_i|\beta^*, \sigma^{2*})$ is Student-t with mean $x_i'\beta^*$, scale parameter σ^{2*}, and ν degrees of freedom. Note that the right-hand side of this expression does not involve the latent λ_i; these have been marginalized out to obtain a Student-t distribution for y. The gth draw from the posterior distribution in the denominator utilizes reduced run samples from $\sigma^2|\beta^*, \lambda^{(g-1)}, y$, which is distributed as $IG(\alpha_1/2, \delta_1^{(g-1)}/2)$, where

$$\delta_1^{(g-1)} = \delta_0 + (y - X\beta^*)'\Lambda^{(g-1)}(y - X\beta^*),$$

and from $\lambda_i|\beta^*, \sigma^{2(g)}, y$, which is distributed as $G(\nu_1/2, \nu_{2i}^{(g)}/2)$, where

$$\nu_{2i}^{(g)} = \nu + \sigma^{-2(g)}\left(y_i - x_i'\beta^*\right)^2.$$

For the Vella–Verbeek data, the Student-t model has a $\log_{10}$ marginal likelihood of -147.95. The resulting Bayes factor in favor of the Student-t model is 4.83, a strong evidence in its favor.

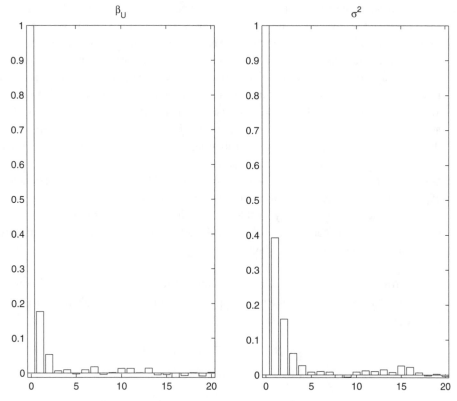

Figure 8.4. Autocorrelations of β_U and σ^2, Student-t errors.

8.2 Limited Dependent Variables

This section takes up several models that have the usual normal linear regression form,

$$y_i^* = x_i'\beta + u_i, \quad u_i \sim N(0, \sigma^2), \tag{8.5}$$

but some or all of the y_i^*, the *latent data*, are not observed. The ways in which the observed y_i depend on the latent data give rise to several models. We consider the Tobit and the binary choice models in the remainder of this chapter and show that the extension to Student-t errors is straightforward.

8.2.1 *Tobit Model for Censored Data*

Censored data are data for which values of y in a given range are reported as a single value; we use the censored regression model, often called the *Tobit model*, for such data. There are two primary examples of this type of data.

8.1 *Top coded data*: the values of y_i are reported when $y_i \leq Y$; the value Y is reported for observation i if $y_i > Y$. This case arises as a result of the sampling scheme. An example is income data, where incomes over some value, say $200,000, are reported as $200,000. The observations in this case are a mixture of data that are modeled continuously for $y_i \leq Y$ and of a mass of probability at the point Y. In this model, it is assumed that the covariate vector x_i is observed for all i. Data sets in which neither y_i nor x_i are observed when $y_i > Y$ are called *truncated data*. A third type of data structure, *incidentally truncated* data, is discussed in Section 11.3. In that setup, y_i and the selection variable s_i have a joint distribution, y_i is observed only when $s_i > 0$, and at least some of the x_i are observed for all i.

8.2 *Corner solution outcomes*: the values of y_i are bounded by a constraint. As examples, expenditures on durable goods are nonnegative, and the demand for tickets at a ball game is limited by the capacity of the stadium. In the former case, a large number of households report zero expenditures on durable goods; in the latter, the capacity attendance is reported on sellout days.

In what follows we discuss data with a lower limit at zero; the modifications for an upper constraint or for lower and upper constraints are straightforward. The model is written as

$$y_i = \begin{cases} x_i'\beta + u_i, & \text{if } x_i'\beta + u_i > 0, \\ 0, & \text{otherwise,} \end{cases}$$

where $u_i \sim N(0, \sigma^2)$ and $i = 1, \ldots, n$. The model can be written as $y_i = y_i^* 1(x_i'\beta + u_i > 0)$ or as $y_i = \max(0, x_i'\beta + u_i)$. Let the set of observations for which $y_i = 0$ be denoted by $C = \{i : y_i = 0\}$. The likelihood function is

$$f(y|\beta, \sigma^2) = \prod_{i \in C} \Phi(-x_i'\beta/\sigma) \prod_{i \in C^c} \phi([y_i - x_i'\beta]/\sigma),$$

where $\phi(\cdot)$ and $\Phi(\cdot)$ are the p.d.f. and d.f., respectively, of the standard normal distribution. Since the model is very similar to the linear regression model, the normal prior for β and inverse gamma prior for σ^2 can be justified for the reasons discussed before. With these assumptions about the priors and likelihood function, you should verify that the form of the posterior distribution is very complex. But there is a way to specify the likelihood function that greatly simplifies the problem of designing an algorithm.

To do so, the latent data are included in the sampler as in Chib (1992). These are denoted by y_{Ci}^* and are defined only for $i \in C$. We also define the scalars

$$y_i^* = \begin{cases} y_{Ci}^*, & \text{if } i \in C, \\ y_i, & \text{if } i \in C^c, \end{cases}$$

and the vectors y_C^*, which contains the y_{Ci}, and $y^* = (y_1^*, \ldots, y_n^*)'$. The likelihood contribution of the ith observation is

$$f(y_i|\beta, \sigma^2, y_{Ci}^*) = 1(y_i = 0)1(y_{Ci}^* \leq 0) + 1(y_i > 0)N(y_i|x_i'\beta, \sigma^2),$$

where $N(\cdot|\mu, \sigma^2)$ is the density function of the $N(\mu, \sigma^2)$ distribution. The joint prior for the parameters and y_C^* is

$$\pi(\beta, \sigma^2, y_C^*) = \pi(y_C^*|\beta, \sigma^2)\pi(\beta)\pi(\sigma^2),$$

where

$$\pi(y_C^*|\beta, \sigma^2) = \prod_{i \in C} N(y_{Ci}^*|x_i'\beta, \sigma^2).$$

The prior distributions for β and σ^2 are the usual conditionally conjugate priors, $\beta \sim N(\beta_0, B_0)$ and $\sigma^2 \sim \text{IG}(\alpha_0/2, \delta_0/2)$.

We can now write the posterior distribution,

$$\pi(\beta, \sigma^2, y_C^*|y) = \prod_i^n [1(y_i = 0)1(y_{Ci}^* \leq 0) + 1(y_i > 0)N(y_i|x_i'\beta, \sigma^2)]$$

$$\times \pi(y_C^*|\beta, \sigma^2)\pi(\beta)\pi(\sigma^2)$$

$$= \prod_i^n [1(y_i = 0)1(y_{Ci}^* \leq 0) + 1(y_i > 0)]N(y_i^*|x_i'\beta, \sigma^2)$$

$$\times \pi(\beta)\pi(\sigma^2)$$

$$\propto \prod_i^n [1(y_i = 0)1(y_{Ci}^* \leq 0) + 1(y_i > 0)]$$

$$\times \left(\frac{1}{\sigma^2}\right)^{n/2} \exp\left[-\frac{1}{2\sigma^2}(y^* - X\beta)'(y^* - X\beta)\right]$$

$$\times \exp\left[-\frac{1}{2}(\beta - \beta_0)'B_0^{-1}(\beta - \beta_0)\right] \left(\frac{1}{\sigma^2}\right)^{\alpha_0/2-1} \exp\left[-\frac{\delta_0}{2\sigma^2}\right],$$

$$(8.6)$$

since $\pi(y_{Ci}^*|\beta, \sigma^2) = N(y_i^*|x_i'\beta, \sigma^2)$. The posterior distribution for the parameters of interest, β and σ^2, can be recovered by integrating out y_C^*. This is done by ignoring their draws.

From (8.6), we can derive the full conditional distributions. For β and σ^2, these are (8.2) and (8.3), respectively, with y^* in place of y. Note that β and σ^2 are independent of the observations y, given y^*. To complete the Gibbs sampler we need $\pi(y_C^*|\beta, \sigma^2)$. From (8.6) we see that y_{Ci}^* is $N(x_i'\beta, \sigma^2)$ truncated to the range $(-\infty, 0]$. (See Section A.1.13.) Sampling from this distribution is easily accomplished with the result in (5.1).

In algorithmic form,

Algorithm 8.2: Tobit model

At the gth step,

8.1 Draw $\beta^{(g)}$ from $N_K(\bar{\beta}^{(g)}, B_1^{(g)})$, where

$$B_1^{(g)} = \left[\sigma^{-2(g-1)}X'X + B_0^{-1}\right]^{-1},$$
$$\bar{\beta}^{(g)} = B_1^{(g)}\left[\sigma^{-2(g-1)}X'y^{*(g-1)} + B_0^{-1}\beta_0\right].$$

8.2 Draw $\sigma^{2(g)}$ from $\mathrm{IG}(\alpha_1/2, \delta_1^{(g)}/2)$, where

$$\alpha_1 = \alpha_0 + n,$$
$$\delta_1^{(g)} = \delta_0 + \left(y^{*(g-1)} - X\beta^{(g)}\right)'\left(y^{*(g-1)} - X\beta^{(g)}\right).$$

8.3 Draw $y_i^{*(g)}$ for $i \in C$ from $\mathrm{TN}_{(-\infty,0]}(x_i'\beta^{(g)}, \sigma^{2(g)})$.

The Student-t version of this model is specified by assuming $y_i = y_i^* 1(y_i^* > 0)$, $y_i^* \sim N(x_i'\beta, \lambda_i^{-1}\sigma^2)$, and $\lambda_i \sim G(\nu/2, \nu/2)$. As mentioned before, ν may be specified or a hierarchical setup may be employed. With the usual priors on β and σ^2, Algorithm 8.2 is easily modified to handle this case.

As an example, we analyze the Mroz (1987) data set, which consists of data for 753 married women from the University of Michigan Panel Study of Income Dynamics. The response variable is hours worked in the year 1975, and 428 reported nonzero hours worked. A Tobit model is desirable because of the large number of women who worked zero hours. The original study is concerned with important issues of endogeneity and sample selection, but these are neglected here to provide a simple example. We return to these data in Section 11.3 as an example of a model that accounts for sample selection. In addition to the constant, the covariates are a dummy variable for children less than 6 years old at home (childl6), a dummy variable for children 6 years old or more (childge6), the woman's age (age), and the husband's hourly wage (huswage).

We next specify the prior distributions. First, β_1 is hours worked for someone with no children and huswage of zero, if age is neglected. On the assumption that such a person works virtually full time, the prior mean of β_1 is set to 2,000, and a rather large standard deviation of 400 is assumed. Since having young children present is likely to reduce hours, we set $\beta_{02} = -500$, with a variance of 2,000 to reflect considerable uncertainty. The presence of older children also reduces hours, but not as much; accordingly, we set $\beta_{03} = -300$, with a variance of 2,000. For the effect of age, consider a person with no children present as she ages from 50 to 60. We assume this results in reduction of 500 hours, implying $\beta_{04} = -50$, and

Table 8.1. *Summary of Posterior Distribution: Tobit Model, Mroz Data.*

Coefficient	Mean	S.D.	n.s.e.	Lower	Upper
β_1	2,079.264	116.237	1.321	1,846.449	2,303.242
β_2	−556.363	41.093	0.456	−637.937	−477.806
β_3	−191.708	28.894	0.331	−248.486	−136.099
β_4	−27.159	3.338	0.041	−33.630	−20.588
β_5	−29.732	11.825	0.151	−53.298	−6.642
σ	1,293.170	47.017	0.823	1,205.395	1,389.020

set a large variance of 2,000. Finally, consider a husband's wage increasing from $5 to $10 per hour. We assume this change reduces labor input by 500 hours, so that $\beta_{05} = -50$. The variance is again set at 2,000 to reflect uncertainty. For σ^2 we assume a standard deviation of 1,200 yielding $E(\sigma^2) = 1,400,000$, and $\text{Var}(\sigma^2) = 100,000$. Since the parameters are $\alpha/2$ and $\beta/2$, the result in (A.2) is modified to $\alpha = 2[E(\sigma^2)]^2/\text{Var}(\sigma^2)$ and $\delta = 2E(\sigma^2)/\text{Var}(\sigma^2)$. Given the aforementioned numbers, we have $\alpha = 39,200,000$ and $\delta = 28$.

Results are in Table 8.1 and Figure 8.5. Coefficient means are consistent with our expectations, and their distributions seem relatively symmetric. Note that none of the 95% credibility bounds include zero, which suggests that all of the covariates contribute to the explanation of the response variable. The autocorrelations, which are not reported, drop off quickly, indicating that the chain converged.

It is instructive to examine the predictive distribution implied by the Tobit model for these data. We generate y^* for two sets of covariates: $x'_{l6} = (1, 1, 0, 40, 7.5)$ and $x'_{g6} = (1, 0, 1, 40, 7.5)$. The first describes a 40-year-old woman with children under 6 years of age present and no children 6 years old or older, whose husband earns $7.50 hourly. The second has children 6 or more years of age present, with the same age and husband's wage as the first. The predictive distribution, given the first set of covariates, is found by generating G observations, with the gth drawn from

$$y_{l6}^{*(g)} \sim N\left(x'_{l6}\beta^{(g)}, \sigma^{2(g)}\right), \quad g = 1, \ldots, G,$$

and the predictive distribution for the second set is found analogously. The hours worked for i is set to zero if negative values of $y_{l6}^{*(g)}$ or $y_{g6}^{*(g)}$ are generated. The results are summarized in Figure 8.6. The probability of working zero hours for women with younger children is estimated to be 0.431 compared to 0.328 for women with older children. (Note that zero hours are combined with small numbers of hours in the histograms.) The overall average hours worked is about 214 for women with small children and about 587 for women with older children, a difference approximately equal to $\bar{\beta}_2 - \bar{\beta}_3$. If we condition on working positive hours, the

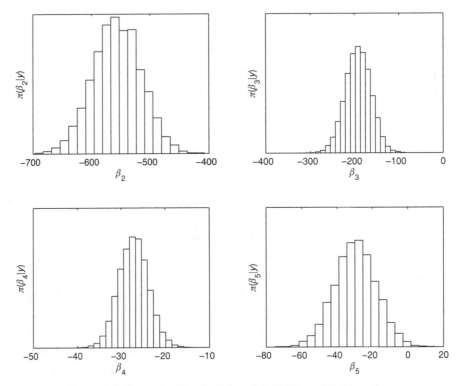

Figure 8.5. Posterior distributions of β: Tobit model, Mroz data.

mean is about 1,284 h for women with small children and 1,105 for women with older children. In summary, having older rather than younger children increases the probability of working positive hours by about 0.100, and, for those who work, the average number of hours is increased by about 180 h.

8.2.2 Binary Probit Model

The binary probit model is designed to deal with situations in which y_i can take one of two values, coded as 0 and 1. For example, if y denotes union membership, let $y_i = 0$ if person i does not belong to a union and $y_i = 1$ if he or she does. Or y_i could denote a choice of one of the parties in a two-party election. Finally, y_i might equal 1 if subject i receives a treatment and 0 if not. Since y has the character of a Bernoulli variable, we model its probability mass function, $p(y)$, rather than y itself.

There is an interesting relationship between the linear regression model and a model for binary data. The linear regression model assumes $E(y_i) = x_i'\beta$. This assumption can be generalized to what statisticians call the *generalized linear model* (GLM) by specifying $E(y_i) = G(x_i'\beta)$, where $G(\cdot)$ is called the *link function*

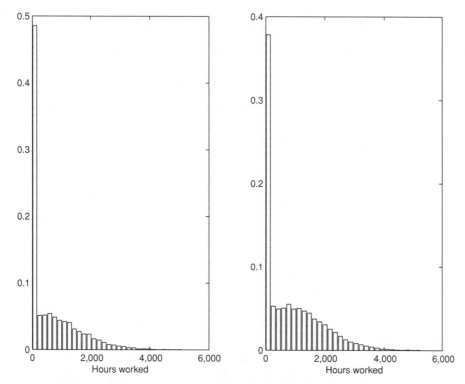

Figure 8.6. Predictive distributions of hours worked: Tobit model, Mroz data. Left: women with young children; right: women with older children.

and is chosen to reflect the nature of the data being modeled. The linear regression model for continuous data is the special case in which $G(\cdot)$ is the identity function; that is, $G(x'_i\beta) = x'_i\beta$. When y is a binary variable, $E(y) = P(y = 1)$. In this case, the identity link function is not suitable for the binary probit model, because $x'_i\beta$ is not restricted to the $(0, 1)$ interval required for a probability.

A convenient way to restrict $0 \leq G(x'_i\beta) \leq 1$ is to choose $G(\cdot)$ to be a distribution function. The binary probit version of this model assumes

$$P(y_i = 1) = \Phi(x'_i\beta), \tag{8.7}$$

where $\Phi(z)$, the link function, is the d.f. of the standard normal distribution evaluated at z; we explain next why $\sigma^2 = 1$. This model is a GLM with $G(\cdot) = \Phi(\cdot)$.

The model can be written with latent data to simplify the design of an algorithm:

$$y_i^* = x'_i\beta + u_i, \quad u_i \sim N(0, 1), \tag{8.8}$$

$$y_i = \begin{cases} 0, & \text{if } y_i^* \leq 0, \\ 1, & \text{otherwise,} \end{cases} \tag{8.9}$$

or $y_i = 1(y_i^* > 0)$. You should verify that the latent data form of the model is equivalent to (8.7). The latent data formulation makes clear why we assume $u_i \sim N(0, 1)$, rather than the more general assumption $N(0, \sigma^2)$. Since it is only the sign of y_i^* that determines the observed y_i, both sides of (8.8) can be multiplied by any nonnegative constant and still be consistent with the observed data, which shows that the pair (β, σ^2) is not identified. A simple way to achieve identification is to set $\sigma^2 = 1$.

Determining the prior distribution for β is not as straightforward as it is in the linear regression case, where β_k is interpreted as $\frac{\partial E(y)}{\partial x_k}$ for continuous data. In general,

$$\frac{\partial E(y_i^*)}{\partial x_{ik}} = \beta_k \frac{\partial G(x_i'\beta)}{\partial x_{ik}},$$

and for the Gaussian link function,

$$\frac{\partial E(y_i^*)}{\partial x_{ik}} = \beta_k \phi(x_i'\beta),$$

where $\phi(\cdot)$ is the p.d.f. of the Gaussian distribution. The effect of x_{ik} on $E(y_i)$ therefore depends on the vector x_i and all of the elements of β. One way to approach the problem of assigning a prior distribution for β is to consider the value of $x_i'\beta$ at which x_{ik} has the largest effect on y_i. For the normal distribution, this occurs at $x_i'\beta = 0$, where $\phi(\cdot)$ is maximized. Since $\phi(0) = 1/\sqrt{2\pi} = 0.3989$, the largest effect of x_k on y is approximately $0.4\beta_k$; this fact may help to put a prior mean and variance on β. Note that $P(y_i = 1|\beta) = 0.5$ at $x_i'\beta = 0$. Another approach is to think about $P(y_i = 1|\beta)$ at various values of the covariates and set parameter values accordingly. This approach is illustrated in the example described later.

To specify a Gibbs algorithm for this problem, we add the latent data y^* to the sampler as in Albert and Chib (1993b) and write the likelihood contribution of the ith observation as

$$p(y_i|y_i^*) = 1(y_i = 0)1(y_i^* \leq 0) + 1(y_i = 1)1(y_i^* > 0),$$

because $y_i = 0 \iff y_i^* \leq 0$. Assuming the usual Gaussian prior distribution for β, we can write the posterior distribution of β and $y^* = (y_1^*, \ldots, y_n^*)'$ as

$$\begin{aligned}
\pi(\beta, y^*|y) &= \prod p(y_i|y_i^*) f(y_i^*|\beta) \pi(\beta) \\
&= \prod [1(y_i = 0)1(y_i^* \leq 0) + 1(y_i = 1)1(y_i^* > 0)] \\
&\quad \times N_n(y^*|X\beta, I) N_K(\beta|\beta_0, B_0).
\end{aligned}$$

In algorithmic form, we have the following.

Algorithm 8.3: Gibbs algorithm for binary probit

8.1 Choose a starting value $\beta^{(0)}$.

8.2 At the gth iteration, draw

$$
y_i^{*(g)} \sim \begin{cases} \text{TN}_{(-\infty,0]}(x_i'\beta^{(g-1)}, 1), & \text{if } y_i = 0, \\ \text{TN}_{(0,\infty)}(x_i'\beta^{(g-1)}, 1), & \text{if } y_i = 1, \end{cases} \quad i = 1, \ldots, n,
$$

$$
\beta^{(g)} \sim N_K(\bar{\beta}^{(g)}, B_1),
$$

where

$$
B_1 = \left[X'X + B_0^{-1} \right]^{-1},
$$

$$
\bar{\beta}^{(g)} = B_1 \left[X'y_i^{*(g)} + B_0^{-1}\beta_0 \right].
$$

Note that B_1 is not updated, because $\sigma^2 = 1$.

Before turning to an example, we consider a model in which the link function is the Student-t distribution with ν degrees of freedom. From our discussion in Section 8.1.2, it should be clear that this can be accomplished by the model

$$
y_i^* = x_i'\beta + u_i, \quad u_i \sim N\left(0, \lambda_i^{-1}\right), \quad \lambda_i \sim G(\nu/2, \nu/2).
$$

The analysis proceeds by including λ_i and y_i^* in the sampler.

We illustrate the probit model for binary data by applying it to computer ownership data collected by the U.S. Census Bureau and the Bureau of Labor Statistics from a survey of a large number of U.S. households. This survey contains information on whether the household owns a computer, $y_i = 1$, and detailed demographic information about the household. We extracted a random sample of 500 households from the large number contained in this survey. The first task is to specify the covariates for the model. We assume that computer ownership is influenced by whether the person is a college graduate and the household's income, measured as the weekly wage of the household in thousands of dollars. We therefore define the covariates x_{i2} as the weekly wage of household i and $x_{i3} = 1$ if the head of household i is a college graduate and zero if not. Since the observations are a random sample of households, it is reasonable to assume that they are independent. Accordingly, the likelihood function is the product of the likelihood functions for each household.

The next step is to specify the prior distribution of β. Consider a household with a zero weekly wage headed by a person who did not graduate college. We assume a low probability, 0.10, that such a household contains a computer. Accordingly, $\int_{-\infty}^{\beta_1} \phi(t)\, dt = 0.10$. This implies $\beta_1 = -1.2816$, which we take as β_{01}. On the assumption that this probability is very likely to be less than 0.3, we solve $\int_{-\infty}^{\beta_1} \phi(t)\, dt = 0.3$ to find $\beta_1 = -0.5244$. Interpreting "very likely" to mean a probability of 0.95, we have $(-0.5244 + 1.2816)/\sqrt{B_{0,11}} = 1.96$, or $B_{0,11} = 0.1492$.

For β_{02}, consider a household that earns \$2,000 weekly, in which the head is not a college graduate. We assume a probability of 0.8 that such a household has a computer. Setting $\beta_1 = \beta_{01}$, we solve $\int_{-\infty}^{-1.2816+2\beta_{02}} \phi(t)\,dt = 0.8$ and find $\beta_{02} = 1.0616$. We further assume it very likely that the probability is at least 0.6 that such a household owns a computer. Accordingly, we solve $\int_{-\infty}^{-1.2816+2\beta_2} \phi(t)\,dt = 0.6$ to find $\beta_2 = .7674$, and then find $B_{0,22} = 0.0225$. To specify a prior for β_3, we assume the probability that a household with zero weekly wage is 0.4 for a household with a college degree and have previously assumed the probability is 0.1 for a household without a college degree. Computations similar to those mentioned before imply $\beta_{03} = 1.0283$ and $B_{0,33} = 0.2752$. To summarize,

$$\beta_0 = \begin{pmatrix} \beta_{01} \\ \beta_{02} \\ \beta_{03} \end{pmatrix} = \begin{pmatrix} -1.2816 \\ 1.0616 \\ 1.0283 \end{pmatrix},$$

and

$$B_0 = \begin{pmatrix} 0.1492 & 0 & 0 \\ 0 & 0.0225 & 0 \\ 0 & 0 & 0.2752 \end{pmatrix}.$$

We generated 10,000 draws from the joint posterior distribution and analyzed the last 9,000. The summary statistics in Table 8.2 and Figure 8.7 point to positive effects for both covariates. The coefficient of weekly wage is determined rather precisely.

8.2.3 Binary Logit Model

The binary logit model is another model for binary data. It is based on

$$P(y_i = 1) = P_i = \frac{\exp[x_i'\beta]}{1 + \exp[x_i'\beta]},$$

Table 8.2. *Summary of Posterior Distribution: Probit Model, Computer Example.*

Coefficient	Mean	S.D.	n.s.e	Lower	Upper
β_1	−0.705	0.074	0.001	−0.853	−0.558
β_2	0.879	0.106	0.002	0.669	1.086
β_3	0.524	0.154	0.002	0.222	0.824

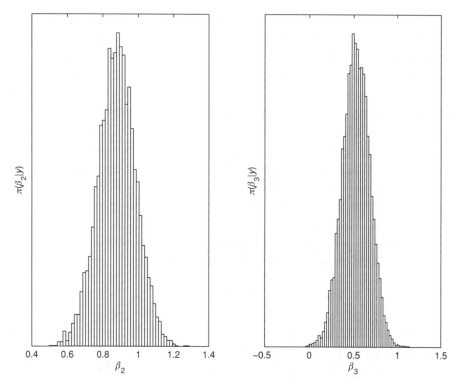

Figure 8.7. Posterior distributions of β: computer ownership example, probit model.

which implies the link function $G(x_i'\beta) = \exp[x_i'\beta]/(1 + \exp[x_i'\beta])$. This model can be written in the form of latent data as

$$y_i^* = x_i'\beta + u_i,$$

where u_i has the *logistic* distribution, $P(U_i \leq u_i) = \Lambda(u_i) = e^{u_i}/(1 + e^{u_i})$ and density function $\lambda(u_i) = e^{u_i}/(1 + e^{u_i})^2$.

This model has the interesting property that

$$\text{logit}(P_i) \equiv \log\left(\frac{P(y_i = 1)}{P(y_i = 0)}\right) = \log\left(\frac{P_i}{1 - P_i}\right) = x_i'\beta,$$

that is, the logarithm of the odds ratio is a linear function of the covariates. This feature may be useful for setting prior distributions because it implies that $\frac{\partial \text{logit}(P_i)}{\partial x_{ik}} = \beta_k$, which permits the use of subject-matter based knowledge about the effect on the log odds ratio of a change in a covariate. In addition, the general result $\frac{\partial P_i}{\partial x_{ik}} = \beta_k \frac{\partial G(x_i'\beta)}{\partial x_{ik}}$ implies that $\frac{\partial P_i}{\partial x_{ik}} = \beta_k P_i(1 - P_i)$ for the logit model. Since this expression is maximized at $P_i = 1/2$, the largest effect of covariate k on the probability is $\beta_k/4$, a fact that may be helpful in specifying a prior distribution for β_k. This calculation also allows a rough comparison between the coefficients of a probit and logit model fit to the same data. We saw in Section 8.2.2 that $\frac{\partial P_i}{\partial x_{ik}}$ is maximized at $0.4\beta_{pk}$, where β_{pk} is the coefficient from a probit equation. Equating the maximum effects, we have $0.4\beta_{pk} = \beta_{lk}/4$, or the logit coefficient $\beta_{lk} = 1.6\beta_{pk}$. This approximation should be reasonably good in the neighborhood of $x_i'\beta = 0$.

Placing a normal prior on β results in a model that is not conditionally conjugate; see Exercise 8.8. Since the conditional posterior distribution of β is not a standard form, we utilize the general form of the MH algorithm to approximate it. A possible proposal generator is the random walk, in which a scaled normal or Student-t variable is added to the current value; another possibility is an independence chain, where the proposal density is a Student-t distribution centered at the maximum of the posterior distribution with scale matrix proportional to the negative of the inverted Hessian at the maximum.

We illustrate the logit model by returning to the computer ownership data discussed earlier. That discussion leads us to specify the likelihood function

$$P_i = \frac{\exp[\beta_1 + \beta_2 x_{i2} + \beta_3 x_{i3}]}{1 + \exp[\beta_1 + \beta_2 x_{i2} + \beta_3 x_{i3}]},$$

where the covariates are defined earlier. The likelihood function for the sample is again the product of the individual likelihoods.

To specify prior distributions for the β_k, we start with the result that $\text{logit}(P_i) = x_i'\beta$ and consider a household with zero income and a head of household who is not a college graduate. In that case $\text{logit}(P_i) = \beta_1$. We assume that such a household has a small probability of owning a computer, say 0.1, implying that $\log(1/9) = -2.1972$, which is taken as the mean of the prior distribution for β_1. If we consider it very unlikely that the probability is greater than 0.3, $\log(3/7) = -0.8473$ is taken to be the upper end of the interval that contains 95% of the probability distribution of β_1. This implies a prior standard deviation of β_1 of $\sqrt{B_{0,11}} = [-0.8473 - (-2.1972)]/1.96 = 0.6887$, or a variance $B_{0,11} = 0.4743$.

For β_2, let us consider a household with a weekly wage of \$2,000 and a head of household who is not a college graduate. We assume the probability is 0.8 that such a household owns a computer. Since the wage is measured in thousands, $\log(8/2) = -2.1972 + 2\beta_2$, which implies $\beta_{02} = 1.7917$. If we take 0.6 as the lower limit of a 95% credibility interval for the probability that a household earning \$2,000 per week owns a computer, we find that the variance of the prior density of β_2, $B_{0,22}$, is 0.2504.

The last coefficient gives the effect of being a college graduate. Assume again a household with a weekly income of zero and consider the logit of a household in which the head has a college degree, $\beta_1 + \beta_3$, compared to one in which the head does not have a degree, β_1. We have taken the latter to be $1/9$ and assume the former to be 0.4; these imply that $\beta_3 = 0.3$. On the assumption that this effect is not likely to be greater than 0.5, we find an implied standard deviation of one. Accordingly, $B_{0,33} = 1$.

In summary, under the assumption that the parameters are independent and normally distributed, our prior distribution is

$$\pi(\beta_0) = N(\beta | \beta_0, B_0), \tag{8.10}$$

where

$$\beta_0 = \begin{pmatrix} \beta_{01} \\ \beta_{02} \\ \beta_{03} \end{pmatrix} = \begin{pmatrix} -2.1972 \\ 1.7917 \\ 0.3000 \end{pmatrix},$$

and

$$B_0 = \begin{pmatrix} 0.4743 & 0 & 0 \\ 0 & 0.2504 & 0 \\ 0 & 0 & 1.000 \end{pmatrix}.$$

We generate a sample of 10,000 from the posterior distribution and discard 1,000 as the burn-in. The autocorrelations are very low, resulting in values of both r.n.e. and autocorrelation time close to one. A summary of the output is in Table 8.3, and Figure 8.8 presents histograms of the posterior distributions of β_2 and β_3. The sample results yield $P(\beta_2 > 0|y) = 0.98$ and $P(\beta_3 > 0|y) = 0.88$, which suggests that income almost certainly has an effect but that the positive effect on computer ownership of being a college graduate is less clear.

8.3 Further Reading and References

Chapter 8 Appendix B contains comments on computer programs for performing the computations discussed in this chapter.

Section 8.1.1 Special algorithms have been devised to deal with the problem of model selection when a researcher contemplates a linear regression model with a large number of possible covariates and little prior information about which of these to include. The overall model in this case includes a possibly large number of

Table 8.3. *Summary of Posterior Distribution: Logit Model, Computer Example.*

Coefficient	Mean	S.D.	n.s.e.	Lower	Upper
β_1	−1.081	0.382	0.004	−1.818	−0.305
β_2	1.299	0.636	0.007	0.027	2.557
β_3	0.786	0.745	0.007	−0.703	2.230

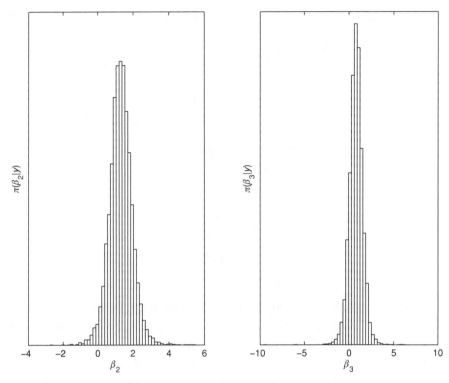

Figure 8.8. Posterior distributions of β: computer ownership example, logit model.

submodels. An algorithm that samples from such models must allow for sampling within and across submodels, which presents special problems. The *reversible jump* algorithm has been developed to deal with such cases; it is particularly associated with P. J. Green; see, for example, Green (1995). A thorough discussion of this algorithm and others is in Robert and Casella (2004, chap. 11).

Section 8.1.2 The use of Student-t errors is one of several possible ways to generalize the assumption of Gaussian errors in regression models. The t errors allow thicker tails than does the normal and is more general in the sense that it is close to the normal distribution for large degrees of freedom. The relationship between the normal and t is an example of a more general idea, that of representing a distribution by continuous mixtures of another family of distributions; the concept was discussed in Section 5.2 in connection with simulation. In the more general case, $f(y) = \int g(y|\theta)\lambda(\theta)\,d\theta$, where $f(y)$ is represented as a mixture of $g(y|\theta)$ and the weights for the values of θ are determined by $\lambda(\theta)$. Another approach is to represent a random variable by a finite mixture, for example $f(y_i) = \sum_j \lambda_j p_j(y_i|\theta_j)$, where λ_i is the probability that the observation y_i is drawn from "state" j with probability λ_j. Finite mixtures of normal distributions with different means and variances can display a wide variety of shapes. See Gelman et al. (2004, chap. 18) and Geweke (2005, sec. 6.4) for more discussion of such mixtures. The latter discusses estimation of the model by procedure "fmn_ullm" in BACC.

Another general approach to modeling error terms flexibly is the Dirichlet mixture process. See Escobar and West (1995) for a discussion and references and an MCMC approach to simulation. A method of computing the marginal likelihood for such models is presented in Basu and Chib (2003).

Section 8.2 Greene (2003, chaps. 21 and 22) presents the Tobit and binary probit models in a frequentist setting, including explicit formulas for the Hessian matrices and a comparison of the coefficients of probit and logit models. Wooldridge (2002, chaps. 15 and 16) also covers these models in great detail. He points out an important difference between the top-coded and boundary solution versions of the Tobit model: the values of β are of interest in the former because $E(y^*|x) = x'\beta$ can be interpreted as an expectation in the absence of top coding, and so β has its usual interpretation as a partial derivative. In contrast, for the boundary solution case, interest usually centers on $E(y|x)$, $E(y|x, y > 0)$, or $P(y = 0|x)$, rather than β, because values of $y^* < 0$ have no meaning. An exception arises in the utility maximization model, where β may depend on parameters of the utility function. The probit and logit models are thoroughly covered by Train (2003), who includes a Bayesian analysis of the latter.

Tanner and Wong (1987) introduce the idea of introducing missing data in a two-block Gibbs sampling algorithm. In the first application of MCMC methods to econometrics, Chib (1992) analyzes the Tobit model. The use of latent data in a Gibbs algorithm by Albert and Chib (1993b) for the binary probit model and the ordered probit and Student-t versions of the model has become the standard approach to categorical responses from a Bayesian perspective. Chib and Greenberg (1998) show how the approach extends to correlated binary data.

An interesting variation of the binary probit model appears in the political science literature in the form of the spatial voting model, which is equivalent to the two-parameter item response model used in educational testing. The statistical model takes the form

$$P(y_{ij} = 1) = \Phi(\beta'_j x_i - \alpha_j), \tag{8.11}$$

where y_{ij} is 1 if legislator i votes yea on issue j and 0 otherwise, $i = 1, \ldots, n$, $j = 1, \ldots, m$. The $d \times 1$ vector x_i represents i's "ideal point," which is the primary object of interest of the analysis. The only data observed are the y_{ij}, and $d(d + 1)$ restrictions must be imposed on $X = (x'_1, \ldots, x'_n)'$ to identify the remainder of X, the β_j, and the α_j. The Bayesian approach to the spatial voting model is explained in Clinton et al. (2004) who assume Gaussian priors for the x_i, β_j, and α_j. A dynamic version of this model is analyzed in Martin and Quinn (2002), where the ideal points are given a time index, x_{it}, and are allowed to evolve. Models in which parameters evolve over time are discussed in Section 10.3.

Generalizations of the binary probit and logit models to data sets in which an individual chooses among three or more possibilities are discussed in Section 9.4.

8.4 Exercises

8.1 Download the data in "Birth weight II" from the StatLabs Web site, www.stat.berkeley. edu/users/statlabs/labs.html. The variables are birth weight (ounces, 999 unknown), gestation (length of pregnancy in days, 999 unknown), parity (0 = firstborn, 9 is unknown), age (mother's age in years), height (mother's height in inches), weight (mother's prepregnancy weight in pounds), smoke (0 not now, 1 yes now, 9 = unknown).

Specify a linear regression, where the response variable is birth weight, and the covariates are a constant and the remaining variables in the data set. Eliminate observations for which you do not have complete information on the variables. Specify prior distributions for the coefficients and the variance (or precision). Summarize the results for the dummy variable for smoking. Does smoking by the mother appear to affect the baby's birth weight?

8.2 Verify that specifying the model of (8.4) by a Student-t likelihood function on ν degrees of freedom for y, a normal prior for β, and an inverse gamma prior for σ^2 does not permit use of the Gibbs algorithm. Verify that a Student-t likelihood function on ν degrees of freedom for y and a Student-t prior for β do not yield conditional distributions that permit a Gibbs algorithm.

8.3 Repeat Exercise 8.1 for errors distributed as Student-t with five degrees of freedom. Compute marginal likelihoods and compare the models.

8.4 Study the sensitivity of the results for the union coefficient by varying the prior mean and variance.

8.5 Write out an algorithm to sample for β, σ^2, and λ for the linear regression model with Student-t errors of Section 8.1.2.

8.6 Write out an algorithm to sample for β, σ^2, y_{Ci}^*, and λ for the Tobit model of Section 8.2.1 with Student-t errors.

8.7 Write out an algorithm to sample for β, y^*, and λ for the binary data model with Student-t errors of Section 8.2.2.

8.8 Verify that the posterior distribution of the logit model with a normal prior (Section 8.2.3) has the form

$$\pi(\beta|y) \propto \prod \left(\frac{\exp[x_i'\beta]}{1 + \exp[x_i'\beta]} \right)^{y_i} \left(\frac{1}{1 + \exp[x_i'\beta]} \right)^{1-y_i}$$
$$\times \exp\left[-\frac{1}{2}(\beta - \beta_0)' B_0^{-1}(\beta - \beta_0) \right],$$

and show that including the latent data in the sampler does not simplify the posterior distribution.

8.9 Write out an algorithm to estimate the parameters of (8.11) under the Gaussian prior. Compare your algorithm to the one in Clinton et al. (2004).

8.10 Another type of discrete data is count data, where the observations y_i are equal to zero or a positive integer; that is, $y_i \in \{0, 1, \dots\}$. Such data are often modeled by the Poisson distribution,

$$p(y_i|\theta_i) = \frac{e^{-\theta_i}\theta_i^{y_i}}{y_i!}, \quad \theta_i = \exp(x_i'\beta).$$

The model is discussed in detail from the frequentist viewpoint in Wooldridge (2002, chap. 19) and Winkelmann (1997); the latter also discusses the Bayesian approach. Find an expression for the posterior distribution $\beta|y$ on the assumption that $\pi(\beta) = N(\beta_0, B_0)$, and discuss possible ways to simulate from this distribution. (See Winkelmann, 1997, sec. 5.2.1.)

Chapter 9

Multivariate Responses

IN THIS CHAPTER, we consider three examples of models in which the response variable is a vector, rather than a scalar, random variable: the "seemingly unrelated regression" (SUR) model, the multivariate probit (MVP) model, and a model for panel data.

9.1 SUR Model

The SUR model was introduced in Zellner (1962) and has been applied extensively. Before turning to examples we specify the model formally. Since the response variable is multivariate, the observations and error terms are written with two subscripts:

$$y_{sj} = x_{sj}'\beta_s + u_{sj}, \quad s = 1, \ldots, S, \quad j = 1, \ldots, J, \tag{9.1}$$

where x_{sj} is $K_s \times 1$ and $\beta_s = (\beta_{s1}, \beta_{s2}, \ldots, \beta_{sK_s})'$. The jth observation on the vector of responses is contained in the $S \times 1$ vector $y_j = (y_{1j}, y_{2j}, \ldots, y_{Sj})'$. To specify a model for y_j, we define the $S \times K$ matrix, $K = \sum K_s$,

$$X_j = \begin{pmatrix} x_{1j}' & & \cdots & 0 \\ 0 & x_{2j}' & \cdots & 0 \\ & & \vdots & \\ 0 & 0 & \cdots & x_{Sj}' \end{pmatrix},$$

the $K \times 1$ vector $\beta = (\beta_1', \ldots \beta_S')'$, and the $S \times 1$ vector $u_j = (u_{1j}, u_{2j}, \ldots u_{Sj})'$; these definitions and the model specification imply

$$y_j = X_j\beta + u_j. \tag{9.2}$$

The defining characteristic of the SUR model is the assumption that $u_j|X \sim N_S(0, \Sigma)$, where $X = (X_1, \ldots, X_J)$ and $\Sigma = \{\sigma_{st}\}$. The covariances permit nonzero correlations for disturbances with the same second subscript,

$$\text{Cov}(u_{sj}, u_{tk}|X) = \begin{cases} \sigma_{st}, & \text{if } j = k, \\ 0, & \text{otherwise.} \end{cases}$$

These nonzero covariances explain the phrase "seemingly unrelated." If the co-variances were all zero, each of the equations in (9.2) would be unrelated to the others. But the nonzero covariances tie the individual regressions into a system of equations that can be analyzed together. Finally, note that the model allows the disturbance variances σ_{ss} to differ across firms and that the $u_j|X$ are independent across j, that is,

$$f(u_1, \ldots, u_J|X) = f(u_1|X) \cdots f(u_J|X).$$

Here are examples of data sets to which the model has been applied:

9.1 Let y_{sj} be the investment expenditures of firm s in year j, where all of the firms are in the same industry. In that case, u_{sj} represents unobserved disturbances that affect firm s at time j. Since the firms are in the same industry, it is reasonable to assume that a disturbance in a particular period affects all the firms to some degree, which can be modeled by assuming that the covariance σ_{st} between the disturbances of firms s and t at time j is not zero. Finally, the specification assumes that the disturbances across time for a given firm are independent.

9.2 Let y_{sj} represent the score on the sth of one of several medical or intelligence tests taken by individual j. The specification permits the scores to be correlated for a particular individual, perhaps representing some unobserved genetic factor, but the scores across individuals are independent.

9.3 Let y_{sj} represent the expenditures by household s on product j. The specification allows the disturbance to expenditures across product categories for a particular household to be correlated, but assumes zero correlation across households.

Before turning to the analysis of this model, we note a special case,

$$y_{sj} = x'_{sj}\beta + u_{sj},$$

where x_{sj} is defined as before, but β is a $K \times 1$ vector. This specification differs from (9.1) by assuming that all the β_s are equal to the common value β. The special case is still a SUR model because of the assumption that $\sigma_{st} \neq 0$. By defining

$$X_j = \begin{pmatrix} x'_{1j} \\ x'_{2j} \\ \vdots \\ x'_{Sj} \end{pmatrix},$$

and $\beta = (\beta_1, \ldots, \beta_k)'$, verify that (9.2) is still valid.

From the specification of the SUR model and the definition of the multivariate normal distribution in Section A.1.12, the likelihood function for the data $y = (y_1, \ldots, y_J)$ is

$$f(y|\beta, \Sigma) \propto \frac{1}{|\Sigma|^{J/2}} \exp\left[-\frac{1}{2}\sum_j (y_j - X_j\beta)'\Sigma^{-1}(y_j - X_j\beta)\right]. \qquad (9.3)$$

We next specify a conditionally conjugate prior for this model. The regression coefficients are assumed to have a Gaussian prior, $\beta \sim N_K(\beta_0, B_0)$. For the precision matrix Σ^{-1}, we assume a generalization of the gamma distribution, the Wishart distribution described in Section A.1.16: $\Sigma^{-1} \sim W_S(\nu_0, R_0)$. (We could have equivalently assumed an inverted Wishart distribution for the covariance matrix Σ.)

With these assumptions, the posterior distribution is

$$\pi(\beta, \Sigma|y) \propto \frac{1}{|\Sigma|^{J/2}} \exp\left[-\frac{1}{2}\sum_j (y_j - X_j\beta)'\Sigma^{-1}(y_j - X_j\beta)\right]$$
$$\times \exp\left[-\frac{1}{2}(\beta - \beta_0)'B_0^{-1}(\beta - \beta_0)\right]$$
$$\times \frac{1}{|\Sigma|^{(\nu_0 - S - 1)/2}} \exp\left[-\frac{1}{2}\operatorname{tr}(R_0^{-1}\Sigma^{-1})\right].$$

It is then straightforward to determine the conditional distribution,

$$\beta|y, \Sigma \sim N_K(\bar{\beta}, B_1),$$

where

$$B_1 = \left[\sum_j X_j'\Sigma^{-1}X_j + B_0^{-1}\right]^{-1},$$
$$\bar{\beta} = B_1\left[\sum_j X_j'\Sigma^{-1}y_j + B_0^{-1}\beta_0\right]. \qquad (9.4)$$

To derive the conditional distribution of $\Sigma|y, \beta$ we use the properties of the trace operator $z'Az = \operatorname{tr}(z'Az) = \operatorname{tr}(zz'A)$, where z is a column vector, to obtain

$$\sum_j (y_j - X_j\beta)'\Sigma^{-1}(y_j - X_j\beta) = \operatorname{tr}\sum_j (y_j - X_j\beta)(y_j - X_j\beta)'\Sigma^{-1},$$

from which we immediately have $\Sigma \mid y, \beta \sim W_S(\nu_1, R_1)$, where

$$\nu_1 = \nu_0 + J,$$

$$R_1 = \left[R_0^{-1} + \sum_j (y_j - X_j\beta)(y_j - X_j\beta)' \right]^{-1}. \tag{9.5}$$

In algorithmic form, we have the following.

Algorithm 9.1: Gibbs algorithm for SUR model

9.1 Choose a starting value $\Sigma^{(0)}$.

9.2 At the gth iteration, draw

$$\beta^{(g)} \sim N_K\left(\bar{\beta}^{(g)}, B_1^{(g)}\right)$$

$$\Sigma^{-1(g)} \sim W_S\left(\nu_1, R_1^{(g)}\right),$$

where $\bar{\beta}^{(g)}$ and $B_1^{(g)}$ are given in (9.4) with Σ^{-1} replaced by $\Sigma^{-1(g-1)}$, and ν_1 and $R_1^{(g)}$ are given in (9.5) with β replaced by $\beta^{(g)}$.

As an application of this model, we consider the Grunfeld (1958) study of investment behavior as discussed in Boot and de Wit (1960), where the data may be found. In this model, gross investment including repairs and maintenance (I_t) is the response variable, and the covariates are a constant, the market value of the firm (F_t), and the firm's capital stock (C_t). The variables are deflated by appropriate price indices, and the data are for the years 1935–1954 for five large manufacturing companies: General Motors (GM), Chrysler (C), General Electric (GE), Westinghouse (W), and U.S. Steel (USS). We consider the SUR version of the model M_1, where the β_s differ for each firm and contemporaneous correlations are permitted, and a version M_2 in which the β_s differ, but contemporaneous correlations are forced to equal zero. For a third model, M_3, we assume zero contemporaneous correlations and the same β_s for each firm.

Boot and de Wit (1960, p. 8) offer a few comments about parameter values for β_{sF} and β_{sC} that can be used to form prior distributions. On the basis of their discussion, we assume each $\beta_{sF} \sim N(0, 0.33)$ and each $\beta_{sC} \sim N(0.25, 0.17)$. These imply that $-1 \le \beta_F \le 1.0$ with probability 0.997 and that $0 \le \beta_C \le 1$ with probability 0.997. There is little prior information about the constant term. We assume $\beta_1 \sim N(0, 100)$ as an uninformative prior. To allow for uncertainty in the distribution of Σ, we set $\nu_0 = 6$, and we set $R_0 = 400I_5$ to allow for large variances of the disturbances. For M_2 and M_3, we assume the precision is distributed as $G(1, 1/400)$, and the priors for the β_s are the same as those of M_1.

The results for M_1 in Figures 9.1 and 9.2 and Tables 9.1–9.3 indicate considerable variation in β_F and β_C across firms and values of contemporaneous correlations

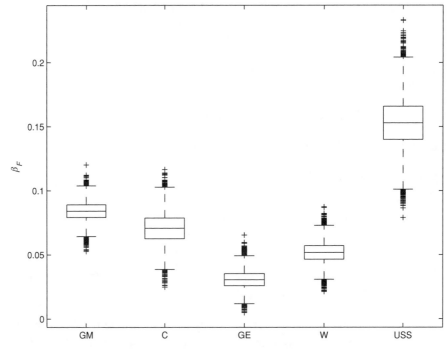

Figure 9.1. Summary of β_F.

ranging in absolute value from 0.029 to 0.599. The β values for M_2 show comparable variation. The marginal likelihood values are -708.60 for M_1, -593.01 for M_2, and -651.75 for M_3. By this criterion, the data strongly favor M_2, a model that allows each firm to have a different set of regression coefficients, but imposes zero contemporaneous correlations. Another model that might be examined is one in that permits different regression coefficients and different variances for each firm. This possibility is included as an exercise.

One reason why M_1 lost so decisively to M_2 may have to do with the number of parameters in the model, as discussed in Section 3.2.4. Both M_1 and M_2 contain 15 regression coefficients, but the former also contains 5 variances and 10 covariances,

Table 9.1. *Summary of Posterior Distribution of β_F: Grunfeld Data, SUR Model.*

Firm	Mean	S.D.	n.s.e.	Lower	Upper
GM	0.084	0.008	0.000	0.069	0.099
C	0.071	0.012	0.000	0.047	0.094
GE	0.030	0.007	0.000	0.017	0.045
W	0.052	0.008	0.000	0.036	0.068
USS	0.153	0.020	0.000	0.114	0.191

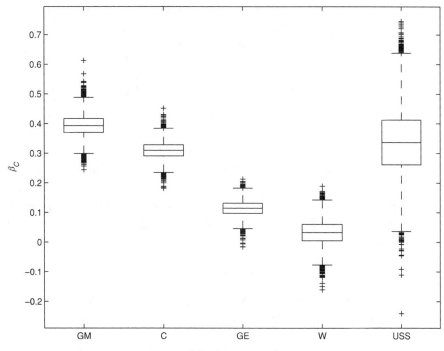

Figure 9.2. Summary of β_C.

whereas M_2 includes only one variance. The latter model therefore entails 14 fewer parameters than does the former. Although we might expect the likelihood ratio to favor the model with more parameters, M_1, the effect from this source was apparently not enough to offset the larger number of parameters. In contrast, M_3, which contains only four parameters, is decisively beaten by M_2 with its 16 parameters.

9.2 Multivariate Probit Model

The multivariate probit (MVP) model is a SUR model in which all response variables are binary choices: $y_{ij} = 1$ indicates that individual i chooses 1 on decision

Table 9.2. *Summary of Posterior Distribution of β_C: Grunfeld Data, SUR Model.*

Firm	Mean	S.D.	n.s.e.	Lower	Upper
GM	0.394	0.037	0.000	0.322	0.469
C	0.309	0.028	0.000	0.254	0.364
GE	0.114	0.026	0.000	0.062	0.163
W	0.032	0.042	0.000	−0.052	0.112
USS	0.337	0.114	0.002	0.116	0.566

Table 9.3. *Means of Posterior Distribution of Contemporaneous*
Correlations: Grunfeld Data, SUR Model.

1.000	0.073	−0.151	−0.370	0.556
0.073	1.000	0.126	0.029	−0.297
−0.151	0.126	1.000	−0.562	−0.091
−0.370	0.029	−0.562	1.000	−0.599
0.556	−0.297	−0.091	−0.599	1.000

j, and $y_{ij} = 0$ indicates that individual i chooses 0 on decision j, $i = 1, \ldots, n$, $j = 1, \ldots, J$. It is applied to data sets in which decision maker i makes binary choices over J decisions that are believed to be related through unobserved random variables. The model is most easily represented and analyzed by the latent variable representation,

$$y_{ij}^* = x_{ij}'\beta_j + u_{ij},$$

where x_{ij} and β_j are $K_j \times 1$, and let $K = \sum K_j$. The observed choices are the y_{ij}, which are related to the latent data through

$$y_{ij} = \begin{cases} 0, & \text{if } y_{ij}^* \leq 0, \\ 1, & \text{otherwise.} \end{cases}$$

Upon defining $y_i^* = (y_{i1}^*, \ldots, y_{iJ}^*)'$,

$$X_i = \begin{pmatrix} x_{i1}' & 0 & \ldots & 0 \\ 0 & x_{i2}' & \ldots & 0 \\ 0 & 0 & \ldots & x_{iJ}' \end{pmatrix},$$

$\beta = (\beta_1', \ldots, \beta_J')'$, and $u_i = (u_{i1}, \ldots, u_{iJ})'$, we can write

$$y_i^* = X_i\beta + u_i.$$

Note that the observations are grouped by the first subscript in contrast to the SUR model, where they were grouped by the second subscript. Grouping by the first subscript simplifies the writing of the likelihood function.

As an example of this model, consider individual i who makes two binary choices: (1) send his or her child to a public or private school and (2) vote for or against a school tax increase. We might expect these choices to be related even after controlling for such covariates as income and family size.

We now continue with the specification of the model. The "probit" in MVP arises from the assumption that $u_i \sim N_J(0, \Sigma)$. The covariance matrix Σ is not identified for the MVP model, because only the signs of the latent variables are identified through the likelihood function. In Section 8.2.2, we resolved the lack of identification by setting $\sigma_{11} = 1$. In the present case, we have J variances that are not identified. One possibility is to set $\sigma_{jj} = 1$, $j = 1, \ldots, J$. If $J = 3$, for example,

$$\Sigma = \begin{pmatrix} 1 & \sigma_{12} & \sigma_{13} \\ \sigma_{12} & 1 & \sigma_{23} \\ \sigma_{13} & \sigma_{23} & 1 \end{pmatrix}.$$

With ones on the main diagonal, Σ is a correlation matrix, and, because it is symmetric, there are $J(J-1)/2$ unique unknown σ_{ij}. We denote these by $\sigma = (\sigma_{12}, \sigma_{13}, \ldots, \sigma_{J-1,J})'$. In addition, the positive definiteness of Σ imposes restrictions on σ.

We assume a Gaussian prior, $\beta \sim N_K(\beta_0, B_0)$. For the elements of σ, we propose a normal prior, truncated to the region C_Σ in which Σ is positive definite, so that $1(\Sigma \in C_\Sigma) = 1$ if Σ is positive definite and 0 otherwise. Then

$$\pi(\sigma) \propto 1(\Sigma \in C_\Sigma) \exp\left[-\frac{1}{2}(\sigma - \sigma_0)' \Sigma_0^{-1}(\sigma - \sigma_0)\right].$$

We can therefore write the posterior distribution as

$$\begin{aligned} \pi(\beta, \Sigma, y^*|y) \propto {} & \frac{1}{|\Sigma|^{n/2}} \exp\left[-\frac{1}{2}\sum_i (y_i^* - X_i\beta)' \Sigma^{-1}(y_i^* - X_i\beta)\right] \\ & \times \prod_{i,j} [1(y_{ij} = 1)1(y_{ij}^* > 0) + 1(y_{ij} = 0)1(y_{ij}^* \leq 0)] \\ & \times \exp\left[-\frac{1}{2}(\beta - \beta_0)' B_0^{-1}(\beta - \beta_0)\right] \\ & \times 1(\Sigma \in C_\Sigma) \exp\left[-\frac{1}{2}(\sigma - \sigma_0)' \Sigma_0^{-1}(\sigma - \sigma_0)\right], \end{aligned}$$

which implies

$$\beta|y, \Sigma, y^*, y \sim N_K(\bar{\beta}, B_1), \tag{9.6}$$

where

$$\begin{aligned} B_1 &= \left[\sum_i X_i' \Sigma^{-1} X_i + B_0^{-1}\right]^{-1}, \\ \bar{\beta} &= B_1 \left[\sum_i X_i' \Sigma^{-1} y_i^* + B_0^{-1}\beta_0\right]. \end{aligned} \tag{9.7}$$

The regression parameter β can therefore be simulated from its conditional distribution in a Gibbs step.

The conditional posterior distribution for σ is

$$\pi(\sigma|y, y^*, \beta) \propto 1(\Sigma \in C_\Sigma) \frac{1}{|\Sigma|^{n/2}} \exp\left[-\frac{1}{2} \sum_i (y_i^* - X_i\beta)' \Sigma^{-1} (y_i^* - X_i\beta)\right]$$

$$\times \exp\left[-\frac{1}{2}(\sigma - \sigma_0)' \Sigma_0^{-1}(\sigma - \sigma_0)\right]. \tag{9.8}$$

This distribution can be sampled by a tailored MH algorithm. The proposal density at the gth iteration is a Student-t distribution with ν degrees of freedom (e.g., $\nu = 5$), with mean at the value of σ that maximizes the logarithm of Equation (9.8) given the current values of β and y^*. The scale matrix is taken to be the negative of the inverse Hessian at the maximum. A draw from the distribution that violates the positive definiteness of Σ is immediately rejected, and the current value of Σ is retained. If the draw results in positive-definite Σ, the proposed value replaces the current value with the usual MH probability. Details are given in the next algorithm.

The y_i^* are drawn from their full conditional posterior distributions, which are independent truncated multivariate normal distributions, $N_J(X_i\beta, \Sigma)$, truncated to the left at zero for j such that $y_{ij} = 1$ and to the right at zero for j such that $y_{ij} = 0$. To make this draw we employ a Gibbs algorithm that cycles through the full conditionals for $i = 1, \ldots, n$,

$$f(y_{i1}^* | y_{i2}^*, \ldots, y_{iJ}^*)$$
$$\vdots$$
$$f(y_{ij}^* | y_{i1}^*, \ldots, y_{i,j-1}^*, y_{i,j+1}^*, \ldots, y_{iJ}^*) \tag{9.9}$$
$$\vdots$$
$$f(y_{i,J}^* | y_{i1}^*, \ldots, y_{i,J-1}^*),$$

where updated values of y_{ij}^* are entered into the conditioning set as they are generated. Each of these is a truncated univariate normal distribution with mean and variance given by the conditional distribution of (A.9).

In algorithmic form, we have

Algorithm 9.2: MH algorithm for MVP model

9.1 Select starting values $y^{*(0)}$ and $\beta^{(0)}$.

9.2 At the gth iteration,

(a) Maximize

$$-\frac{n}{2} \log |\Sigma| - \frac{1}{2} \sum_i \left(y_i^{*(g-1)} - X_i\beta^{(g-1)}\right)' \Sigma^{-1} \left(y_i^{*(g-1)} - X_i\beta^{(g-1)}\right)$$

$$-\frac{1}{2}(\sigma - \sigma_0)' \Sigma_0^{-1}(\sigma - \sigma_0)$$

with respect to σ. Denote the maximizing value by $\hat{\sigma}^{(g)}$ and denote the negative of the inverse Hessian matrix at the maximizing value by $\hat{S}^{(g)}$.

(b) Draw σ^* from $t_{J(J-1)/2}(\nu, \hat{\sigma}^{(g)}, \hat{S}^{(g)})$ and set

$$\alpha(\sigma^{(g-1)}, \sigma^*) = \left(\frac{\prod_i N_J(y_i|X_i\beta, \Sigma^*)}{\prod_i N_J(y_i|X_i\beta, \Sigma^{(g-1)})} \right) \left(\frac{N_{J(J-1)/2}(\sigma^*|\sigma_0, \Sigma_0)}{N_{J(J-1)/2}(\sigma^{(g-1)}|\sigma_0, \Sigma_0)} \right)$$

$$\times \left(\frac{t_{J(J-1)/2}(\sigma^*|\nu, \hat{\sigma}^{(g)}, \hat{S}^{(g)})}{t_{J(J-1)/2}(\sigma^{(g-1)}|\nu, \hat{\sigma}^{(g)}, \hat{S}^{(g)})} \right).$$

In these expressions, $N_J(z|\mu, \Sigma)$ denotes the density function of the J-dimensional normal distribution with mean vector μ and covariance matrix Σ evaluated at z; $t_D(t|\nu, \mu, \Sigma)$ denotes the density function evaluated at t of the D-dimensional Student-t distribution with ν degrees of freedom, location vector μ, and scale matrix Σ; and Σ^* is the covariance matrix obtained from the covariances in σ^*.

(c) Draw U from $U(0, 1)$. If $U \le \alpha(\sigma^{(g-1)}, \sigma^*)$, set $\sigma^{(g)} = \sigma^*$; otherwise, set $\sigma^{(g)} = \sigma^{(g-1)}$. Note that a drawing of σ^* that leads to a Σ that is not positive definite is always rejected.

(d) Draw $\beta^{(g)}$ from (9.6), with $\Sigma = \Sigma^{(g)}$ and $y^* = y^{*(g-1)}$ in (9.7).

(e) Draw $y^{*(g)}|y, \beta^{(g)}, \Sigma^{(g)}$ following the strategy described around (9.9).

As an example, we consider a data set analyzed by Rubinfeld (1977). Ninety-five individuals report on whether they send at least one of their children to a public school (y_{i1}) and whether they voted in favor of a school tax increase (y_{i2}). These decisions are modeled in the multivariate probit form. The covariates for the first decision are a constant, log(income), and log(property taxes); for the second, they are a constant, log(income), log(property taxes), and the number of years the responder has lived in the city.

Some experimentation indicated considerable sensitivity of results to the prior distributions of the parameters. This is not surprising in view of the small sample size. For this reason, we decided to impose highly uninformative priors: $\beta_0 = 0$, $B_0 = 100I_7$, and $\sigma_{12} \sim N(0, 0.5)$. We generated 5,500 observations, of which 500 were discarded, and found autocorrelations at lag 20 to be very small. The prior and posterior distributions are summarized in Table 9.4. The 95% credibility intervals of most parameters range from negative to positive values, except that β_{22} seems clearly positive and β_{23} clearly negative. It appears that a higher income is associated with a higher probability of voting for a tax increase, while a higher property tax works in the opposite direction. Little can be said about the effects of the other covariates in the model.

Table 9.4. *Summary of Prior and Posterior Distributions of β and σ_{12}: Rubinfeld Data.*

Coefficient	Prior		Posterior				
	Mean	S.D.	Mean	S.D.	n.s.e.	Lower	Upper
β_{11}	0.000	10.000	−4.543	3.761	0.230	−12.846	2.304
β_{12}	0.000	10.000	0.129	0.439	0.040	−0.698	0.994
β_{13}	0.000	10.000	0.620	0.607	0.037	−0.627	1.784
β_{21}	0.000	10.000	−0.634	3.762	0.309	−8.145	6.231
β_{22}	0.000	10.000	1.113	0.443	0.044	0.282	1.997
β_{23}	0.000	10.000	−1.437	0.546	0.050	−2.495	−0.367
β_{24}	0.000	10.000	−0.018	0.015	0.000	−0.048	0.013
σ_{12}	0.000	0.707	0.085	0.185	0.023	−0.302	0.455

9.3 Panel Data

Panel data consist of observations on the same unit over several time periods. The response variable is denoted y_{it}, which denotes an observation on unit i at time t. Since the first of the examples of SUR data mentioned in Section 9.1 also involves individual units across time, we discuss how the models differ before presenting the panel data model in detail.

The SUR model is usually applied to data for which the number of time periods is large and the number of units is small, and the panel data model is applied to datasets with a small number of time periods and a large number of units. The first subscript of the response variable in the SUR model is usually associated with an identifiable unit whose behavior is expected to differ from that of other units, and such differences are of interest. In the investment data, for example, the s subscript identifies one of a small number of firms, and differences in the investment behavior of the firms are of interest in the research. The j subscript indicates a year, and it is assumed that there are a large number of observations for the investment expenditures of each firm. In fact, there are usually enough observations to estimate individual regressions for each firm. As we have pointed out, it is the correlation across firms in a particular year that distinguishes the SUR model from other models for multivariate data.

Although our other examples for SUR data do not involve time series cross-section data, they have the same general structure: in the test score example, there are a fairly small number of tests and a large number of individuals, and we assume correlation across test results for a particular individual; we are also likely to believe that each covariate has a different effect on each test, which is indicated by different values of β_s. In the household expenditure example, there are a relatively small number of expenditure categories, indexed by s, and a large number of households, indexed by j, and we expect correlation across categories for a given household; again, the covariates are likely to affect each product differently. These cases have in common the idea that the first subscript of y_{sj} is of particular interest and that the second indexes a relatively large number of observations.

In contrast, a typical panel data set consists of a large number of units, usually firms or households, often over a time period that is too short to estimate a separate regression for each unit. The identity of the individual units is of no inherent interest; they are chosen randomly from a very large population and are regarded as exchangeable. The large number of units makes it impractical to estimate individual variances for each unit and covariances for each pair of units. This model assumes further that the behavior of the units is independent at each time period, but that there are differences across individuals that persist over time. These differences are called *heterogeneity*, and they are modeled by a nonzero covariance between the disturbances of a particular firm or household across time.

Here are a few examples of panel data:

9.1 In a famous study, Mundlak (1961) considered agricultural production functions allowing for the possibility of unobserved differences in the quality of management or land that do not change over time.

9.2 Hausman (1978) considered log wages as a function of demographic variables in a panel of 629 observations over 6 years.

9.3 The Vella and Verbeek (1998) study, discussed in earlier chapters, is based on panel data; the sample includes observations on 545 young men over 8 years.

A general version of the model may be written as

$$y_{it} = x'_{it}\beta + w'_{it}b_i + u_{it}, \quad i = 1, \dots, n, \quad t = 1, \dots, T, \tag{9.10}$$

where x_{it} and β are $K_1 \times 1$ and w_{it} and b_i are $K_2 \times 1$. The i subscript of b_i allows each of the variables in w_{it} to have a different effect on each observation unit; these different effects are a way to model heterogeneity. It is assumed that $u_{it} \sim N(0, h_u^{-1})$ and that $\text{Cov}(u_{it}, u_{js}) = 0$ unless $i = t$ and $j = s$. Note that the distribution of u_{it} has been parameterized in terms of the precision rather than the variance. We assume that the covariates in w_{it} are a subset of those in x_{it}. In the statistical literature, the elements of β, which do not differ across i, are called *fixed effects*, and the b_i, which do differ across i, are called *random effects*. This terminology differs from that found in most econometric discussions of panel data models. In that literature, the b_i are regarded either as random variables and called "random effects," or as nonrandom, but unknown, parameters and called "fixed effects." Since, from the Bayesian viewpoint, both β and the b_i are regarded as random variables, the econometric terminology does not distinguish between the two types of parameters. We therefore adopt the definitions found in the statistics literature.

To illustrate how to apply the Bayesian approach to panel data, we specify a basic model and then discuss several ways in which it may be extended. First, define $y_i = (y_{i1}, \ldots, y_{iT})'$, $X_i = (x_{i1}, \ldots, x_{iT})'$, $u_i = (u_{i1}, \ldots, u_{iT})'$, and $W_i = (w_{i1}, \ldots, w_{iT})'$. Then the basic model is

$$
\begin{aligned}
y_i &= X_i\beta + W_i b_i + u_i, \\
u_i | h_u &\sim N_T(0, h_u^{-1} I_T), \\
\beta &\sim N_{K_1}(\beta_0, B_0), \\
h_u &\sim G(\alpha_0/2, \delta_0/2), \\
b_i | D &\sim N_{K_2}(0, D), \\
D^{-1} &\sim W_{K_2}(\nu_0, D_0).
\end{aligned}
\tag{9.11}
$$

From the result that the posterior distribution is proportional to the likelihood function times the prior distribution, we have

$$
\begin{aligned}
\pi(\beta, b, h_u, D | y) &\propto h_u^{nT/2} \exp\left[-\frac{h_u}{2} \sum (y_i - X_i\beta - W_i b_i)'(y_i - X_i\beta - W_i b_i)\right] \\
&\times \exp\left[-\frac{1}{2}(\beta - \beta_0)' B_0^{-1}(\beta - \beta_0)\right] h_u^{\alpha_0/2-1} \exp\left[-\frac{\delta_0 h_u}{2}\right] \\
&\times |D|^{-K_2/2} \exp\left[-\frac{1}{2} \sum b_i' D^{-1} b_i\right] \\
&\times |D|^{-(\nu_0 - K_2 - 1)/2} \exp\left[-\frac{1}{2} \mathrm{tr}(D_0^{-1} D^{-1})\right],
\end{aligned}
$$

where $b = (b_1, \ldots, b_n)$. It is now straightforward to see that

$$
h_u | y, \beta, b, D \sim G(\alpha_1/2, \delta_1/2),
\tag{9.12}
$$

where

$$
\begin{aligned}
\alpha_1 &= \alpha_0 + nT, \\
\delta_1 &= \delta_0 + \sum (y_i - X_i\beta - W_i b_i)'(y_i - X_i\beta - W_i b_i),
\end{aligned}
$$

and

$$
D^{-1} | b \sim W_{K_2}(\nu_1, D_1),
\tag{9.13}
$$

where

$$\nu_1 = \nu_0 + K_2,$$

$$D_1 = \left[D_0^{-1} + \sum b_i b_i' \right]^{-1}.$$

It is preferable to sample β and b in one block as $\pi(\beta, b|y, h_u, D)$, rather than in two blocks $\pi(\beta|y, b, h_u, D)$ and $\pi(b|y, \beta, h_u, D)$, because of possible correlation between them. This is conveniently done by using

$$\pi(\beta, b|y, h_u, D) = \pi(\beta|y, h_u, D)\pi(b|y, \beta, h_u, D)$$

$$= \pi(\beta|y, h_u, D) \prod \pi(b_i|y, \beta, h_u, D).$$

The first term on the right-hand side can be found by integrating out the b_i from $\pi(\beta, b|y, h_u, D)$. For the second, set $\tilde{y}_i = y_i - X_i\beta$ and complete the square in b_i to obtain

$$b_i|y, \beta, D, h_u \sim N_{K_2}(\bar{b}_i, D_{1i}), \tag{9.14}$$

where $D_{1i} = [h_u W_i' W_i + D^{-1}]^{-1}$ and $\bar{b}_i = D_{1i}[h_u W_i' \tilde{y}_i]$. To find the conditional posterior distribution for β, we write $y_i = X_i\beta + (W_i b_i + u_i)$ and integrate out the b_i and u_i:

$$\text{Cov}(y_i) = E[(W_i b_i + u_i)(W_i b_i + u_i)'] = W_i D W_i' + h_u^{-1} I_T \equiv B_{1i},$$

which implies $y_i|\beta, h_u, D \sim N_T(X_i\beta, B_{1i})$. It follows that

$$\pi(\beta|y, D, h_u) \propto \exp\left[-\frac{1}{2} \sum (y_i - X_i\beta)' B_{1i}^{-1}(y_i - X_i\beta) \right]$$

$$\times \exp\left[-\frac{1}{2}(\beta - \beta_0)' B_0^{-1}(\beta - \beta_0) \right],$$

from which we have

$$\beta|y, h_u, D \sim N_{K_1}(\bar{\beta}, B_1), \tag{9.15}$$

where

$$B_1 = \left[\sum X_{1i}' B_{1i}^{-1} X_i + B_0^{-1} \right]^{-1},$$

$$\bar{\beta} = B_1 \left[\sum X_i' B_{1i}^{-1} y_i + B_0^{-1} \beta_0 \right].$$

The algorithmic form of our sampler for panel data is the following.

Algorithm 9.3: Gibbs sampler for model (9.11)

9.1 Choose $\beta^{(0)}, b^{(0)}$.

9.2 At the gth iteration, sample

$$h_u \sim G(\alpha_1/2, \delta_1^{(g)}/2),$$

$$D^{-1} \sim W_{K_2}(\nu_1, D_1^{(g)}),$$

$$b_i \sim N_{K_2}(\bar{b}_i^{(g)}, D_{1i}^{(g)}), \quad i = 1, \ldots, n,$$

$$\beta \sim N_{K_1}(\bar{\beta}^{(g)}, B_1^{(g)}),$$

where

$$\delta_1^{(g)} = \delta_0 + \sum \left(y_i - X_i \beta^{(g-1)} - W_i b_i^{(g-1)} \right)' \left(y_i - X_i \beta^{(g-1)} - W_i b_i^{(g-1)} \right),$$

$$D_1^{(g)} = \left[D_0^{-1} + \sum b_i^{(g-1)} b_i^{(g-1)'} \right]^{-1},$$

$$D_{1i}^{(g)} = [h_u^{(g)} W_i' W_i + (D^{(g)})^{-1}]^{-1},$$

$$\bar{b}_i^{(g)} = D_{1i}^{(g)} [h_u^{(g)} W_i'(y_i - X_i \beta^{(g-1)})],$$

$$B_{1i}^{(g)} = W_i D^{(g)} W_i' + h_u^{-1} I_T,$$

$$B_1^{(g)} = \left[\sum X_i'(B_{1i}^{(g)})^{-1} X_i + B_0^{-1} \right]^{-1},$$

$$\bar{\beta}^{(g)} = B_1^{(g)} \left[\sum X_i'(B_{1i}^{(g)})^{-1} y_i + B_0^{-1} \beta_0 \right].$$

An approximation to the joint posterior distribution of the parameters of interest, $\pi(\beta, h_u, D | y)$, is provided by the simulated output of those parameters, ignoring the simulated values of b.

This model may be extended in several directions. Consider first the model for $E(b_i)$. The simplest assumption is $E(b_i) = 0$, which assumes exchangeability and the independence of the b_i and the covariates in X_i. Since in many applications this assumption seems overly strong, dependence between b_i and covariates a_i : $r \times 1$, possibly including covariates in X_i, may be introduced in a hierarchical fashion by assuming $b_i \sim N_{K_2}(A_i \gamma, h_b^{-1} D_0)$, where $A_i = I_{K_2} \otimes a_i'$ is $K_2 \times r K_2$, D_0 is $K_2 \times K_2$, and γ is $r K_2 \times 1$. This hierarchical specification is an assumption of exchangeability given a_i. The model specification is completed by placing a prior distribution on γ, for example $\gamma \sim N_{r K_2}(\gamma_0, G_0)$. A second extension is to specify hierarchical prior distributions, rather than values, for some or all of the hyperparameters with a subscript of zero. Another possible extension is to substitute a Student-t distribution for the Gaussian. This can be done in the usual way, by assuming $u_i | h_u, \lambda_i \sim N_T(0, (\lambda_i h_u)^{-1} I_T)$ and then adding the λ_i to the sampler. Similarly, the normal distribution for b_i can be replaced by a Student-t distribution by assuming $b_i | D, \eta_i \sim N_{K_2}(b_0, \eta_i^{-1} D)$ and a gamma distribution for

Table 9.5. *Summary of Posterior Distribution: Panel Data Model, Vella–Verbeek Data.*

Coefficient	Mean	S.D.	n.s.e.	Lower	Upper
β_U	0.090	0.044	0.000	0.006	0.179
σ_u^2	1.527	2.121	0.049	0.280	6.379
Mean(b_2)	0.058	0.010	0.000	0.038	0.078
D_{22}	12.568	37.340	0.449	1.340	61.473

η_i; see Exercise 9.3. Finally, it may be desirable to model the time series features of y_i, a topic taken up in Section 10.4.

We conclude with an example based on the Vella–Verbeek data discussed in Sections 4.4 and 8.1.1. The intercept and the experience variable are assigned to W_i (random effects), and the remaining covariates, including the union membership dummy variable, are placed in X_i (fixed effects). The results are summarized in Table 9.5 and Figure 9.3. The coefficient on the union dummy variable based on all 8 years of data is somewhat smaller than that based on only the 1987 data. Mean(b_2) indicates the mean of the n values of b_{i2}, the random effect of experience. On average, a year of experience adds about 6% to wage, but the likely effect varies between 3.85 and 7.82%.

9.4 Further Reading and References

Section 9.2 The sampling of the MVP model is explained in more detail in Chib and Greenberg (1998); it is based on the latent data approach of Albert and Chib (1993b).

In contrast to the MVP model, which models data where an individual makes more than one binary choice, are models for data in which an individual makes one choice from more than two possibilities. These models generalize the binary probit and logit models discussed in Sections 8.2.2 and 8.2.3. One version, called the ordered probit model, arises when the choices have a natural order such as the rating assigned to a corporate bond. An MCMC algorithm for this case is presented in Chib (2001, pp. 3606–7).

For unordered data, we model the probability that decision maker i chooses alternative j, $P(y_i = j|x_i)$, where $j \in \{0, 1, \ldots, J\}$ and x_i is a vector of covariates. Since $\sum_{j=0}^{J} P(y_i = j|x_i) = 1$, we need model only J probabilities. There are several variants of this model, depending on the nature of the data. In the *multinomial probit model*, the covariates are the same for all choices, but specific to an individual. For example, the alternatives are occupational choices, and the

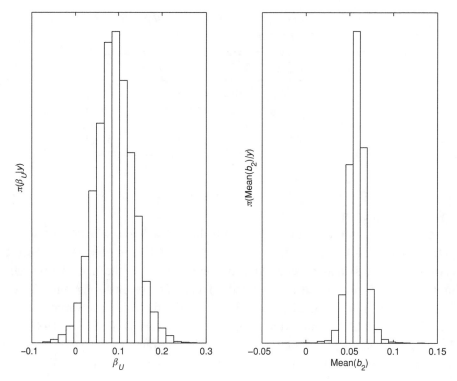

Figure 9.3. Posterior distributions of β_U and mean(b_2).

covariates include the individual's years of education and race. The latent data for this model are specified as $y_{ij}^* = x_i' \beta_j + u_{ij}$, $j = 1, \dots, J$, and $u_i \sim N_J(0, \Sigma)$, where $u_i = (u_{i1}, \dots, u_{iJ})$, and the observed data

$$y_{ij} = \begin{cases} 1, & \text{if } \max\{y_{i1}^*, \dots, y_{iJ}^*\} = y_{ij}^* > 0, \\ 0, & \text{if } \max\{y_{i1}^*, \dots, y_{iJ}^*\} \le 0. \end{cases}$$

In the *conditional probit model*, the covariates are individual and choice specific. For example, an individual chooses between taking a bus, taking a train, or driving a car to work, and the covariates might include the commuting time for individual i when taking transportation choice j or the cost to i when choosing j. The latent data are specified as $y_{ij}^* = x_{ij}' \beta + u_{ij}$, $j = 1, \dots, J$, and $u_i \sim N_J(0, \Sigma)$, where u_i and y_{ij} are defined as in the multinomial probit model. The model is called a *mixed probit model* when data for both types of covariate are available. A clear explanation of the various models appears in Kennedy (2003, sec. 15.2). For other authors, such as Train (2003), the word "mixed" refers to models that include individual-specific parameters as discussed in Section 9.3.

An algorithm for the multinomial probit model requires drawing from an inverted Wishart distribution under the constraint, required for identification, that $\sigma_{11} = 1$.

It is possible to do the simulation as a Gibbs algorithm by setting $Y_{11} = \sigma_{11} = 1$ and applying (A.15). See McCulloch et al. (2000) for details. Also see Rossi et al. (2006, sec 4.2).

The logit model may also be extended to more than two choices. The ordered logit model, which is applicable when the choices have a natural ordering, is discussed from the frequentist viewpoint in Train (2003, sec. 7.4). Conditional logit, multinomial logit, and mixed logit models are specified as the corresponding probit versions. As in the case of the mixed probit model, some authors reserve the mixed logit model to refer to models in which individual-specific effects appear. The various models differ in the way identification constraints are introduced, and the references mentioned before discuss this issue in more detail. The multinomial logit model is analyzed from a Bayesian viewpoint in Chib and Jeliazkov (2005).

Section 9.3 Excellent recent books on panel data, primarily from the frequentist view, are Arellano (2003), Hsiao (2003), and Baltagi (2001); Hsiao's book also contains some Bayesian material. From the Bayesian viewpoint, Chib (in press-b) discusses panel data in great detail and presents more general models than those we have considered, and Chib and Carlin (1999) introduce Algorithm 9.3 and suggest alternative blocking strategies for panel data models.

9.5 Exercises

9.1 Show that the SUR model with multivariate t errors can be analyzed by introducing latent data. Specifically, consider the model

$$y_j = X_j\beta + u_j, \quad u_j | \Sigma, \lambda_j \sim N_S\left(0, \lambda_j^{-1}\Sigma\right), \quad \lambda_j \sim G(\nu/2, \nu/2).$$

By integrating out λ_j, show that $y_j | X_j, \beta, \Sigma \sim t_S(\nu, X_j\beta, \Sigma)$. Let the prior distributions for β and Σ be those in Section 9.1. Specify a Gibbs algorithm to sample from this model.

9.2 Explain how to analyze a panel data set where the response variable is binary, that is, $y_{it} \in \{0, 1\}$, the latent data are determined by $y_{it}^* = x_{it}'\beta + w_{it}'b_i + u_{it}$, and the remainder of the specification is given in (9.11). (Note: Chib and Carlin (1999) provide several algorithms for this model.)

9.3 The basic panel data model of Equation (9.11) can be modified to specify Student-t errors for either or both of u_i and b_i. To do so for both, make the following changes and additions to those equations:

$$u_i | h_u, \lambda_i \sim N_T(0, (\lambda_i h_u)^{-1} I_T),$$
$$\lambda_i \sim G(\nu_l/2, \nu_l/2),$$
$$b_i | D, \eta_i \sim N_{K_2}(0, \eta_i^{-1} D),$$
$$\eta_i \sim G(\nu_h/2, \nu_h/2).$$

Show that, in the modified model,

$$u_i | h_u \sim t_T(\nu_l, 0, I_T) \quad \text{and} \quad b_i | D \sim t_{K_2}(\nu_h, 0, D).$$

Develop an algorithm to sample from $\pi(\beta, h_u, D | y)$.

9.4 Explain how to analyze panel and SUR data sets when the response variable is censored, as in Section 8.2.1. Use a latent data formulation.

9.5 Specify a multivariate logit model and discuss estimation.

Chapter 10

Time Series

THE ANALYSIS OF TIME SERIES data has generated a vast literature from both frequentist and Bayesian viewpoints. We consider a few standard models to illustrate how they can be analyzed with MCMC methods. Section 10.5 provides references to more detailed explanations and additional models.

10.1 Autoregressive Models

This section is concerned with models of the general form

$$y_t = x_t'\beta + \epsilon_t,$$
$$\epsilon_t = \phi_1\epsilon_{t-1} + \phi_2\epsilon_{t-2} + \cdots + \phi_p\epsilon_{t-p} + u_t, \tag{10.1}$$

where $t = 1, \ldots, T$ and $u_t \sim N(0, \sigma_u^2)$. The disturbance ϵ_t is said to be *autoregressive of order p*, denoted by $\epsilon_t \sim \mathrm{AR}(p)$. We assume that the stochastic process defining ϵ_t is second-order stationary, which implies that the mean $E(\epsilon_t)$ and all covariances $E(\epsilon_s\epsilon_t)$ of the process are finite and independent of t and s, although the covariances may depend on $|t - s|$. Note that the variance is the special case of the covariance where $t = s$ and is therefore finite and independent of time.

The stationarity property imposes restrictions on the ϕs. To state these, we define the *lag operator L*. It operates on time-subscripted variables as $Lz_t = z_{t-1}$, which implies that $L^r z_t = z_{t-r}$ for integer values of r. We can now write ϵ_t in terms of the *polynomial in the lag operator*

$$\Phi_p(L) = 1 - \phi_1 L - \cdots - \phi_p L^p,$$

as $\Phi_p(L)\epsilon_t = u_t$. The stationary restriction implies that all roots of the polynomial $\Phi(z)$ lie outside the unit circle. A simple example is the AR(1) model, which leads to the first-order polynomial $\Phi(z) = 1 - \phi_1 z$. Its single root is the solution to $1 - \phi_1 z = 0$, or $z = 1/\phi_1$. Stationarity requires $|1/\phi_1| > 1$, or $|\phi_1| < 1$. Although in the AR(1) model there is a clear connection between the root of the equation and the parameter of the model, the connection is less obvious for autoregressive models of higher order.

This model is a way to capture the possibility that disturbances in a particular time period continue to affect y in later time periods, a property that characterizes many time series in economics and other areas. A special case of some importance is one in which there are no covariates; that is, $y_t = \epsilon_t$, from which we have

$$y_t = \phi_1 y_{t-1} + \cdots + \phi_p y_{t-p} + u_t,$$

in which case $y_t \sim \text{AR}(p)$. It is easy to accommodate a constant term. If

$$z_t = \mu + \phi_1 z_{t-1} + \cdots + \phi_p z_{t-p} + u_t, \qquad (10.2)$$

then

$$E(z_t) = \mu + \phi_1 E(z_{t-1}) + \cdots + \phi_p E(z_{t-p}).$$

But, by stationarity, $E(z_t) = E(z_{t-1}) = \cdots = E(z_{t-p})$, which implies that

$$E(z_t) = \frac{\mu}{1 - \phi_1 - \cdots - \phi_p},$$

if $\sum \phi_i \neq 1$. After subtracting this expression for $E(z_t)$ from both sides of (10.2) and defining $y_t = z_t - E(z_t)$, you can verify that $y_t \sim \text{AR}(p)$ and $E(y_t) = 0$.

We now return to the model with covariates specified in (10.1). Given a sample of T observations, we want the posterior distribution of β, $\phi = (\phi_1, \ldots, \phi_p)'$, and σ_u^2. The likelihood function may be written as

$$f(y_1, \ldots, y_T) = f(Y_p) f(y_{p+1} \mid Y_p) f(y_{p+2} \mid Y_{p+1}) \cdots f(y_T \mid Y_{T-1}),$$

where $Y_r = (y_r, y_{r-1}, \ldots, y_{r-p+1})$. To implement an MCMC algorithm, we first write the likelihood function so that β appears as a regression coefficient given ϕ and then write it so that ϕ appears as a regression coefficient given β.

To isolate β, multiply both sides of (10.1) by $\Phi_p(L)$:

$$\begin{aligned} \Phi_p(L) y_t &= \Phi_p(L) x_t' \beta + \Phi_p(L) \epsilon_t \\ &= \Phi_p(L) x_t' \beta + u_t, \end{aligned}$$

or

$$\hat{y}_t = \hat{x}_t' \beta + u_t,$$

where $\hat{y}_t = \Phi_p(L) y_t$ and $\hat{x}_t = \Phi_p(L) x_t$. This expression is valid for $t > p$, for which it implies $\hat{y}_t \mid Y_{t-1}, \beta, \phi, \sigma^2 \sim N(\hat{x}_t' \beta, \sigma^2)$, but it is not valid for the p observations in Y_p, because observations in periods before $t = 1$ are not available.

The stationarity property can be exploited to find the distribution of Y_p. To do so, we write the model in *state space form*:

$$
\begin{aligned}
y_t &= x_t'\beta + e_1' E_t \quad \text{(observation equation)}, \\
E_t &= GE_{t-1} + e_1 u_t \quad \text{(state equation)},
\end{aligned}
\tag{10.3}
$$

where

$$
G = \begin{pmatrix}
\phi_1 & \phi_2 & \cdots & \phi_p \\
 & & & 0 \\
 & I_{p-1} & & \vdots \\
 & & & 0
\end{pmatrix},
$$

and e_1 is a $p \times 1$ vector with a one in the first row and zeros elsewhere. We can now express Y_p as

$$
Y_p = X_p\beta + E_p,
$$

where, for integer r,

$$
X_r = \begin{pmatrix}
x_p' \\
x_{p-1}' \\
\vdots \\
x_{r-p+1}'
\end{pmatrix}.
$$

It follows that

$$
\begin{aligned}
\Omega_p &\equiv \mathrm{Var}(Y_p) \\
&= \mathrm{Var}(E_p) \\
&= \mathrm{Var}(GE_{p-1} + u_p e_1) \\
&= G\,\mathrm{Var}(E_{p-1})G' + \sigma_u^2 e_1 e_1' \\
&= G\Omega_p G' + \sigma_u^2 e_1 e_1',
\end{aligned}
$$

because $\mathrm{Var}(E_p) = \mathrm{Var}(E_{p-1})$ by stationarity and u_p and E_{p-1} are independent. Finally, it is convenient to define $\Sigma_p = (1/\sigma_u^2)\Omega_p$, implying that $Y_p \sim N_p(X_p\beta, \sigma_u^2\Sigma_p)$. By (A.19) we can write Σ_p explicitly in terms of ϕ:

$$
\begin{aligned}
\mathrm{vec}(\Sigma_p) &= \mathrm{vec}(G\Sigma_p G') + \mathrm{vec}(e_1 e_1') \\
&= (G \otimes G)\,\mathrm{vec}(\Sigma_p) + \mathrm{vec}(e_1 e_1') \\
&= [I - (G \otimes G)]^{-1}\,\mathrm{vec}(e_1 e_1').
\end{aligned}
$$

The joint posterior distribution of the parameters in a form that is convenient for simulating β and σ_u^2 is

$$\pi(\beta, \phi, \sigma_u^2 \mid y) \propto \left(\frac{1}{\sigma_u^2}\right)^{p/2} \frac{1}{|\Sigma_p|^{p/2}} \exp\left[-\frac{1}{2\sigma_u^2}(Y_p - X_p\beta)'\Sigma_p^{-1}(Y_p - X_p\beta)\right]$$

$$\times \left(\frac{1}{\sigma_u^2}\right)^{(T-p)/2} \exp\left[-\frac{1}{2\sigma_u^2}\sum_{p+1}^{T}(\hat{y}_t - \hat{x}_t'\beta)'(\hat{y}_t - \hat{x}_t'\beta)\right]$$

$$\times \pi(\beta)\pi(\sigma_u^2)\pi(\phi).$$

On the assumption $\beta \sim N_K(\beta_0, B_0)$, it is straightforward to show that $\beta \mid y, \sigma_u^2, \phi \sim N_K(\bar{\beta}, B_1)$, where

$$B_1 = \left[\sigma_u^{-2}\left(X_p'\Sigma_p^{-1}X_p + \sum_{p+1}^{T}\hat{x}_t\hat{x}_t'\right) + B_0^{-1}\right]^{-1},$$

$$\bar{\beta} = B_1\left[\sigma_u^{-2}\left(X_p'\Sigma_p^{-1}Y_p + \sum_{p+1}^{T}\hat{x}_t\hat{y}_t\right) + B_0^{-1}\beta_0\right].$$

The derivation of $\pi(\sigma_u^2 \mid y, \beta, \phi)$ is also straightforward on the assumption that the prior distribution for $h_u = 1/\sigma_u^2$ is $G(\alpha_0/2, \delta_0/2)$; then $h_u \mid y, \beta, \phi \sim G(\alpha_1/2, \delta_1/2)$, where

$$\alpha_1 = \alpha_0 + T,$$

$$\delta_1 = \delta_0 + (Y_p - X_p\beta)'\Sigma_p^{-1}(Y_p - X_p\beta) + \sum_{p+1}^{T}(\hat{y}_t - \hat{x}_t'\beta)'(\hat{y}_t - \hat{x}_t'\beta).$$

The conditional posterior distributions of β and σ_u^2 can therefore be simulated by Gibbs steps, but that of ϕ requires an MH step.

We write $\Sigma_p(\phi)$ to reflect the dependence of Σ_p on ϕ and rewrite the likelihood function to make clear the role of ϕ. To do so, let $y_t^* = y_t - x_t'\beta$. Starting again from $\Phi_p(L)y_t = \Phi_p(L)x_t'\beta + u_t$, we find

$$y_t^* = \phi_1 y_{t-1}^* + \cdots + \phi_p y_{t-p}^* + u_t$$

$$= Y_{t-1}^*\phi + u_t.$$

Accordingly, for $t > p$, $y_t^* \sim N(Y_{t-1}^* \phi, \sigma^2)$. The conditional posterior distribution of ϕ is therefore

$$\phi \mid y, \beta, \sigma_u^2 \propto \frac{1}{|\Sigma_p(\phi)|^{T/2}} \exp\left[-\frac{1}{2\sigma_u^2}(Y_p - X_p\beta)' \Sigma_p(\phi)^{-1}(Y_p - X_p\beta) \right]$$

$$\times \exp\left[-\frac{1}{2\sigma_u^2} \sum_{p+1}^{T} (y_t^* - Y_{t-1}^*\phi)'(y_t^* - Y_{t-1}^*\phi) \right]$$

$$\times \pi(\phi) 1(\phi \in S_\phi), \tag{10.4}$$

where S_ϕ is the region in which the process is stationary. This distribution is clearly nonstandard, but it can be sampled with an MH algorithm after specifying the prior distribution of ϕ; for example, $\phi \sim N_p(\phi_0, \Phi_0)$. A possible proposal generating density is the distribution obtained by multiplying $\pi(\phi)$ by the terms involving y_t^*, $t > p$, in (10.4); that distribution is $N(\hat{\phi}, \hat{\Phi})$, where

$$\hat{\Phi} = \left(\sigma_u^{-2} \sum_{p+1}^{T} Y_{t-1}^{*'} Y_{t-1}^* + \Phi_0^{-1} \right)^{-1},$$

$$\hat{\phi} = \hat{\Phi} \left(\sigma_u^{-2} \sum_{p+1}^{T} Y_{t-1}^{*'} y_t^* + \Phi_0^{-1} \phi_0 \right).$$

Draws of ϕ from that distribution are made until one is found that is in the stationary region; it is then subjected to the usual MH acceptance criterion.

As an example, we examine the expectations augmented Phillips curve model as presented in Wooldridge (2006, pp. 390–391). The data are monthly observations on inflation and the unemployment rate for the period 1948 January to 2005 November, and the model is

$$y_t = x_t'\beta + u_t, \tag{10.5}$$

$$u_t = \rho u_{t-1} + \epsilon_t, \tag{10.6}$$

where $\epsilon_t \sim N(0, \sigma^2)$, y_t is the change in inflation rate, and x_t includes a constant and the unemployment rate. We employ the training sample approach to specify hyperparameters for the priors, where the training period is January 1948 to December 1952. The hyperparameters are estimated from a regression of y on x that allows for first-order autocorrelated errors. We set $\alpha_0 = 2.001$ to allow for a large variance and set B_0 at the estimated variance from the training sample.

The results are shown in Table 10.1. The coefficient of unemployment, β_2, is clearly negative; its 95% credibility interval is $(-0.082, -0.036)$, and its mean of -0.059 is in the middle of the interval. The autocorrelation parameter ϕ is clearly positive. Its mean of 0.234, along with the fairly tight credibility interval,

Table 10.1. *Summary of Posterior Distribution: AR(1) Errors.*

Coefficient	Mean	S.D.	n.s.e.	Lower	Upper
β_1	0.343	0.069	0.001	0.206	0.480
β_2	-0.059	0.012	0.000	-0.082	-0.036
σ^2	0.109	0.006	0.000	0.098	0.122
ϕ	0.234	0.037	0.000	0.161	0.308

suggests a moderate amount of autocorrelation. To check this, we ran the same specification without an autocorrelation parameter, where the priors are taken from a regression on the training-sample data, assuming independent errors. The $\log_{10}$ of the marginal likelihood for the AR(1) model is -89.028 compared to -94.543 for the model that assumes independent errors, which is a strong evidence in favor of the autocorrelated model.

10.2 Regime-Switching Models

This section takes up the regime-switching (or hidden Markov) model popularized in econometrics by Hamilton (1989) and first studied from a Bayesian MCMC perspective by Albert and Chib (1993a). We consider the AR(0) version presented in Kim and Nelson (1999, chap. 9). The model is given by

$$y_t = \mu_0 + \mu_1 s_t + u_t, \quad t = 1, \ldots, T,$$

where $u_t \sim N(0, \sigma_{s_t}^2)$. The hidden variable s_t indicates the two states or regimes of the model, 0 and 1. The probability of being in state s_t is given by a Markov process,

$$P(s_t = 0 \mid s_{t-1} = 0) = 1 - a,$$
$$P(s_t = 1 \mid s_{t-1} = 0) = a,$$
$$P(s_t = 0 \mid s_{t-1} = 1) = b,$$
$$P(s_t = 1 \mid s_{t-1} = 1) = 1 - b.$$

The intercept shifts from μ_0 in state 0 to $\mu_0 + \mu_1$, $\mu_1 > 0$, in state 1, while the variance shifts from σ_0^2 to σ_1^2. In a typical macroeconomics application, y_t, the growth rate of GDP, is modeled as being in one of two states – the larger mean of state 1 identifies a period of rapid growth and the smaller mean of state 0 identifies a period of slow growth or recession. The condition $\mu_1 > 0$ is a way to identify the model. If μ_1 could be negative, we could relabel the pair (μ_0, σ_0^2) to be the state 1 parameters and the pair $(\mu_0 + \mu_1, \sigma_1^2)$ to be those of state 0.

The posterior distributions to be estimated are those of $\mu = (\mu_0, \mu_1)$, $P = (a, b)$, $\sigma^2 = (\sigma_0^2, \sigma_1^2)$, and $S = (s_1, \ldots, s_T)$. The values $P(s_t = 1 \mid y)$ estimate the probability that the economy is not in recession for each of the time periods in the sample. The model can be extended by assuming $u \sim \mathrm{AR}(p)$, by including covariates in the form $x_t'\beta$, and by specifying more than two states.

Given S, the likelihood function can be written as the product of terms when the process is in state 0 times the product of terms when the process is in state 1:

$$
f(y \mid S, \mu, \sigma^2) \propto \left(\frac{1}{\sigma_0^2}\right)^{T_0/2} \exp\left[-\frac{1}{2\sigma_0^2} \sum_{t:s_t=0} (y_t - \mu_0)^2\right]
$$

$$
\times \left(\frac{1}{\sigma_1^2}\right)^{T_1/2} \exp\left[-\frac{1}{2\sigma_1^2} \sum_{t:s_t=1} (y_t - \mu_0 - \mu_1)^2\right],
$$

where $T_1 = \sum_t s_t$ and $T_0 = T - T_1$. By assuming the usual conditional conjugate distributions for μ_0 and σ^2 and a truncated normal distribution for μ_1, it is straightforward to devise a sampler for μ and σ^2. Moreover, if we are given S and beta prior distributions for a and b

$$
\pi(a) \propto a^{a_0-1}(1-a)^{a_1-1},
$$

$$
\pi(b) \propto b^{b_0-1}(1-b)^{b_1-1},
$$

then the conditional posterior distributions of a and b are independent of Y_T, and $\pi(a \mid S_T)$ is a beta distribution with parameters $a_0 + S_{01}$ and $a_1 + S_{00}$, where S_{ij} is the number of transitions from state i to state j. An analogous calculation can be made for $\pi(b \mid S_T)$.

The interesting part of the analysis of this model lies in the sampling for S; our discussion follows Chib (1996). The derivations that follow illustrate two important aspects of algorithm design: (1) all of the steps utilize the standard rules of probability and (2) the derivations require considerable ingenuity and care.

Begin by defining $S_t = (s_1, \ldots, s_t)$ and $S^{t+1} = (s_{t+1}, \ldots, s_T)$, and, analogously, Y_t and Y_{t+1}. In addition, let $\theta = (\mu, \sigma^2, P)$. We wish to find $\pi(S_T \mid Y_T, \theta)$. By Bayes theorem,

$$
\pi(S_T \mid Y_T, \theta) = p(s_T \mid Y_T, \theta)p(S_{T-1} \mid Y_T, s_T, \theta)
$$

$$
= p(s_T \mid Y_T, \theta) \times \cdots \times p(s_t \mid Y_T, S^{t+1}, \theta) \times \cdots \times p(s_1 \mid Y_T, S^2, \theta).
$$

$$\tag{10.7}$$

Except for the first, the terms in this expression have the form $p(s_t \mid Y_T, S^{t+1}, \theta)$. Again by Bayes theorem,

$$p(s_t \mid Y_T, S^{t+1}, \theta) \propto p(s_t \mid Y_t, \theta) f(Y^{t+1}, S^{t+1} \mid Y_t, s_t, \theta)$$
$$\propto p(s_t \mid Y_t, \theta) p(s_{t+1} \mid s_t, \theta) f(Y^{t+1}, S^{t+2} \mid Y_t, s_t, s_{t+1}, \theta)$$
$$\propto p(s_t \mid Y_t, \theta) p(s_{t+1} \mid s_t, \theta).$$

The last step follows from the independence of (Y^{t+1}, S^{t+2}) and s_t, given s_{t+1} and θ. Incorporating the proportionality constant, we have

$$p(s_t \mid Y_T, S^{t+1}, \theta) = \frac{p(s_t \mid Y_t, \theta) p(s_{t+1} \mid s_t, \theta)}{\sum_{s_t} p(s_t \mid Y_t, \theta) p(s_{t+1} \mid s_t, \theta)}. \tag{10.8}$$

The next step is to use (10.8) to generate a sample of S_T. The term $p(s_{t+1} \mid s_t, \theta)$ can be evaluated by the Markov model for s_t given a and b, but $p(s_t \mid Y_t, \theta)$ requires a recursion. By the law of total probability,

$$p(s_t \mid Y_{t-1}, \theta) = \sum_k p(s_t \mid s_{t-1} = k, \theta) p(s_{t-1} = k \mid Y_{t-1}, \theta), \tag{10.9}$$

this expression is the "prediction step": it predicts s_t on the basis of information Y_{t-1} available before period t. Next is the "update step," which updates the probability of s_t on the basis of Y_t:

$$p(s_t \mid Y_t, \theta) = \frac{p(s_t \mid Y_{t-1}, \theta) f(y_t \mid Y_{t-1}, s_t, \theta)}{\sum_{s_t} p(s_t \mid Y_{t-1}, \theta) f(y_t \mid Y_{t-1}, s_t, \theta)}.$$

We begin the recursion of (10.9) with $p(s_1 \mid Y_0, \theta)$ by sampling s_1 from the invariant distribution as a function of a and b. In the two-state case, we find the invariant distribution from (6.6),

$$p(s_1 = 0) = \frac{b}{a+b} \quad \text{and} \quad p(s_1 = 1) = \frac{a}{a+b}.$$

We next compute $p(s_2 \mid Y_1, \theta)$ from the prediction step and $p(s_2 \mid Y_2, \theta)$ from the update step. The recursion continues for $t = 3, \ldots, T$. At the last step of this recursion, the "forward" recursion, a value of s_T is simulated from $p(s_T \mid Y_T, \theta)$. Given this value of s_T, the "backward" recursion samples $s_{t-1} \mid Y_T, S^{t+1}, \theta$, for $t = T, T-1, \ldots, 2$, as in (10.7) and (10.8).

As an example, we apply the data to real GDP from the first quarter of 1952 to the third quarter of 1995. Results appear in Table 10.2 and Figure 10.1, where we plot the posterior means of the probability that the economy is in recession, $1 - s_t$. The table indicates a substantial difference in recessionary (μ_0) and nonrecessionary growth rates (μ_1). The results also indicate an asymmetry in the probability of changing states: an economy in recession has a probability of 0.742 of remaining in recession, but an economy that is not in recession has a probability of 0.926 of

Table 10.2. *Parameter Estimates for GDP Data.*

Parameter	Mean	S. D.	Median
μ_0	-0.353	0.266	-0.339
μ_1	1.334	0.232	1.322
σ^2	0.579	0.076	0.572
$1-a$	0.742	0.085	0.751
$1-b$	0.926	0.034	0.930

not going into recession. The figure suggests a fairly clear-cut distinction between recessionary and nonrecessionary periods since only a few of the 175 observations are around 0.5.

10.3 Time-Varying Parameters

The model discussed in this section assumes that regression coefficients evolve randomly through time. It is written in state–space form and consists of the *observation*

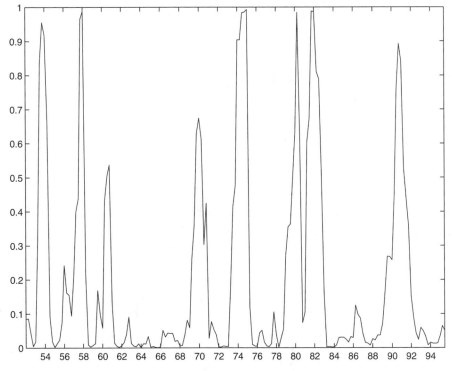

Figure 10.1. Probability of recession.

equation

$$y_t = x_t'\beta_t + u_t, \tag{10.10}$$

and the *transition equation*

$$\beta_t = \beta_{t-1} + \epsilon_t, \tag{10.11}$$

where $t = 1, \ldots, T$, y_t and u_t are scalars, x_t, β_t, and ϵ_t are $K \times 1$ vectors, $u_t \sim N(0, \sigma^2)$, and $\epsilon_t \sim N_K(0, \Sigma)$. We further assume that the u_t and ϵ_t are independent of each other and through time. The initial state β_0 can be given a fixed value or can be assumed to have a normal distribution with known mean and variance. Another possibility is to specify a hierarchical model for β_0. For simplicity, we take β_0 to be a known vector. This model can be generalized to a vector autoregression by allowing y_t to be a vector.

To analyze this model we define

$$Y = (y_T, y_{T-1}, \ldots, y_1)',$$

$$\beta = (\beta_T, \beta_{T-1}, \ldots, \beta_1)',$$

$$u = (u_T, u_{T-1}, \ldots, u_1),$$

$$\epsilon = (\epsilon_T, \epsilon_{T-1}, \ldots, \epsilon_1)',$$

$$X = \begin{pmatrix} x_T' & 0 & 0 & 0 \\ 0 & x_{T-1}' & \cdots & 0 \\ \vdots & \vdots & \ddots & 0 \\ 0 & 0 & \cdots & x_1' \end{pmatrix}.$$

The likelihood function is

$$f(y \mid \beta, \sigma^2) \propto \left(\frac{1}{\sigma^2}\right)^{T/2} \exp\left[-\frac{1}{2\sigma^2}(y - X\beta)'(y - X\beta)\right].$$

The transition equation leads to a prior distribution for β: by defining the $KT \times KT$ matrix H

$$H = \begin{pmatrix} I_K & -I_K & 0 & \cdots & 0 \\ 0 & I_K & -I_K & \cdots & 0 \\ \vdots & 0 & I_K & \ddots & 0 \\ \vdots & 0 & \ddots & \ddots & 0 \\ 0 & 0 & 0 & 0 & I_K \end{pmatrix},$$

we can write $H\beta = \tilde{\beta}_0 + \epsilon$, where $\tilde{\beta}_0$ is a $TK \times 1$ vector with β_0 in the last K rows and zeros elsewhere. It follows that $\beta = H^{-1}\tilde{\beta}_0 + H^{-1}\epsilon$, from which we conclude that

$$\beta \sim N_K(H^{-1}\tilde{\beta}_0, H^{-1}(I_T \otimes \Sigma)(H^{-1})').$$

We adopt standard priors for the remaining parameters: $1/\sigma^2 \sim G(\alpha_0/2, \delta_0/2)$ and $\Sigma^{-1} \sim W_K(\nu_0, S_0)$. The joint posterior distribution is

$$\pi(\beta, \sigma^2, \Sigma \mid y) \propto \left(\frac{1}{\sigma^2}\right)^{T/2} \exp\left[-\frac{1}{2\sigma^2}(y - X\beta)'(y - X\beta)\right] \frac{1}{|\Sigma|^{T/2}}$$

$$\times \exp\left[-\frac{1}{2}(\beta - H^{-1}\tilde{\beta}_0)'H'(I_T \otimes \Sigma^{-1})H(\beta - H^{-1}\tilde{\beta}_0)\right]$$

$$\times \left(\frac{1}{\sigma^2}\right)^{\alpha_0/2-1} \exp\left[-\frac{\delta_0}{2\sigma^2}\right] \frac{1}{|\Sigma|^{(\nu_0-K-1)/2}} \exp\left[-\frac{1}{2}\mathrm{tr}(S_0^{-1}\Sigma^{-1})\right],$$

where we have used $|H'(I_T \otimes \Sigma^{-1})H| = |H'||I_T \otimes \Sigma^{-1}||H|$, $|H| = 1$, and (A.20).

A Gibbs algorithm can be used because the conditional posterior distributions are available for sampling:

$$\beta|y, \sigma^2, \Sigma \sim N_{TK}(\bar{\beta}, B_1),$$

$$(1/\sigma^2)|y, \beta, \Sigma \sim G(\nu_1/2, \delta_1/2),$$

$$\Sigma^{-1} \sim W_K(\nu_1, S_1),$$

where

$$B_1 = \left[(1/\sigma^2)X'X + H'(I_T \otimes \Sigma^{-1})H\right]^{-1},$$

$$\bar{\beta} = B_1\left[(1/\sigma^2)X'y + H'(I_T \otimes \Sigma^{-1})\tilde{\beta}_0\right],$$

$$\alpha_1 = \alpha_0 + T,$$

$$\delta_1 = \delta_0 + (y - X\beta)'(y - X\beta),$$

$$\nu_1 = \nu_0 + T,$$

$$S_1 = \left[S_0^{-1} + \sum_{t=1}^{T}(\beta_t - \beta_{t-1})(\beta_t - \beta_{t-1})'\right]^{-1}.$$

The expression for S_1 follows from

$$(\beta - H^{-1}\tilde{\beta}_0)'H'(I_T \otimes \Sigma^{-1})H(\beta - H^{-1}\tilde{\beta}_0) = (H\beta - \tilde{\beta}_0)'(I \otimes \Sigma^{-1})(H\beta - \tilde{\beta}_0)$$

$$= \begin{pmatrix} \beta_T - \beta_{T-1} \\ \vdots \\ \beta_1 - \beta_0 \end{pmatrix}' \begin{pmatrix} \Sigma^{-1} & 0 & 0 & 0 \\ 0 & \Sigma^{-1} & 0 & 0 \\ \vdots & & \ddots & \vdots \\ 0 & 0 & 0 & \Sigma^{-1} \end{pmatrix} \begin{pmatrix} \beta_T - \beta_{T-1} \\ \vdots \\ \beta_1 - \beta_0 \end{pmatrix}$$

$$= \sum_{t=1}^{T} (\beta_t - \beta_{t-1})'\Sigma^{-1}(\beta_t - \beta_{t-1})$$

$$= \mathrm{tr}\left[\sum_{t=1}^{T} (\beta_t - \beta_{t-1})(\beta_t - \beta_{t-1})'\Sigma^{-1}\right].$$

This algorithm must be modified for large KT because B_1 is the inverse of a $KT \times KT$ matrix that may be too large to invert rapidly and accurately. The matrix inversion can be avoided by sampling β_t with the same type of recursive scheme utilized in sampling for s_t in Section 10.2.

As an example of this model, we return to the Phillips curve model discussed in Section 10.1, but we now assume that β_t follows a random walk, rather than being constant, and that u_t is not autocorrelated. The model is that of Equations (10.10) and (10.11), where y_t is the change in the inflation rate and x_t consists of a constant and the unemployment rate. The priors are again based on the first 5 years of data employed as a training sample, and β_t is taken as a constant over the training sample to specify the hyperparameters.

Table 10.3 and Figure 10.2 contain results, where the lower and upper limits refer to a 90% credibility interval. Results are based on 20,000 draws from the posterior distribution after 1,000 burn-in iterations. The $\log_{10}$ marginal likelihood value is -92.506. The AR(1) model has a larger marginal likelihood despite the large variation in the values of β_t displayed in Figure 10.2.

Table 10.3. *Summary of Posterior Distribution: Time Varying Parameter Model.*

Coefficient	Mean	S.D.	Lower	Upper
σ_{11}	0.006	0.003	0.003	0.010
σ_{12}	-0.001	0.001	-0.002	-0.001
σ_{22}	0.000	0.000	0.000	0.000
σ^2	0.103	0.006	0.096	0.111

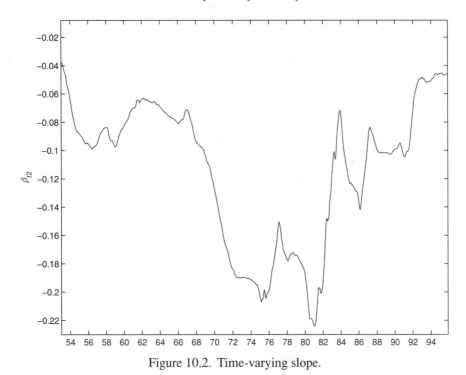

Figure 10.2. Time-varying slope.

10.4 Time Series Properties of Models for Panel Data

A number of models have been proposed to capture the time series nature of panel data; we examine two of these. For both models, we set $i = 1, \ldots, n$, and $t = 1, \ldots, T$.

First, consider the dynamic panel model

$$y_{it} = \beta_1 y_{i,t-1} + b_i + u_{it}, \quad |\beta_1| < 1, \quad u_{it} \sim N(0, \sigma^2). \tag{10.12}$$

For simplicity, we condition on y_{i1} rather than specify its distribution. The likelihood function for $y_{i2}, \ldots, y_{iT}$ can be written as

$$f(y_{i2}, \ldots, y_{iT} \mid y_{i1}) = f(y_{i2} \mid y_{i1}) f(y_{i3} \mid y_{i2}) \cdots f(y_{iT} \mid y_{i,T-1})$$

$$\propto \left(\frac{1}{\sigma^2}\right)^{(T-1)/2} \exp\left[-\frac{1}{2\sigma^2} \sum_{t=2}^{} (y_{it} - \beta_1 y_{i,t-1} - b_i)^2\right].$$

By defining $y_i = (y_{i2}, \ldots, y_{iT})'$, $X_i = (y_{i1}, \ldots, y_{i,T-1})'$, $\beta = \beta_1$, $w_{it} = 1$, and $u_i = (u_{i2}, \ldots, u_{iT})'$, the dynamic model (10.12) is equivalent to the static panel model of (9.11), along with the prior distributions specified there and the added requirement that $|\beta_1| < 1$. Accordingly, the algorithm specified for the earlier model is applicable, except that the sampling for β_1 is from a normal distribution truncated to $(-1, 1)$.

Second, consider a model that includes unit-specific regression coefficients and an AR(1) disturbance term:

$$y_{it} = x_{it}'\beta + w_{it}'b_i + \epsilon_{it}, \quad \epsilon_{it} = \rho\epsilon_{i,t-1} + u_{it}, \quad |\rho| < 1, \tag{10.13}$$

where $u_{it} \sim N(0, \sigma^2)$ independent over i and t. A standard analysis shows that

$$\text{Cov}(\epsilon_{it}, \epsilon_{i,t-s}) = \frac{\sigma^2}{1 - \rho^2}\rho^s,$$

which implies that $y_i \mid \beta, b_i, \rho, \sigma^2 \sim N(X_i\beta + W_ib_i, \frac{\sigma^2}{1-\rho^2}\Omega)$, where

$$\Omega = \begin{pmatrix} 1 & \rho & \rho^2 & \cdots & \rho^{T-1} \\ \rho & 1 & \rho & \cdots & \rho^{T-2} \\ \vdots & \vdots & \vdots & \cdots & \vdots \\ \rho^{T-1} & \rho^{T-2} & \cdots & \rho & 1 \end{pmatrix}.$$

We may again utilize the specification in (9.11) by adding a prior distribution for ρ, say $\rho \sim \text{TN}_{(-1,1)}(\rho_0, R_0)$, and modifying the likelihood function to

$$f(y \mid \beta, b, \sigma^2, \rho) \propto \left(\frac{\sigma^2}{1 - \rho^2}\right)^{-T/2} \frac{1}{|\Omega|^{T/2}}$$

$$\times \exp\left[-\frac{1 - \rho^2}{2\sigma^2} \sum_i (y_i - X_i\beta - W_ib_i)'\Omega^{-1}(y_i - X_i\beta - W_ib_i)\right].$$

We leave the details of the algorithm as an exercise.

10.5 Further Reading and References

Chapter 10 Useful sources for time series, primarily from the frequentist viewpoint, are Hamilton (1994) and Harvey (1989). Such standard texts as Greene (2003, chaps. 12, 20) also cover the basic ideas.

Secton 10.1 Chib (1993) considers the AR(p) model conditioned on the first p observations in which case all the updates are in closed form and no MH step is required. The general ARMA(p, q) model without conditioning is covered from the Bayesian viewpoint in Chib and Greenberg (1994). The Phillips curve example was estimated with the "AR" model in the BACC program. See Geweke (2005, sec. 7.1) for details.

Section 10.2 State–space models are discussed from a Bayesian viewpoint by Carlin et al. (1992b), Carter and Kohn (1994), Frühwirth-Schnatter (1994), de Jong and Shephard (1995), Chib and Greenberg (1995a), and Kim and Nelson (1999); the latter provide downloadable Gauss software. The results contained in the text were computed with their program GIBS_MS0.PRG. Further discussion of the hidden Markov model from the Bayesian viewpoint may be found in Chib (2001, sec. 8.8), which builds on Albert and Chib (1993a) and Chib (1996).

The regime-switching model is a mixture model,

$$y_t \sim P(s_t = 0)N(\mu_0, \sigma_0^2) + P(s_t = 1)N(\mu_0 + \mu_1, \sigma_1^2).$$

As noted before, this model is not identified without a restriction such as $\mu_1 > 0$, because the state labels and all parameters could be switched. The restriction has the effect of forcing the mean of the distribution in state 1 to be greater than the mean in state 0. Without such a restriction, the sampler would generate a bimodal distribution for the means and variances. More generally, the question of how to deal with label switching has been studied extensively. While the solution we have adopted works well in the regime-switching model, the question of how to deal with models with more states and more parameters is not settled. For an introduction, suggested solutions, and further references, see Celeux et al. (2000) and Frühwirth-Schnatter (2001).

Section 10.3 More details and references to an MCMC algorithm for this model is in Chib (2001, sec. 8.9); a discussion and downloadable programs are in Kim and Nelson (1999, chap. 9). A model that combines regime switching and time-varying parameters, along with downloadable programs, is described in Kim and Nelson (1999, chap. 10).

Section 10.4 The panel data model with correlated errors is discussed in Chib (in press-b).

10.6 Exercises

10.1 Verify that the state–space form (10.3) reproduces the AR(p) model of (10.1).

10.2 Explain how to find the predictive distribution for y_{T+1} if $y_t \sim$ AR(p), given a sample of draws from the posterior distributions of β, ϕ, and σ_u^2.

10.3 Provide the details of an algorithm to analyze the model of (10.13).

10.4 Modify the SUR model to include first-order autocorrelation, and describe an algorithm for estimating parameters.

Chapter 11

Endogenous Covariates and Sample Selection

THIS CHAPTER IS CONCERNED with data sets for which the assumption made about the exogeneity of covariates in Chapter 4 and subsequent chapters is untenable. Covariates that are correlated with the disturbance term are called *endogenous variables* in the econometrics literature. We take up three types of models in which endogeneity may be present: treatment models, unobserved covariates, and sample selection subject to incidental truncation.

11.1 Treatment Models

Treatment models are used to compare responses of individuals who belong either to a treatment or a control group. If the assignment to a group is random, as in many of the clinical trials that arise in biostatistical applications, the assignment may be regarded as independent of any characteristics of the individual. But in many economic applications and in clinical trials in which compliance is not guaranteed, whether an individual is in the treatment or control group may depend on unobserved covariates that are correlated with the response variable. Such unobserved covariates are called *confounders* in the statistical literature; in the econometrics literature, the treatment assignment is called endogenous when it is not independent of the response variable. As an example, let the response variable be wages and the treatment be participation in a job training program. We might expect that people with sufficient motivation to participate in training would earn higher wages, even without participating in the program, than those with less motivation. The problem may be less serious if individuals are randomly assigned to the training program, but there may still be confounding. For example, individuals assigned to the program may choose not to participate, and individuals not assigned to the program may find a way to participate. Inferences drawn from models that ignore confounding may yield misleading results.

To model this situation, we suppose that the response variable is related to the covariates and the treatment assignment through

$$y_{0i} = x_i'\beta_0 + u_{0i},$$
$$y_{1i} = x_i'\beta_1 + u_{1i}, \qquad (11.1)$$

where x_i is a K_1 vector of covariates, a 0 subscript indicates assignment to the control group, and 1 indicates assignment to the treatment group. The group assignment is determined by the binary variable s_i,

$$s_i = \begin{cases} 0, & \text{if } i \text{ is assigned to control group,} \\ 1, & \text{if } i \text{ is assigned to treatment group.} \end{cases}$$

An important objective of such studies is to determine the effect of the treatment on the response. The *average treatment effect* is a measure of this effect; it is defined as

$$\text{ATE} = E(y_{1i} - y_{0i}|x_i) = x_i'(\beta_1 - \beta_0).$$

Because an individual is assigned to either the treatment or control group, however, only one of y_{0i} and y_{1i} are observed. In the presence of confounding, the data provide information about $E(y_{1i}|s_i = 1)$ and $E(y_{0i}|s_i = 0)$, but the difference between these is not the ATE, because of the correlation between y_{0i} and s_i and between y_{1i} and s_i:

$$E(y_{1i}|s_i = 1) - E(y_{0i}|s_i = 0) = x_i'(\beta_1 - \beta_0) + [E(u_{1i}|s_i = 1) - E(u_{0i}|s_i = 0)],$$

and the bracketed term is not equal to zero in the presence of confounding.

One approach to solving the problem caused by confounders is to model the assignment decision. We consider a method that uses one or more *instrumental variables* (IVs). These are variables that have two properties:

11.1 They are independent of u_{0i} and u_{1i}.
11.2 They are not independent of s_i.

In the wage–job training program example, a possible IV is the score on an intelligence test: we would not expect the test score itself to affect wages, and we would not expect the decision to participate to be independent of intelligence. By their independence from the confounders, the IVs introduce an element of randomization into data that were not generated by random assignment. In particular, we assume

$$s_i^* = x_i'\gamma_1 + z_i'\gamma_2 + v_i,$$
$$s_i = \begin{cases} 1, & \text{if } s_i^* > 0, \\ 0, & \text{if } s_i^* \leq 0, \end{cases} \qquad (11.2)$$

and set

$$y_i = (1 - s_i)y_{0i} + s_i y_{1i}, \tag{11.3}$$

where z_i is a $K_2 \times 1$ vector of instrumental variables. The latent data value s_i^* for the treatment indicator s_i is modeled as a binary probit variable. Confounding or endogeneity appears in this model if there is a correlation between u_{0i} and v_i and between u_{1i} and v_i. We regard the correlation as arising from an unobserved covariate that affects both the observed response y_i and whether or not i receives the treatment. The covariance matrices are

$$\text{Cov}(u_{0i}, v_i) \equiv \Sigma_0 = \begin{pmatrix} \sigma_{00} & \sigma_{0v} \\ \sigma_{0v} & 1 \end{pmatrix}, \qquad \text{Cov}(u_{1i}, v_i) \equiv \Sigma_1 = \begin{pmatrix} \sigma_{11} & \sigma_{1v} \\ \sigma_{1v} & 1 \end{pmatrix},$$

where $\sigma_{vv} = 1$ because of the probit specification.

We now develop a Gibbs algorithm to draw a sample from the posterior distribution of the parameters. First, some definitions and notation. For the remainder of the section, $j = 0, 1$ indicates the untreated and treated groups, respectively. Let $\beta = (\beta_0', \beta_1', \gamma_1', \gamma_2')'$, $\gamma = (\gamma_1', \gamma_2')'$,

$$X_{ji} = \begin{pmatrix} (1 - j)x_i' & jx_i' & 0 & 0 \\ 0 & 0 & x_i' & z_i' \end{pmatrix},$$

y, X, Z, respectively, are the observations on y_i, x_i, and z_i, s^* represents the latent data s_i^*, $N_0 = \{i : s_i = 0\}$, $N_1 = \{i : s_i = 1\}$, and n_0 and n_1, respectively, are the number of observations in N_0 and N_1. We assume a Gaussian prior distribution for $\beta \sim N_p(b_0, B_0)$, where $p = 3K_1 + K_2$. To expedite the simulation, we reparameterize the variances in Σ_j as $\omega_{jj} = \sigma_{jj} - \sigma_{jv}^2$, which is positive because $\omega_{jj} = |\Sigma_j|$ and Σ_j is positive definite. We define $\psi_j = (\omega_{jj}, \sigma_{jv})$ and specify the prior distributions

$$\begin{aligned} \pi(\psi_j) &= \pi(\omega_{jj})\pi(\sigma_{jv}|\omega_{jj}) \\ &= \text{IG}(v_{j0}/2, d_{j0}/2)N(m_{j0}, \omega_{jj}M_{j0}). \end{aligned}$$

The posterior distribution has the form

$$\begin{aligned} \pi(\beta, \psi_0, \psi_1, s^*|y, s) &= \pi(\beta)\pi(\psi_0)\pi(\psi_1)\prod_i [[1(s_i = 0)1(s_i^* \leq 0) + 1(s_i = 1) \\ &\times 1(s_i^* > 0)]N_2(y_i, s_i^*|X_{0i}\beta, \Sigma_0))^{1-s_i}(N_2(y_i, s_i^*|X_{1i}\beta, \Sigma_1))^{s_i}], \end{aligned}$$

and the Gibbs algorithm proceeds in four blocks: ψ_0, ψ_1, β, and s^*.

The ψ_j blocks may be sampled by the method of composition,

$$\pi(\psi_j|\beta, s^*, y, X, Z) = \pi(\sigma_{jv}|\omega_{jj}, \beta, s^*, y, X, Z)\pi(\omega_{jj}|\beta, s^*, y, X, Z).$$

For the first of these, you will be asked to show in Exercise 11.1 that

$$y_{ji}|s_i^*, \beta_j, \gamma, \psi_j \sim N(x_i'\beta_j + \sigma_{jv}e_i, \omega_{jj}), \qquad (11.4)$$

where $e_i = s_i^* - x_i'\gamma_1 - z_i'\gamma_2$. Let Y_j, X_j, Z_j, S_j^*, and E_j, respectively, contain the values of y_{ji}, x_i, z_i, s_i^*, and e_i for $i \in N_j$. Then

$$Y_j|S_j^*, \beta_j, \gamma, \psi_j \sim N_{n_j}(X_j\beta_j + \sigma_{jv}E_j, \omega_{jj}I_{n_j}). \qquad (11.5)$$

Because σ_{jv} appears in (11.5) as a regression parameter, its conditional posterior distribution is easily obtained. The next step is to obtain the conditional posterior distribution of ω_{jj} after marginalizing out σ_{jv} with respect to its prior distribution. From (11.5), you will verify in Exercise 11.2 that

$$E(Y_j|S_j^*, \beta_j, \gamma, \omega_{jj}) = X_j\beta_j + m_{j0}E_j, \qquad (11.6)$$

$$\text{Var}(Y_j|S_j^*, \gamma, \omega_{jj}) = \omega_{jj}(I_{n_j} + E_jM_{j0}E_j'). \qquad (11.7)$$

Equation (11.5) is multiplied by the prior distribution of ω_{jj} to obtain its conditional posterior distribution, which has the form of an inverse gamma distribution.

In the second block, we sample for β conditioned on all other parameters and the data. This step uses the SUR setup of Section 9.1. In the third block, s^* is sampled from the usual truncated normal distributions. You are asked to supply the details of the distributions in Exercise 11.4.

In algorithmic form, we have the following.

Algorithm 11.1: Gibbs algorithm for treatment model (Chib, in press-a)

11.1 Sample ψ_j conditioned on (y, s^*, X, Z, β)

(a) Drawing ω_{jj} marginalized over σ_{jv} from

$$\text{IG}\left(\frac{\nu_{j0} + n_j}{2}, \frac{d_{j0} + d_j}{2}\right),$$

where

$$d_j = (Y_j - X_j\beta_j - m_{j0}E_j)'(I_{n_j} + E_jM_{j0}E_j')^{-1}(Y_j - X_j\beta_j - m_{j0}E_j),$$

(b) Drawing σ_{jv} conditioned on ω_{jj} from $N(c_j, \omega_{jj}C_j)$, where

$$c_j = C_j[M_{j0}^{-1}m_{j0} + E_j'(Y_j - X_j\beta_j)],$$
$$C_j = (M_{j0}^{-1} + E_j'E_j)^{-1}.$$

11.2 Sample β conditioned on (y, s^*, ψ_0, ψ_1) from $N_p(\hat{\beta}, B)$, where

$$\hat{\beta} = B\left(B_0^{-1}b_0 + \sum_{i \in N_0} X_{0i}'\Sigma_0^{-1}y_i^* + \sum_{i \in N_1} X_{1i}'\Sigma_1^{-1}y_i^*\right),$$

$$B = \left(B_0^{-1} + \sum_{i \in N_0} X_{0i}'\Sigma_0^{-1}X_{0i} + \sum_{i \in N_1} X_{1i}'\Sigma_1^{-1}X_{1i}\right)^{-1},$$

and $y_i^* = (y_i, s_i^*)'$.

11.3 Sample s^* conditioned on $(y, X, Z, \beta, \psi_0, \psi_1)$ by drawing

$$s_i^* \text{ from } \begin{cases} \text{TN}_{(-\infty,0)} \left(\mu_{0i}, \phi_0^2 \right), & \text{if } s_i = 0, \\ \text{TN}_{(0,\infty)} \left(\mu_{1i}, \phi_1^2 \right), & \text{if } s_i = 1, \end{cases}$$

where

$$\mu_{ji} = x_i' \gamma_1 + z_i' \gamma_2 + \sigma_{jv} \sigma_{jj}^{-1} (y_{ji} - x_i' \beta_j),$$
$$\phi_j^2 = 1 - \sigma_{jv}^2 \sigma_{jj}^{-1}.$$

We compute the marginal likelihood for this model by the Chib method of Section 7.1.2; it uses the fact that the log of the marginal likelihood $m(y, s | X, Z)$ can be written as

$$\log m(y, s | X, Z) = \log f(y, s | X, Z, \beta^*, \psi_0^*, \psi_1^*) + \log \pi(\beta^*, \psi_0^*, \psi_1^*)$$
$$- \log \pi(\beta^*, \psi_0^*, \psi_1^* | y, s, X, Z),$$

where $(\beta^*, \psi_0^*, \psi_1^*)$ is, say, the posterior mean of the parameters from the MCMC run, the first term is the log likelihood, the second is the log prior, and the third is the log posterior, and all are evaluated at $(\beta^*, \psi_0^*, \psi_1^*)$. The second term is available directly. The first term is

$$\sum_{i \in N_0} \log f(y_{0i}, s_i = 0 | x_i, z_i, \beta^*, \psi_0^*) + \sum_{i \in N_1} \log f(y_{1i}, s_i = 1 | x_i, z_i, \beta^*, \psi_1^*).$$

For $j = 0$, we have

$$f(y_{0i}, s_i = 0 | x_i, z_i, \beta, \psi_0) = f(y_{0i} | x_i, z_i, \beta, \psi_0) \int_{-\infty}^{0} f(s_i^* | y_{0i}, x_i, z_i, \beta, \psi_0) \, ds_i^*$$
$$= N(y_{0i} | x_i' \beta_0, \sigma_{00}) \Phi \left(-\frac{\mu_{0i}}{\phi_0} \right).$$

A similar analysis for $j = 1$ (see Exercise 11.3), shows that both cases can be written as

$$f(y_{ji}, s_i = j | x_i, z_i, \beta, \psi_j) = N(y_{ji} | x_i' \beta_j, \sigma_{jj}) \Phi \left((2j - 1) \frac{\mu_{ji}}{\phi_j} \right). \tag{11.8}$$

The third term can be estimated by decomposing it as

$$\pi(\beta^*, \psi_0^*, \psi_1^* | y, s, X, Z) = \pi(\psi_0^*, \psi_1^* | y, s, X, Z) \pi(\beta^* | y, s, X, Z, \psi_0^*, \psi_1^*),$$

from which $\pi(\psi_0^*, \psi_1^* | y, s, X, Z)$ is obtained by averaging the product of the inverse gamma and normal densities in step 1 of Algorithm 11.1 over the MCMC draws and $\pi(\beta^* | y, s, X, Z, \psi_0^*, \psi_1^*)$ is obtained by fixing (ψ_0, ψ_1) at (ψ_0^*, ψ_1^*), running the MCMC algorithm with the remaining unknowns, and averaging the normal density in step 2 over the resulting draws.

11.2 Endogenous Covariates

In the econometrics literature, the endogenous covariate is often continuous, rather than binary as in the treatment variables discussed in the previous section. We examine a simple example to understand the nature of the problems caused by the presence of endogenous covariates. Let

$$y_i = x_i'\beta_1 + \beta_s x_{is} + u_i, \quad i = 1, \ldots, n,$$

and suppose that the K_1 covariates in x_i are independent of u_i, but that u_i and x_{is} have a joint normal distribution,

$$\begin{pmatrix} u_i \\ x_{is} \end{pmatrix} \sim N_2 \left(\begin{pmatrix} 0 \\ E(x_{is}) \end{pmatrix}, \begin{pmatrix} \sigma_{11} & \sigma_{12} \\ \sigma_{12} & \sigma_{22} \end{pmatrix} \right),$$

where $\sigma_{12} \neq 0$. Equation (A.9) implies that the distribution of $y_i | x_i, x_{is}$ is Gaussian with parameters

$$E(y_i | x_i, x_{is}) = x_i'\beta_1 - \frac{\sigma_{12}}{\sigma_{22}} E(x_{is}) + \left(\beta_s + \frac{\sigma_{12}}{\sigma_{22}} \right) x_{is},$$

$$\text{Var}(y_i) = \sigma_{11} - \frac{\sigma_{12}^2}{\sigma_{22}}.$$

This result has an important implication. Since $\frac{\partial E(y_i)}{\partial x_{is}} = \beta_s + \frac{\sigma_{12}}{\sigma_{22}}$, the likelihood function contains information about $\beta_s + \frac{\sigma_{12}}{\sigma_{22}}$, not β_s; equivalently, in the absence of observations on u_i, β_s is not identifiable. We have no way of separating β_s from $\beta_s + \frac{\sigma_{12}}{\sigma_{22}}$.

As an example of how this situation may arise, let y_i be the hourly wage of individual i, x_i be a vector of covariates that control for demographic and economic factors, and x_{is} be i's years of schooling. Let us assume that an unobserved variable, call it intelligence, affects both wages and schooling; that is, an individual with higher intelligence would tend to earn a higher wage for any level of schooling and attain a higher level of education ($\sigma_{12} > 0$) than an individual with lower intelligence. In that case, the coefficient on education measures both the direct effect of schooling through β_s and the indirect effect through the relationship between schooling and intelligence $\frac{\sigma_{12}}{\sigma_{22}}$.

If the relation between education and intelligence is ignored, the effect of education on wages of schooling is overestimated by $\frac{\sigma_{12}}{\sigma_{22}}$. This may be important for public policy. Suppose it is decided to choose people randomly from the population to receive an additional year of schooling. Being chosen randomly, some of the people receiving the additional year will be of lower intelligence levels than those in the first sample who made their schooling decisions without the policy intervention. The increase in wages for the group will be closer to β_s than to $\beta_s + \frac{\sigma_{12}}{\sigma_{22}}$, and the policy may appear to be unsuccessful. It is thus important to find a way to estimate β_s more accurately.

As was done before, we employ IVs to model the endogenous variable x_{is}. Consider the system

$$y_i = x_i'\beta_1 + \beta_s x_{is} + u_i, \tag{11.9}$$

$$x_{is} = x_i'\gamma_1 + z_i'\gamma_2 + v_i, \tag{11.10}$$

where the K_2 covariates in z_i are the instrumental variables, assumed to be exogenous to the system in the sense that they are independent of u_i and v_i. On the assumption that $(u_i, v_i) \sim N_2(0, \Sigma)$, where $\Sigma = \{\sigma_{ij}\}$, this system, conditional on x_i and z_i, reproduces the correlation between u_i and x_{is} specified before.

The next step is to devise an MCMC algorithm to sample the parameters $\beta = (\beta_1', \beta_s)'$, $\gamma = (\gamma_1', \gamma_2')'$, and Σ. We begin with the latter and adopt a Wishart prior for $\Sigma^{-1} \sim W_2(v_0, R_0)$. Since $(u_i, v_i) \sim N_2(0, \Sigma)$, we may write

$$\pi(\Sigma|\beta, \gamma, y) \propto |\Sigma|^{-n/2} \exp\left[-\frac{1}{2}\sum(y_i - X_i'\beta, x_{is} - Z_i'\gamma)\Sigma^{-1}\left(\begin{array}{c} y_i - X_i'\beta \\ x_{is} - Z_i'\gamma \end{array}\right)\right]$$

$$\times |\Sigma|^{-(v_0-3)/2}\exp\left[-\frac{1}{2}\mathrm{tr}\left(R_0^{-1}\Sigma^{-1}\right)\right],$$

where $X_i' = (x_i', x_{is})$ and $Z_i' = (x_i', z_i')$.

To sample β, we use $f(y_i, x_{is}|\theta) = f(x_{is}|\theta)f(y_i|x_{is}, \theta)$, where $\theta = (\beta, \gamma, \Sigma)$, and specify a Gaussian prior $N_{K+1}(\beta_0, B_0)$. By the properties of conditional distributions of normal distributions, we have

$$y_i|x_{is}, \theta \sim N\left(X_i'\beta + \frac{\sigma_{12}}{\sigma_{22}}(x_{is} - Z_i'\gamma), \omega_{11}\right),$$

where $\omega_{11} = \sigma_{11} - \sigma_{12}^2/\sigma_{22}$. From these considerations, we may write

$$\pi(\beta|\gamma, \Sigma, y) \propto \exp\left[-\frac{1}{2\omega_{11}}\sum\left(y_i - \frac{\sigma_{12}}{\sigma_{22}}(x_{is} - Z_i'\gamma) - X_i'\beta\right)^2\right]$$

$$\times \exp\left[-\frac{1}{2}(\beta - \beta_0)'B_0^{-1}(\beta - \beta_0)\right].$$

To obtain the posterior distribution for γ, we make use of the decomposition $f(y_i, x_{is}|\theta) = f(y_i|\theta)f(x_{is}|y_i, \theta)$ and note that γ appears only in the second expression. The standard results for conditional distributions of joint normal distributions yield

$$x_{is}|y_i, \theta \sim N\left(Z_i'\gamma + \frac{\sigma_{12}}{\sigma_{11}}(y_i - X_i'\beta), \omega_{22}\right),$$

where $\omega_{22} = \sigma_{22} - \sigma_{12}^2/\sigma_{11}$. We specify a Gaussian prior $N_{K_1+K_2}(\gamma_0, G_0)$ and obtain

$$\pi(\gamma|\beta, \Sigma, y) \propto \exp\left[-\frac{1}{2\omega_{22}}\sum\left(x_{is} - \frac{\sigma_{12}}{\sigma_{11}}(y_i - X_i'\beta) - Z_i'\gamma\right)^2\right]$$
$$\times \exp\left[-\frac{1}{2}(\gamma - \gamma_0)'G_0^{-1}(\gamma - \gamma_0)\right].$$

It is now straightforward to derive the conditional posterior distributions for specifying a Gibbs algorithm:

$$\Sigma \sim W_2(\nu_1, R_1),$$
$$\beta \sim N(\bar{\beta}, B_1),$$
$$\gamma \sim N(\bar{\gamma}, G_1),$$

where

$$\nu_1 = \nu_0 + n,$$
$$R_1 = \left[R_0^{-1} + \sum \begin{pmatrix} y_i - X_i'\beta \\ x_{is} - Z_i'\gamma \end{pmatrix}(y_i - X_i'\beta, x_{is} - Z_i'\gamma)\right]^{-1},$$
$$B_1 = \left[B_0^{-1} + \omega_{11}^{-1}\sum X_i X_i'\right]^{-1},$$
$$\bar{\beta} = B_1\left(B_0^{-1}\beta_0 + \omega_{11}^{-1}\sum X_i\left[y_i - \frac{\sigma_{12}}{\sigma_{22}}(x_{is} - Z_i'\gamma)\right]\right),$$
$$G_1 = \left[G_0^{-1} + \omega_{22}^{-1}\sum Z_i Z_i'\right]^{-1},$$
$$\bar{\gamma} = G_1\left(G_0^{-1}\gamma_0 + \omega_{22}^{-1}\sum Z_i\left[x_{is} - \frac{\sigma_{12}}{\sigma_{11}}(y_i - X_i'\beta)\right]\right).$$

11.3 Incidental Truncation

Incidental truncation arises when the response variable y_i is not observed for all units, and whether it is observed depends on the value of a "selection" variable s_i. Part or all of the covariate data x_i are observed for all sample units. A well-known example of this situation is a model designed to explain the wage rate of married women on the basis of demographic and economic variables, where no wage rate is observed for women who do not work in the time period of observation, but part or all of the demographic and economic variables may be observed. The factors determining the decision to work, which is the binary variable $s_i = 1$ if individual i works and 0 otherwise, may not be independent of the wage rate, so that including in the sample only those women who work is likely to result in a poor estimate of the effects of the covariates of interest. As another example, s_i may be a Tobit-type variable rather than a binary variable, where y_i is observed when $s_i > 0$. In the wage rate example, s_i may be the hours worked, which is bounded below at zero, rather than a binary variable for labor force participation. In other cases, y_i may be a binary variable. For continuous y_i, we assume

$$y_i = x_i'\beta_1 + u_i,$$

where x_i is a K_1 vector observed for all i, and y_i is not observed if $s_i = 0$ and is observed if $s_i = 1$. For the units that are observed,

$$E(y_i|x_i, s_i = 1) = x_i'\beta_1 + E(u_i|x_i, s_i = 1).$$

The last term on the right may not equal zero, because of correlation between u_i and s_i, and a model based on the specification of a zero expected value is misspecified.

To deal with sample selection, we assume that we have K_2 instrumental variables contained in the vector z_i and that z_i and x_i are observed for all units. The model is specified by

$$y_i = x_i'\beta_1 + u_i,$$
$$s_i^* = x_i'\gamma_1 + z_i'\gamma_2 + v_i,$$
$$s_i = \begin{cases} 0, & \text{if } s_i^* \leq 0, \\ 1, & \text{if } s_i^* > 0, \end{cases}$$

where $(u_i, v_i) \sim N_2(0, \Sigma)$ and

$$\Sigma = \begin{pmatrix} \sigma_{11} & \sigma_{12} \\ \sigma_{12} & 1 \end{pmatrix}.$$

The restriction $\sigma_{22} = 1$ arises from the binary probit model for s_i; see Section 8.2.2.

Letting $N_0 = \{i : s_i = 0\}$, $N_1 = \{i : s_i = 1\}$, and θ denote the parameters of the model, we can write the contribution of $i \in N_0$ to the posterior distribution as

$$\pi(s_i^*, \theta|s_i = 0) \propto P(s_i = 0|s_i^*, \theta)\pi(s_i^*|\theta)\pi(\theta)$$
$$\propto 1(s_i = 0)1(s_i^* \leq 0)\pi(s_i^*|\theta)\pi(\theta),$$

and of $i \in N_1$,

$$\pi(s_i^*, \theta|s_i = 1, y_i) \propto f(s_i = 1, y_i|\theta, s_i^*)\pi(s_i^*|\theta)\pi(\theta)$$
$$\propto f(s_i = 1, y_i, s_i^*|\theta)\pi(\theta)$$
$$\propto f(y_i, s_i^*|\theta)P(s_i = 1|s_i^*, y_i, \theta)\pi(\theta)$$
$$\propto f(y_i, s_i^*|\theta)1(s_i = 1)1(s_i^* > 0)\pi(\theta).$$

The posterior distribution is therefore

$$\pi(s^*, \theta|s, y) \propto \pi(\theta) \prod_{i \in N_0} \pi(s_i^*|\theta)1(s_i = 0)1(s_i^* \leq 0)$$
$$\times \prod_{i \in N_1} f(y_i, s_i^*|\theta)1(s_i = 1)1(s_i^* > 0). \qquad (11.11)$$

We begin the development of an MCMC algorithm to approximate the posterior distribution by deriving the conditional posterior distribution of $\beta = (\beta_1', \gamma_1', \gamma_2')'$. Defining

$$\eta_i = \begin{cases} (0, s_i^*)', & i \in N_0, \\ (y_i, s_i^*)', & i \in N_1, \end{cases}$$

$$X_i = \begin{pmatrix} x_i' & 0 & 0 \\ 0 & x_i' & z_i' \end{pmatrix}, \quad J = \begin{pmatrix} 0 & 0 \\ 0 & 1 \end{pmatrix},$$

we may write the likelihood terms involving β in SUR form as

$$\pi(\beta | y, s^*, \Sigma) \propto \exp\left[-\frac{1}{2} \sum_{i \in N_0} (\eta_i - X_i \beta)' J' J (\eta_i - X_i \beta) \right]$$

$$\times \exp\left[-\frac{1}{2} \sum_{i \in N_1} (\eta_i - X_i \beta)' \Sigma^{-1} (\eta_i - X_i \beta) \right].$$

Note that the first row of $\eta_i - X_i \beta$ is zero after premultiplication by J. With the prior distribution $\beta \sim N_{K_1 + K_2}(\beta_0, B_0)$, we have

$$\beta | y, s^*, \Sigma \sim N_{K_1 + K_2}(\bar{\beta}, B_1),$$

where

$$B_1 = \left[\sum_{i \in N_0} X_i' J X_i + \sum_{i \in N_1} X_i' \Sigma^{-1} X_i + B_0^{-1} \right]^{-1},$$

$$\bar{\beta} = B_1 \left[\sum_{i \in N_0} X_i' J \eta_i + \sum_{i \in N_1} X_i' \Sigma^{-1} \eta_i + B_0^{-1} \beta_0 \right],$$

and we have used $J' J = J$.

We next turn to the sampling of the covariance matrix parameters σ_{12} and $\omega_{11} = \sigma_{11} - \sigma_{12}^2$, which appear in the likelihood function only for $i \in N_1$. Sampling for ω_{11} is restricted to positive values and automatically yields a positive $\sigma_{11} = \omega_{11} + \sigma_{12}^2$. We assume the prior distribution $\omega_{11}^{-1} \sim G(\alpha_0/2, \delta_0/2)$ and write $f(y_i, s_i^* | \theta) = f(y_i | s_i^*, \theta) f(s_i^* | \theta)$ to find

$$\pi(\omega_{11} | y, \beta, \sigma_{12}) \propto \left(\frac{1}{\omega_{11}} \right)^{n_1/2} \exp\left[-\frac{1}{2\omega_{11}} \sum_{i \in N_1} [y_i - x_i' \beta_1 - \sigma_{12}(s_i^* - x_i' \gamma_1 - z_i' \gamma_2)]^2 \right]$$

$$\times \left(\frac{1}{\omega_{11}} \right)^{\alpha_0/2 - 1} \exp\left[-\frac{\delta_0}{2\omega_{11}} \right],$$

since ω_{11} does not appear in $f(s_i^* | \theta)$. This implies $\omega_{11}^{-1} | y, \beta, \sigma_{12} \sim G(\alpha_1/2, \delta_1/2)$, where

$$\alpha_1 = \alpha_0 + n_1,$$
$$\delta_1 = \delta_0 + \sum_{i \in N_1} [y_i - x_i' \beta_1 - \sigma_{12}(s_i^* - x_i' \gamma_1 - z_i' \gamma_2)]^2.$$

To sample $\sigma_{12}|y, \beta, \omega_{11}$ we assume the prior distribution $\sigma_{12} \sim N(s_0, S_0)$ and find

$$\pi(\sigma_{12}|y, \beta, \omega_{11}) \propto \exp\left[-\frac{1}{2\omega_{11}} \sum_{i \in N_1} [y_i - x_i'\beta_1 - \sigma_{12}(s_i^* - x_i'\gamma_1 - z_i'\gamma_2)]^2\right]$$

$$\times \exp\left[-\frac{1}{2S_0}(\sigma_{12} - s_0)^2\right],$$

which implies $\sigma_{12}|y, \beta, \omega_{11} \sim N(\hat{s}, \hat{S})$, where

$$\hat{S} = \left[\omega_{11}^{-1} \sum (s_i^* - x_i'\gamma_1 - z_i'\gamma_2)^2 + S_0^{-1}\right]^{-1},$$

$$\hat{s} = \hat{S}\left[\omega_{11}^{-1} \sum (s_i^* - x_i'\gamma_1 - z_i'\gamma_2)(y_i - x_i'\beta_1) + S_0^{-1}s_0\right].$$

To sample the s_i^*, use (11.11) and write, for $i \in N_1$,

$$\prod_{i \in N_1} f(y_i, s_i^*|\theta)1(s_i = 1)1(s_i^* > 0) = \prod_{i \in N_1} f(s_i^*|y_i, \theta)f(y_i|\theta)1(s_i = 1)1(s_i^* > 0),$$

which implies that the s_i^* are drawn from truncated normal distributions:

$$s_i^* \sim \begin{cases} \text{TN}_{(-\infty,0]}(x_i'\gamma_1 + z_i'\gamma_2, 1), & \text{for } i \in N_0, \\ \text{TN}_{(0,\infty)}\left(x_i'\gamma_1 + z_i'\gamma_2 + \dfrac{\sigma_{12}}{\omega_{11} + \sigma_{12}^2}(y_i - x_i'\beta_1), \dfrac{\omega_{11}}{\omega_{11} + \sigma_{12}^2}\right), & \text{for } i \in N_1. \end{cases}$$

Although the sampler generates values of the latent data s_i^*, it does not generate values of the "missing" y_i for $i \in N_0$.

As an example, we utilize the Mroz data described in Section 8.2.1. In this example, we treat hours of work as a binary variable for whether an individual is in ($s_i = 1$) or out ($s_i = 0$) of the labor force. The response variable y_i is log(wage), which is observed only for employed women. We follow the specification of Wooldridge (2002, pp. 468, 565) in setting

$$x' = (\text{constant, educ, experience, experience squared}),$$

$$z' = (\text{nwifeinc, age, childlt6, childge6}),$$

where educ is the wife's education and nwifeinc is household income other than that earned by the wife.

Except for the constant terms in β we set prior means of 0 and variances of 1 in the belief that the effect of each of these variables on log(wages) would be fairly small and knowing that the mean log wage for the sample is slightly larger than 1. We set a 0 mean and variance of 10 for the constant terms because of greater uncertainty. The variance of log(wages) in the sample is slightly over 0.5, suggesting that $\sigma_{11} = \omega_{11} + \sigma_{12}^2$ is of order of magnitude 1, which we split between the two components equally to obtain a value of 0.5 for ω_{11}. With a gamma prior

Table 11.1. *Summary of Posterior Distribution: Probit Selection Model, Mroz Data.*

Coefficient	Mean	SD	Lower	Upper	Corr time
β_{11}	-0.529	0.263	-1.035	-0.004	7.357
β_{12}	0.108	0.015	0.078	0.137	2.389
β_{13}	0.042	0.015	0.012	0.071	4.512
β_{14}	-0.001	0.000	-0.002	0.000	2.955
γ_{11}	0.226	0.502	-0.756	1.207	2.990
γ_{12}	0.132	0.025	0.083	0.181	3.154
γ_{13}	0.124	0.019	0.087	0.161	3.202
γ_{14}	-0.002	0.001	-0.003	-0.001	3.042
γ_{21}	-0.012	0.005	-0.022	-0.002	3.566
γ_{22}	-0.052	0.008	-0.069	-0.036	3.437
γ_{23}	-0.856	0.119	-1.090	-0.626	3.419
γ_{24}	0.037	0.043	-0.048	0.122	3.186
ω_{11}	0.444	0.031	0.386	0.507	1.514
σ_{11}	0.454	0.032	0.396	0.520	1.406
ρ_{12}	0.009	0.147	-0.292	0.279	14.353

distribution on $1/\omega_{11} \approx 2$, from (A.1) we have $E(1/\omega_{11}) = 2.0 = \alpha/\delta$, and a small value of δ is associated with a larger variance. Accordingly, we set $\delta = 2$, or $\delta_0 = 4$ to obtain a large variance and $\alpha = 4$, or $\alpha_0 = 8$ to obtain the desired mean. We assumed $\sigma_{12} \sim N(0, 1)$ to take a neutral stance on its sign and to set a fairly large variance. For the simulation, we set a burn-in of 10,000 and keep 40,000 generated values. A large number of iterations is chosen because of the complexity of the model.

Summary results are in Table 11.1, and Figure 11.1 displays histograms of the coefficient β_{12} of education on log(wages) and $\rho_{12} = \sigma_{12}/\sqrt{\sigma_{11}}$. The means of the marginal posterior distributions are very similar to the estimates obtained by Wooldridge in the work cited earlier. We note that the distribution of β_{12} appears symmetric, and its mean of 0.108 summarizes it well. It is clearly positive in view of the 95% credibility interval of (0.078, 0.137). The distribution of ρ_{12} is rather uninformative about the possibility of a sample selection bias. Its mean is close to zero, and its 95% credibility interval includes negative and positive values fairly symmetrically about zero. The relatively large correlation time of ρ_{12} suggests that the algorithm did not mix well for this parameter.

11.4 Further Reading and References

Section 11.1 The econometric literature on treatment effects in connection with the implementation of public policy was pioneered by James J. Heckman. A recent

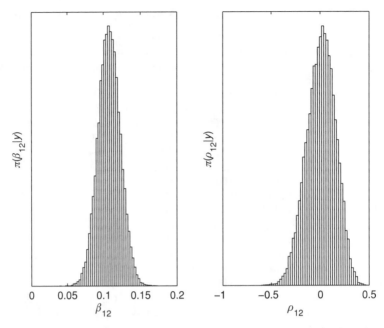

Figure 11.1. Selected coefficients: incidental truncation model, Mroz data.

convenient reference is Heckman and Vytlacil (2005), which includes many references to the literature and definitions of other treatment effects. The Bayesian specification in this section is based on Chib (in press-a), which also treats more general cases. One feature of Chib's approach is that it does not model the correlation between u_i and v_i. This is desirable because y_{i0} and y_{i1} cannot be observed for the same individual, which implies that there is no sample information that can identify those correlations. Poirier and Tobias (2003) argue that the positive definiteness constraint on the joint distribution of (u_{0i}, u_{1i}, v_i) provides information about the unidentified covariance between u_{0i} and u_{1i} and present an algorithm to sample the regression coefficients and the 3×3 covariance matrix.

Section 11.2 The frequentist approach to this model is developed in Wooldridge (2002, chap. 5).

Section 11.3 The model for incidental truncation is estimated from the frequentist viewpoint in Heckman (1979). Wooldridge (2002, chap. 17) is an informative discussion from the frequentist viewpoint with many references to the literature.

11.5 Exercises

11.1 Verify (11.4).
11.2 Verify (11.6) and (11.7).

11.3 Verify (11.8).

11.4 Verify the conditional posterior distributions used in Algorithm 11.1.

11.5 Show how to analyze the model of Section 11.1 if the response variables y_{0i} and y_{1i} are binary variables, modeled by a binary probit formulation. Equation (11.1) specifies latent data in that case.

11.6 Redo the model of Section 11.2 on the assumption that y_i is a binary variable.

11.7 Redo the model of Section 11.2 with Student-t errors.

11.8 Redo the model of Section 11.3 on the assumption that the selection variable is censored as in a Tobit model.

Appendix A

Probability Distributions and Matrix Theorems

A.1 Probability Distributions

THE STANDARD DISTRIBUTIONS are described in most textbooks in mathematical statistics. We recommend DeGroot and Schervish (2002). Other excellent sources are Zellner (1971, apps. A and B), Press (1972), and Berger (1985, app. 1). For the distributions that arise in Bayesian econometrics, we particularly recommend Zellner (1971) and Press (1972). The matricvariate normal distribution and related distributions are discussed in Drèze and Richard (1983, app. A). In consulting these or other references, you should be aware that some authors parameterize distributions differently from the way they are parameterized here.

A.1.1 Bernoulli

The variable x has the Bernoulli distribution with parameter θ, $x \sim \text{Be}(\theta)$, if $x = \{0, 1\}, 0 \leq \theta \leq 1$, and $p(x|\theta) = \theta^x (1 - \theta)^{1-x}$.

Then $E(x) = \theta$ and $\text{Var}(x) = \theta(1 - \theta)$.

A.1.2 Binomial

Let $x_i, i = 1, \ldots, n$, be independently distributed, and $x_i \sim \text{Be}(\theta)$. Then $y = \sum x_i$ has the binomial distribution, $y \sim \text{Bi}(n, \theta)$, if

$$p(y|n, \theta) = \binom{n}{y} \theta^y (1 - \theta)^{n-y}, \quad y = 0, 1, \ldots, n.$$

For the binomial distribution,

$$E(y) = n\theta \quad \text{and} \quad \text{Var}(y) = n\theta(1 - \theta).$$

Note that n is regarded as fixed, and the random variable is the number of trials y for which $x_i = 1$. For the negative binomial distribution described next, y is taken as fixed and the random variable is the number of trials required to obtain y.

A.1.3 Negative Binomial

Let $n = r, r + 1, \ldots$, and let $p(x_i = 1|\theta) = \theta$. Assume the x_i are independent. Then n has the negative binomial distribution, $n \sim \text{NB}(r, \theta)$, if n trials are required to achieve r successes. The probability mass function is

$$p(n|r, \theta) \;=\; \binom{n-1}{r-1} \theta^r (1 - \theta)^{n-r},$$

$$E(n) \;=\; \frac{r(1 - \theta)}{\theta} \quad \text{and} \quad \text{Var}(n) = \frac{r(1 - \theta)}{\theta^2}.$$

As mentioned before, in contrast to the binomial distribution, the number of successes is fixed and the number of trials is the random variable.

A.1.4 Multinomial

The variable $x = (x_1, \ldots, x_p)$ has the multinomial distribution, $x \sim \text{MN}(n; \theta_1, \ldots, \theta_p)$, if $x_i \in \{0, 1\}$, $i = 1, \ldots, p$, $\sum \theta_i = 1$, $\sum x_i = n$, and

$$p(x|n; \theta_1, \ldots, \theta_p) = \binom{n}{x_1, \ldots, x_p} \theta_1^{x_1} \theta_2^{x_2} \cdots \theta_p^{x_p}.$$

The marginal distribution of each x_i is $\text{Bi}(n, \theta_i)$.

A.1.5 Poisson

The variable x has the Poisson distribution with parameter $\theta > 0$, $x \sim P(\theta)$, if

$$p(x|\theta) = \frac{e^{-\theta} \theta^x}{x!}, \quad x = 0, 1, \ldots .$$

The first two moments are

$$E(x) = \theta \quad \text{and} \quad \text{Var}(x) = \theta.$$

A.1.6 Uniform

The variable x has the uniform distribution with parameters α and β, $\beta > \alpha$, denoted by $x \sim U(\alpha, \beta)$, if

$$f(x) = \frac{1}{\beta - \alpha}, \quad \alpha \leq x \leq \beta.$$

Then $E(x) = (\alpha + \beta)/2$ and $\text{Var}(x) = (\beta - \alpha)^2/12$.

A.1.7 Gamma

The gamma function $\Gamma(\alpha, \beta)$ is defined by

$$\int_0^\infty x^{\alpha-1} e^{-\beta x} \, dx = \frac{\Gamma(\alpha)}{\beta^\alpha}, \quad \alpha, \beta > 0,$$

where $\Gamma(\alpha) \equiv \Gamma(\alpha, 1)$. The random variable x has the gamma distribution, $x \sim G(\alpha, \beta)$, if $0 \leq x$ and

$$f(x|\alpha, \beta) = \frac{\beta^\alpha}{\Gamma(\alpha)} x^{\alpha-1} e^{-\beta x}.$$

For the gamma distribution,

$$\begin{aligned} E(x) &= \frac{\alpha}{\beta}, \\ \text{Var}(x) &= \frac{\alpha}{\beta^2}. \end{aligned} \tag{A.1}$$

Alternatively, we may determine α and β from $E(x)$ and $\text{Var}(x)$:

$$\begin{aligned} \alpha &= [E(x)]^2 / \text{Var}(x), \\ \beta &= E(x) / \text{Var}(x). \end{aligned} \tag{A.2}$$

A special case of the gamma distribution is the χ^2 distribution with ν degrees of freedom, χ_ν^2. We say that $x \sim \chi_\nu^2$ if $x \sim G(\nu/2, 1/2)$.

Another special case is the exponential distribution, $G(1, \beta)$: $x \sim \text{Exp}(\beta)$ if

$$f(x|\beta) = \beta e^{-\beta x}, \quad \beta > 0, \quad x > 0. \tag{A.3}$$

If $x \sim \text{Exp}(\beta)$, then $E(x) = 1/\beta$ and $\text{Var}(x) = 1/\beta^2$.

A.1.8 Inverted or Inverse Gamma

Let $x \sim G(\alpha, \beta)$ and $y = 1/x$. Then y has the inverted gamma distribution, $y \sim \text{IG}(\alpha, \beta)$, and

$$f(y|\alpha, \beta) = \frac{\beta^\alpha}{\Gamma(\alpha)} \frac{1}{y^{\alpha+1}} e^{-\beta/y}, \quad y > 0.$$

The first two moments are

$$\begin{aligned} E(y) &= \frac{\beta}{\alpha - 1}, \quad \text{if } \alpha > 1, \\ \text{Var}(y) &= \frac{\beta^2}{(\alpha - 1)^2(\alpha - 2)}, \quad \text{if } \alpha > 2, \end{aligned} \tag{A.4}$$

or

$$\alpha = \frac{[E(y)]^2}{\text{Var}(y)} + 2,$$

$$\beta = E(y)\left(\frac{[E(y)]^2}{\text{Var}(y)} + 1\right). \tag{A.5}$$

A.1.9 Beta

The beta function is defined as

$$B(\alpha, \beta) = \int_0^1 x^{\alpha-1}(1-x)^{\beta-1}\,dx, \quad \alpha, \beta > 0.$$

It can be shown that the beta function is related to the gamma function by

$$B(\alpha, \beta) = \frac{\Gamma(\alpha)\Gamma(\beta)}{\Gamma(\alpha+\beta)}.$$

The variable x has the beta distribution, $x \sim \text{Beta}(\alpha, \beta)$, if $0 \le x \le 1$ and

$$f(x|\alpha, \beta) = \frac{1}{B(\alpha, \beta)} x^{\alpha-1}(1-x)^{\beta-1}.$$

$$= \frac{\Gamma(\alpha+\beta)}{\Gamma(\alpha)\Gamma(\beta)} x^{\alpha-1}(1-x)^{\beta-1}.$$

For the beta distribution

$$E(x) = \frac{\alpha}{\alpha+\beta},$$

$$\text{Var}(x) = \frac{\alpha\beta}{(\alpha+\beta)^2(\alpha+\beta+1)}, \tag{A.6}$$

or

$$\alpha = \frac{E(x)[E(x)(1-E(x)) - \text{Var}(x)]}{\text{Var}(x)},$$

$$\beta = \frac{(1-E(x))[E(x)(1-E(x)) - \text{Var}(x)]}{\text{Var}(x)}. \tag{A.7}$$

A.1.10 Dirichlet

The Dirichlet distribution generalizes the beta distribution. Let $x = (x_1, x_2, \ldots, x_p)$, $0 \le x_i \le 1$, $\sum x_i = 1$. Then $x \sim D(\alpha_1, \ldots, \alpha_p)$ if

$$f(x|\alpha_1, \alpha_2, \ldots, \alpha_p) = \frac{\Gamma\left(\sum \alpha_i\right)}{\prod \Gamma(\alpha_i)} x_1^{\alpha_1-1} x_2^{\alpha_2-1} \cdots x_p^{\alpha_p-1}, \quad \alpha_i > 0.$$

Marginally, $x_i \sim B(\alpha_i, \sum_{k \neq i} \alpha_k)$.

A.1.11 Normal or Gaussian

The variable $x \sim N(\mu, \sigma^2)$ if

$$f(x|\mu, \sigma^2) = \frac{1}{\sqrt{2\pi\sigma^2}} \exp\left[-\frac{1}{2\sigma^2}(x - \mu)^2\right].$$

Then

$$E(x) = \mu \quad \text{and} \quad \text{Var}(x) = \sigma^2.$$

The case $\mu = 0$ and $\sigma^2 = 1$ is called the standard normal distribution; its p.d.f. is denoted by $\phi(x)$ and its d.f. by $\Phi(x)$.

A.1.12 Multivariate and Matricvariate Normal or Gaussian

Let $x = (x_1, \ldots, x_p)$. Then x has the p-dimensional multivariate normal or Gaussian distribution, $x \sim N_p(\mu, \Sigma)$, if

$$f(x|\mu, \Sigma) = \frac{1}{(2\pi)^{p/2}|\Sigma|^{1/2}} \exp\left[-\frac{1}{2}(x - \mu)'\Sigma^{-1}(x - \mu)\right],$$

where $\mu = (\mu_1, \mu_2, \ldots, \mu_p)'$ is the mean vector and Σ is the symmetric, positive-definite covariance matrix,

$$\Sigma = \begin{pmatrix} \sigma_{11} & \sigma_{12} & \cdots & \sigma_{1p} \\ \sigma_{21} & \sigma_{22} & \cdots & \sigma_{2p} \\ \vdots & \vdots & \vdots & \vdots \\ \sigma_{p1} & \sigma_{p2} & \cdots & \sigma_{pp} \end{pmatrix}.$$

The standard multivariate normal is the special case $\mu = 0$ and $\Sigma = I_p$.

The $p \times q$ matrix X has the matricvariate normal distribution, $X \sim \text{MN}_{p \times q}(\bar{X}, \Omega \otimes P)$ if

$$f_{\text{MN}}^{p \times q}(X|\bar{X}, \Omega \otimes P) = \left[(2\pi)^{pq}|\Omega|^p|P|^q\right]^{-1/2}$$
$$\times \exp\left[-\frac{1}{2}\text{tr}\{\Omega^{-1}(X - \bar{X})'P^{-1}(X - \bar{X})\}\right].$$

The multivariate normal distribution is the special case $q = 1$ of the matricvariate distribution.

Marginal Distributions

Let $x_{(1)}$ be a p_1 vector, $p_1 < p$, containing the first p_1 variables in x, where $x \sim N_p(\mu, \Sigma)$. (By renumbering the variables in x we may include any of the variables in $x_{(1)}$.) Then the marginal distribution of $x_{(1)}$ is $N_{p_1}(\mu_1, \Sigma_{11})$, where μ_1 contains the first p_1 rows of μ and the matrix Σ_{11} is the $p_1 \times p_1$ submatrix implicitly defined by

$$\Sigma = \begin{pmatrix} \Sigma_{11} & \Sigma_{12} \\ \Sigma_{21} & \Sigma_{22} \end{pmatrix}. \tag{A.8}$$

Conditional Distributions

To specify the conditional distributions, define $x_{(1)}$ as before and let $x_{(2)}, (p - p_1) \times 1$, be the remaining elements of x. Then the conditional distribution, $x_{(1)}|x_{(2)}$ is

$$N_{p_1}\left(\mu_1 + \Sigma_{12}\Sigma_{22}^{-1}(x_{(2)} - \mu_2), \Sigma_{11} - \Sigma_{12}\Sigma_{22}^{-1}\Sigma_{21}\right), \tag{A.9}$$

where μ_2 contains the last $p - p_1$ elements of μ and the remaining matrices are defined in (A.8).

Completing the Square

The standard form of the multivariate normal distribution has in its exponent the quadratic form $(x - \mu)'\Sigma^{-1}(x - \mu)$. When computing the posterior distribution for a normal likelihood and a normal prior distribution, it is necessary to combine terms from the likelihood and the prior, a process known as *completing the square*. To see how this is done, we expand the quadratic form to obtain

$$(x - \mu)'\Sigma^{-1}(x - \mu) = x'\Sigma^{-1}x - 2x'\Sigma^{-1}\mu + \mu'\Sigma^{-1}\mu.$$

From this expression, we note that Σ^{-1} is the expression between x' and x and that μ is Σ^{-1} times the coefficient of $-2x'$. To find μ, we therefore premultiply the coefficient of $-2x'$ by Σ.

For example, if $x \sim N_p(\mu, \Sigma)$, $\mu \sim N(\mu_0, B_0)$, and Σ is known, the posterior distribution $\pi(\mu|\Sigma, x)$ is

$$\pi(\mu|\Sigma, x) \propto \exp\left[-\frac{1}{2}(x - \mu)'\Sigma^{-1}(x - \mu)\right] \exp\left[-\frac{1}{2}(\mu - \mu_0)'B_0^{-1}(\mu - \mu_0)\right].$$

Consider the expressions in the exponentials (ignoring the $-1/2$ term):

$$(x - \mu)'\Sigma^{-1}(x - \mu) + (\mu - \mu_0)'B_0^{-1}(\mu - \mu_0)$$
$$= x'\Sigma^{-1}x - 2\mu'\Sigma^{-1}x + \mu'\Sigma^{-1}\mu + \mu'B_0^{-1}\mu - 2\mu'B_0^{-1}\mu_0 + \mu_0'B_0^{-1}\mu_0$$
$$= \mu'\left(\Sigma^{-1} + B_0^{-1}\right)\mu - 2\mu'\left(\Sigma^{-1}x + B_0^{-1}\mu_0\right) + x'\Sigma^{-1}x + \mu_0'B_0^{-1}\mu_0. \tag{A.10}$$

Since we are concerned with the distribution of μ and Σ is assumed to be known, all terms that do not involve μ are absorbed into the proportionality constant. Applying the idea of completing the square to (A.10), we have

$$\pi(\mu|\Sigma, x) \sim N_p(\mu_1, B_1), \tag{A.11}$$

where $B_1 = (\Sigma^{-1} + B_0^{-1})^{-1}$ and $\mu_1 = B_1(\Sigma^{-1}x + B_0^{-1}\mu_0)$.

A.1.13 Truncated Normal

The scalar random variable x has the truncated normal distribution with mean μ and variance σ^2, truncated to the region (a, b), if

$$f(x) = \left(\frac{1}{H(b) - H(a)}\right)\left(\frac{1}{\sqrt{2\pi\sigma^2}}\right)\exp\left(-\frac{1}{2\sigma^2}(y - \mu)^2\right), \quad a \leq x \leq b,$$

or $x \sim \text{TN}_{(a,b)}(\mu, \sigma^2)$, where $H(z)$ is the d.f. of $N(\mu, \sigma^2)$ evaluated at z. Note that μ and σ^2 are parameters of the untruncated normal distribution; expressions for the mean and variance of x may be found in Greene (2003, p. 759).

A.1.14 Univariate Student-t

The scalar random variable x has the Student-t distribution with $v > 0$ degrees of freedom, location parameter μ, and scale parameter $\sigma^2 > 0$, $x \sim t(v, \mu, \sigma^2)$ if

$$f(t|v, \mu, \sigma^2) = \frac{\Gamma[(v + 1)/2]}{(\sigma^2 v\pi)^{1/2}\Gamma(v/2)}\left(1 + \frac{(x - \mu)^2}{v\sigma^2}\right)^{-(v+1)/2}.$$

The first two moments are

$$E(x) = \mu, \quad \text{if } v > 1 \quad \text{and} \quad \text{Var}(x) = \frac{v\sigma^2}{v - 2}, \quad \text{if } v > 2.$$

The case $\mu = 0$ and $\sigma^2 = 1$ is the standard Student-t distribution.

A.1.15 Multivariate t

This distribution generalizes the univariate t. The p-dimensional vector $x = (x_1, \ldots, x_p)'$ has the multivariate t distribution (MVT) with $v > 0$ degrees of freedom, location parameter $\mu = (\mu_1, \ldots, \mu_p)'$, and positive definite scale matrix Σ, $x \sim t_p(v, \mu, \Sigma)$, if

$$f(x|v, \mu, \Sigma) = \frac{\Gamma[(v + p)/2]}{|\Sigma|^{1/2}(v\pi)^{p/2}\Gamma(v/2)}\left(1 + \frac{1}{v}(x - \mu)'\Sigma^{-1}(x - \mu)\right)^{-(v+p)/2}.$$

The mean vector and covariance matrix are

$$E(x) = \mu, \quad \text{if } v > 1 \quad \text{and} \quad \text{Var}(x) = \frac{v}{v-2}\Sigma, \quad \text{if } v > 2.$$

Marginal Distributions

Let $x_{(1)}$ be a p_1 vector, $p_1 < p$, containing the first p_1 variables in x, where $x \sim t_p(v, \mu, \Sigma)$. (By renumbering the variables in x we may include any of the variables in $x_{(1)}$.) Also let $\mu_{(1)}$ be the first p_1 rows of μ. Then

$$x_{(1)} \sim t_{p_1}\left(v, \mu_{(1)}, \Sigma_{11} - \Sigma_{12}\Sigma_{22}^{-1}\Sigma_{21}\right), \tag{A.12}$$

where Σ is partitioned as in (A.8), and

$$E\left(x_{(1)}\right) = \mu_{(1)}, \quad v > 1, \tag{A.13}$$

$$\text{Var}\left(x_{(1)}\right) = \frac{v}{v-2}\left(\Sigma_{11} - \Sigma_{12}\Sigma_{22}^{-1}\Sigma_{21}\right), \quad v > 2. \tag{A.14}$$

From (A.17) you should recognize $\Sigma_{11} - \Sigma_{12}\Sigma_{22}^{-1}\Sigma_{21}$ as the inverse of the first p_1 rows and columns of Σ^{-1}.

Conditional distributions may be found in Zellner (1971, App. B.2).

A.1.16 Wishart

Let $X = \{x_{ij}\}$ be a $p \times p$ symmetric positive definite matrix. Then X has the p-dimensional Wishart distribution with $v \geq p$ degrees of freedom and symmetric positive definite scale matrix R, $X \sim W_p(v, R)$, if

$$f(X|v, R) \propto \frac{|X|^{(v-p-1)/2}}{|R|^{v/2}} \exp\left[-\frac{1}{2}\text{tr}(R^{-1}X)\right].$$

The first two moments of the x_{ij} are given by

$$E(x_{ij}) = v\sigma_{ij},$$
$$\text{Var}(x_{ij}) = v\left(\sigma_{ij}^2 + \sigma_{ii}\sigma_{jj}\right),$$
$$\text{Cov}(x_{ij}, x_{kl}) = v(\sigma_{ik}\sigma_{jl} + \sigma_{il}\sigma_{jk}).$$

For $p = 1$, $X \sim G(v/2, R^{-1}/2)$.

Marginal Distributions

Partition X and R as

$$X = \begin{pmatrix} X_{11} & X_{12} \\ X_{21} & X_{22} \end{pmatrix} \quad \text{and} \quad R = \begin{pmatrix} R_{11} & R_{12} \\ R_{21} & R_{22} \end{pmatrix},$$

where X_{11} and R_{11} are $p_1 \times p_1$, X_{12} and R_{12} are $p_1 \times p_2$, X_{21} and R_{21} are $p_2 \times p_1$, and X_{22} and R_{22} are $p_2 \times p_2$. Then

$$X_{11} \sim W_{p_1}(\nu, R_{11}).$$

A.1.17 Inverted or Inverse Wishart

The $p \times p$ symmetric positive definite matrix Y has the p-dimensional inverted Wishart distribution with $\nu \geq p$ degrees of freedom and symmetric positive definite scale matrix R, $Y \sim \mathrm{IW}_p(\nu, R)$, if

$$f(Y|\nu, R) \propto \frac{|R|^{\nu/2}}{|Y|^{(\nu+p+1)/2}} \exp\left[-\frac{1}{2}\mathrm{tr}(Y^{-1}R)\right].$$

There is an important relationship between the Wishart and inverted Wishart distributions. If $X \sim W_p(\nu, R)$, then $Y = X^{-1} \sim \mathrm{IW}_p(\nu + p + 1, R^{-1})$.

For $p = 1$, $Y \sim \mathrm{IG}(\nu/2, R/2)$.

Marginal and Conditional Distributions

Partition Y and R as

$$Y = \begin{pmatrix} Y_{11} & Y_{12} \\ Y_{21} & Y_{22} \end{pmatrix} \quad \text{and} \quad R = \begin{pmatrix} R_{11} & R_{12} \\ R_{21} & R_{22} \end{pmatrix},$$

where Y_{11} and R_{11} are $p_1 \times p_1$, Y_{12} and R_{12} are $p_1 \times p_2$, Y_{21} and R_{21} are $p_2 \times p_1$, and Y_{22} and R_{22} are $p_2 \times p_2$. Then

$$Y_{11} \sim \mathrm{IW}_{p_1}(R_{11}, \nu - p_2).$$

Moreover, let $Y_{22.1} = Y_{22} - Y_{21}Y_{11}^{-1}Y_{12}$ and $R_{22.1} = R_{22} - R_{21}R_{11}^{-1}R_{12}$. Then

$$f\left(Y_{11}, Y_{11}^{-1}Y_{12}, Y_{22.1}\right) = f(Y_{11})f\left(Y_{11}^{-1}Y_{12}|Y_{22.1}\right)f(Y_{22.1}), \tag{A.15}$$

where $Y_{11} \sim \mathrm{IW}_{p_1}(R_{11}, \nu - p_2)$, $Y_{11}^{-1}Y_{12}|Y_{22.1} \sim \mathrm{MN}_{p_1 \times p_2}(R_{11}^{-1}R_{12}), R_{22.1} \otimes R_{11}^{-1})$, and $Y_{22.1} \sim \mathrm{IW}_{p_2}(R_{22.1}, \nu)$.

A.1.18 Multiplication Rule of Probability

Let $f(x_1, x_2, \ldots, x_n)$ be the joint distribution for the x_i. The multiplication rule tells us that, for example,

$$f(x_1, x_2, \ldots, x_n) = f(x_1)f(x_2|x_1)f(x_3|x_1, x_2) \cdots f(x_n|x_1, \ldots, x_{n-1}).$$

A more general statement of the theorem is

$$f(x_1, x_2, \ldots, x_n) = f\left(x_{i_1}\right) f\left(x_{i_2}|x_{i_1}\right) f\left(x_{i_3}|x_{i_1}, x_{i_2}\right) \cdots f\left(x_{i_n}|x_{i_1}, \ldots, x_{i_{n-1}}\right),$$

(A.16)

where $(x_{i_1}, x_{i_2}, \ldots, x_{i_n})$ is any rearrangement of the variables in x. That is, you can write $f(x)$ as a product of the marginal of any of the x_i times the appropriate conditionals, as long as you condition on any of the x_i that already appear in the product.

A.2 Matrix Theorems

A good source for matrix algebra relevant for statistics is Schott (1997).

A.1 If

$$A = \begin{pmatrix} A_{11} & A_{12} \\ A_{21} & A_{22,} \end{pmatrix},$$

then

$$A^{-1} = \begin{pmatrix} G_1 & -A_{22}^{-1} A_{21} G_1 \\ -G_1 A_{12} A_{22}^{-1} & A_{22}^{-1}\left(I + A_{21} G_1 A_{12} A_{22}^{-1}\right) \end{pmatrix},$$

(A.17)

where $G_1 = (A_{11} - A_{12} A_{22}^{-1} A_{21})^{-1}$.

A.2 If A and C are nonsingular, then

$$[A + BCB']^{-1} = A^{-1} - A^{-1} B [C^{-1} + B' A^{-1} B]^{-1} B' A^{-1},$$

(A.18)

where all matrices are conformable.

A.3 The vec operator $\text{vec}(A)$ applied to the $m \times n$ matrix A produces the $mn \times 1$ vector a,

$$\text{vec}(A) = a = \begin{pmatrix} a_1 \\ a_2 \\ \vdots \\ a_n \end{pmatrix},$$

where a_i is the ith column of A. Then

$$\text{vec}(\alpha A + \beta B) = \alpha \, \text{vec}(A) + \beta \, \text{vec}(B)$$
$$\text{vec}(ABC) = (C' \otimes A) \, \text{vec}(B),$$

(A.19)

where α and β are scalars and all matrices are conformable for addition or multiplication.

A.4 Let A be $p \times p$ and B be $m \times m$. Then

$$|A \otimes B| = |A|^m |B|^p.$$

(A.20)

Appendix B

Computer Programs for MCMC Calculations

THE MODELS DISCUSSED in this book are rather easy to program, and students are encouraged to do some or all of the exercises by writing their own programs. The GAUSS and MATLAB programs are good choices.

If you program in MATLAB, you should be aware of a few differences between the program and our presentation.

B.1 The inverted gamma function is not available. Instead, sample for $1/\sigma^2$, which has a gamma distribution with the same parameters.

B.2 The MATLAB version of the gamma function defines the second parameter as the inverse of our version; that is, in our notation, $G(\alpha, \delta_1)$, is interpreted by MATLAB as $G(\alpha, \delta_2)$ where $\delta_2 = 1/\delta_1$.

B.3 In the univariate normal distribution, MATLAB expects $N(\mu, \sigma)$; that is, it expects the standard deviation as the second argument rather than the variance. (In MATLAB's multivariate normal function, the second argument is the covariance matrix.)

A number of free programs are available through the Internet that implement the Gibbs sampler for some of the models studied in this book. We mention three:

- BACC is supported by the National Science Foundation. Its authors request that the following acknowledgments and reference be included.

  Computations reported in this paper were undertaken [in part] using the Bayesian Analysis, Computation and Communication software (http://www.econ.umn.edu/ bacc) described in Geweke (1999, with discussion and rejoinder).

  The Web site provides detailed instructions for downloading, installing, and running the program. Versions are available for Linux/Unix S-PLUS and R, Windows S-PLUS and R, and MATLAB.

  BACC is described extensively in Geweke (2005). See also Geweke (1999), Koop (1999), and McCausland (2004).

- WinBUGS is available through the Web site http://www.mrc-bsu.cam.ac.uk/bugs/ welcome.shtml.

  BUGS code for many models is provided in Congdon (2001, 2003, 2005).

There are a few other implementations of the BUGS language. One that runs easily and compiles on Unix is JAGS, http://www-fis.iarc.fr/ martyn/software/jags/.

There is also another project called OpenBUGS, http://mathstat.helsinki.fi/openbugs/.

- Econometrics Toolbox by James P. LeSage is available at http://www.spatial-econometrics.com/. It runs on MATLAB.

Andrew Martin maintains a Web site that reviews Bayesian software written in R, which has become the primary program for Bayesian work in political science, sociology, and much of applied statistics: http://cran.r-project.org/src/contrib/Views/Bayesian.html

Two packages for model fitting in R are as follows:

- bayesm, by P. E. Rossi, G. Allenby, and R. McCulloch. It is available at http://gsbwww.uchicago.edu/fac/peter.rossi/research/bsm.html. See also Rossi, Allenby, and McCulloch (2006).
- MCMCpack is available at http://mcmcpack.wustl.edu. It is Andrew Martin's NSF supported package, which contains some of the models discussed in this book as well as some additional measurement and ecological inference models of interest to political scientists. See http://adm.wustl.edu/working/RnewsWorking.pdf.

Bibliography

Albert, J. H. and Chib, S. (1993a). Bayes inference via Gibbs sampling of autoregressive time series subject to Markov mean and variance shifts. *Journal of Business and Economic Statistics 11,* 1 (January), 1–15.

Albert, J. H. and Chib, S. (1993b). Bayesian analysis of binary and polychotomous response data. *Journal of the American Statistical Association 88,* 422 (June), 669–679.

Arellano, M. (2003). *Panel Data Econometrics* (Oxford University Press, Oxford).

Baltagi, B. H. (2001). *Econometric Analysis of Panel Data,* 2nd edn. (John Wiley & Sons, New York).

Basu, S. and Chib, S. (2003). Marginal likelihood and Bayes factors for Dirichlet process mixture models. *Journal of the American Statistical Association 98,* 461 (March), 224–235.

Berger, J. O. (1985). *Statistical Decision Theory and Bayesian Analysis,* 2nd edn. Springer Series in Statistics (Springer-Verlag, New York).

Bernardo, J. M. and Smith, A. F. M. (1994). *Bayesian Theory* (John Wiley & Sons, New York).

Berry, D. A. (1996). *Statistics: A Bayesian Perspective* (Wadsworth Publishing Company, Belmont, CA).

Bhattacharya, R. N. and Waymire, E. C. (1990). *Stochastic Processes with Applications.* Wiley Series in Probabilty and Mathematical Statistics – Applied Probability and Statistics (John Wiley & Sons, New York).

Billingsley, P. (1986). *Probability and Measure,* 2nd edn. (John Wiley & Sons, New York).

Bolstad, W. M. (2004). *Introduction to Bayesian Statistics* (John Wiley & Sons, Hoboken, NJ).

Boot, J. C. G. and de Wit, G. M. (1960). Investment demand: An empirical contribution to the aggregation problem. *Inernational Economic Review 1,* 1 (January), 3–30.

Carlin, B. P. and Louis, T. A. (2000). *Bayes and Empirical Bayes Methods for Data Analysis,* 2nd edn. Texts in Statistical Science, vol. 47 (Taylor & Francis/CRC, London).

Carlin, B. P., Gelfand, A. E., and Smith, A. F. M. (1992a). Hierarchical Bayesian analysis of changepoint problems. *Applied Statistics 41,* 2, 389–405.

Carlin, B. P., Polson, N. G., and Stoffer, D. S. (1992b). A Monte Carlo approach to nonnormal and nonlinear state–space modeling. *Journal of the American Statistical Association 87,* 418 (June), 493–500.

Carter, C. K. and Kohn, R. (1994). On Gibbs sampling for state space models. *Biometrika 81,* 3 (August), 541–553.

Celeux, G., Hurn, M., and Robert, C. P. (2000). Computational and inferential difficulties with mixture posterior distributions. *Journal of the American Statistical Association 95,* 451 (September), 957–970.

Chib, S. (1992). Bayes inference in the Tobit censored regression model. *Journal of Econometrics 51,* 1–2 (January–February), 79–99.

Chib, S. (1993). Bayes regression with autoregressive errors: A Gibbs sampling approach. *Journal of Econometrics 58,* 3 (August), 275–294.

Chib, S. (1995). Marginal likelihood from the Gibbs output. *Journal of the American Statistical Association 90,* 432 (December), 1313–1321.

Chib, S. (1996). Calculating posterior distributions and modal estimates in Markov mixture models. *Journal of Econometrics 75,* 1 (November), 79–97.

Chib, S. (1998). Estimation and comparison of multiple change-point models. *Journal of Econometrics 86,* 2 (October), 221–241.

Chib, S. (2001). Markov chain Monte Carlo methods: Computation and inference. In *Handbook of Econometrics,* vol. 5, J. J. Heckman and E. Leamer, eds. (North-Holland, Amsterdam), pp. 3569–3649.

Chib, S. (in press-a). Analysis of treatment response data without the joint distribution of potential outcomes. *Journal of Econometrics.*

Chib, S. (in press-b). Panel data modeling and inference: A Bayesian primer. In *The Econometrics of Panel Data: Fundamentals and Recent Developments in Theory,* 3rd edn., L. Mátyás and P. Sevestre, eds. (Springer, Boston).

Chib, S. and Carlin, B. P. (1999). On MCMC sampling in hierarchical longitudinal models. *Statistics and Computing 9,* 1 (April), 17–26.

Chib, S. and Greenberg, E. (1994). Bayes inference in regression models with ARMA(p, q) errors. *Journal of Econometrics 64,* 1–2 (September–October), 183–206.

Chib, S. and Greenberg, E. (1995a). Analysis of SUR models with extensions to correlated serial errors and time-varying parameter models. *Journal of Econometrics 68,* 2 (August), 339–360.

Chib, S. and Greenberg, E. (1995b). Understanding the Metropolis–Hastings algorithm. *The American Statistician 49,* 4 (November), 327–335.

Chib, S. and Greenberg, E. (1998). Analysis of multivariate probit models. *Biometrika 85,* 2 (June), 347–361.

Chib, S. and Jeliazkov, I. (2001). Marginal likelihood from the Metropolis–Hastings output. *Journal of the American Statistical Association 96,* 453 (March), 270–281.

Chib, S. and Jeliazkov, I. (2005). Accept–reject Metropolis–Hastings sampling and marginal likelihood estimation. *Statistica Neerlandica 59,* 1 (February), 30–44.

Christensen, R. (2005). Testing Fisher, Neyman, Pearson, and Bayes. *The American Statistican 59,* 2 (May), 121–126.

Clinton, J., Jackman, S., and Rivers, D. (2004). The statistical analysis of roll call data. *American Political Science Review 98,* 2 (May), 355–370.

Congdon, P. (2001). *Bayesian Statistical Modelling* (John Wiley & Sons, New York).

Congdon, P. (2003). *Applied Bayesian Modelling* (John Wiley & Sons, New York).

Congdon, P. (2005). *Bayesian Models for Categorical Data* (John Wiley & Sons, New York).

de Finetti, B. (1990). *Theory of Probability.* Wiley Classics Library, vol. 1 (John Wiley & Sons, Chichester).

de Jong, P. and Shephard, N. (1995). The simulation smoother for time series models. *Biometrika 82,* 2 (June), 339–350.

DeGroot, M. H. and Schervish, M. J. (2002). *Probability and Statistics*, 3rd edn. (Addison-Wesley, Boston).

Devroye, L. (1986). *Non-Uniform Random Variate Generation* (Springer-Verlag, New York).

Drèze, J. H. and Richard, J.-F. (1983). Bayesian analysis of simultaneous equation systems. In *Handbook of Econometrics*, vol. 1, Z. Griliches and M. D. Intriligator, eds. (North-Holland Publishing Company, Amsterdam), Chapter 9, pp. 517–598.

Escobar, M. D. and West, M. (1995). Bayesian density estimation and inference using mixtures. *Journal of the American Statistical Association 90,* 430 (June), 577–588.

Frühwirth-Schnatter, S. (1994). Data augmentation and dynamic linear models. *Journal of Time Series Analysis 15,* 2 (March), 183–202.

Frühwirth-Schnatter, S. (2001). Markov chain Monte Carlo estimation of classical and dynamic switching and mixture models. *Journal of the American Statistical Association 96,* 453 (March), 194–209.

Garthwaite, P. H., Kadane, J. B., and O'Hagan, A. (2005). Statistical methods for eliciting probability distributions. *Journal of the American Statistical Association 100,* 470 (June), 680–700.

Gelfand, A. E. and Smith, A. F. M. (1990). Sampling based approaches to calculating marginal densities. *Journal of the American Statistical Association 85,* 410 (June), 398–409.

Gelman, A., Carlin, J. B., Stern, H. S., and Rubin, D. B. (2004). *Bayesian Data Analysis*, 2nd edn. Texts in Statistical Science (Chapman & Hall/CRC, Boca Raton).

Gentle, J. E. (2003). *Random Number Generation and Monte Carlo Methods*, 2nd edn. (Springer-Verlag, New York).

Geweke, J. (1989). Bayesian inference in econometric models using Monte Carlo integration. *Econometrica 57,* 6 (November), 1317–1339.

Geweke, J. (1993). Bayesian treatment of the independent Student-t linear model. *Journal of Applied Econometrics 8,* Supplement (December), S19–S40.

Geweke, J. (1999). Using simulation methods for Bayesian econometric models: Inference, development, and communication. *Econometric Reviews 18,* 1 (February), 1–126.

Geweke, J. (2005). *Contemporary Bayesian Econometrics and Statistics*. Wiley Series in Probability and Statistics (John Wiley & Sons, Hoboken, NJ).

Geweke, J. and Keane, M. (2001). Computational intensive methods for integration in econometrics. In *Handbook of Econometrics*, vol. 5, J. J. Heckman and E. E. Leamer, eds. (North-Holland, Amsterdam), pp. 3465–3568.

Geyer, C. J. (1992). Practical Markov chain Monte Carlo. *Statistical Science 7,* 4 (November), 473–483.

Green, P. J. (1995). Reversible jump MCMC computation and Bayesian model determination. *Biometrika 82,* 4 (December), 711–732.

Greene, W. H. (2003). *Econometric Analysis*, 5th edn. (Pearson Education, Inc., Upper Saddle River, NJ).

Grunfeld, Y. (1958). The determinants of corporate investment. Ph.D. thesis, University of Chicago.

Hacking, I. (2001). *An Introduction to Probability and Inductive Logic* (Cambridge University Press, Cambridge).

Hamilton, J. D. (1989). A new approach to the economic analysis of nonstationary time series and the business cycle. *Econometrica 57*, 2 (March), 357–384.

Hamilton, J. D. (1994). *Time Series Analysis* (Princeton University Press, Princeton).

Harvey, A. C. (1989). *Forecasting, Structural Time Series Models and the Kalman Filter* (Cambridge University Press, Cambridge).

Hastings, W. K. (1970). Monte Carlo sampling methods using Markov chains and their applications. *Biometrika 57*, 1 (April), 97–109.

Hausman, J. A. (1978). Specification tests in econometrics. *Economerica 46*, 6 (November), 1251–1271.

Heckman, J. J. (1979). Sample selection bias as a specification error. *Econometrica 47*, 1 (January), 153–161.

Heckman, J. J. and Vytlacil, E. (2005). Structural equations, treatment effects, and econometric policy evaluation. *Econometrica 73*, 3 (May), 669–738.

Hitchcock, D. B. (2003). A history of the Metropolis–Hastings algorithm. *The American Statistician 57*, 4 (November), 254–257.

Howie, D. (2002). *Interpreting Probability: Controversies and Developments in the Early Twentieth Century* (Cambridge University Press, Cambridge).

Howson, C. and Urbach, P. (1993). *Scientific Reasoning: The Bayesian Approach*, 3rd edn. (Open Court Publishing Company, Chicago).

Hsiao, C. (2003). *Analysis of Panel Data* (Cambridge University Press, Cambridge).

Jaynes, E. T. (2003). *Probability Theory: The Logic of Science* (Cambridge University Press, Cambridge).

Jeffreys, H. (1961). *Theory of Probability*, 3rd edn. (Clarendon Press, Oxford).

Kadane, J. B. and Lazar, N. A. (2004). Methods and criteria for model selection. *Journal of the American Statistical Association 99*, 465 (March), 279–290.

Kemeny, J. G., Snell, J. L., and Knapp, A. W. (1976). *Denumerable Markov Chains*. Graduate Texts in Mathematics (Springer-Verlag, New York).

Kennedy, P. (2003). *A Guide to Econometrics*, 5th edn. (The MIT Press, Cambridge).

Kim, C.-J. and Nelson, C. R. (1999). *State–Space Models with Regime Switching: Classical and Gibbs-Sampling Approaches with Applications* (The MIT Press, Cambridge).

Koop, G. (1999). Bayesian analysis, computation and communication software. *Journal of Applied Econometrics 14*, 6 (November–December), 677–689.

Koop, G. (2003). *Bayesian Econometrics* (John Wiley & Sons, New York).

Lancaster, T. (2004). *An Introduction to Modern Bayesian Econometrics* (Blackwell, Malden, MA).

Lee, P. M. (1997). *Bayesian Statistics: An Introduction*, 2nd edn. (Arnold, London).

Martin, A. D. and Quinn, K. M. (2002). Dynamic ideal point estimation via Markov chain Monte Carlo for the U.S. Supreme Court, 1953–1999. *Political Analysis 10*, 2, 134–153.

McCausland, W. J. (2004). Using the BACC software for Bayesian inference. *Computational Economics 23*, 3 (April), 201–218.

McCulloch, R. E., Polson, N. G., and Rossi, P. E. (2000). A Bayesian analysis of the multinomial probit model with fully identified parameters. *Journal of Econometrics 99*, 1 (November), 173–193.

Metropolis, N., Rosenbluth, A. W., Rosenbluth, M. N., Teller, A. H., and Teller, E. (1953). Equations of state calculations by fast computing machines. *Journal of Chemical Physics 21*, 1087–1092.

Meyn, S. P. and Tweedie, R. L. (1993). *Markov Chains and Stochastic Stability* (Springer-Verlag, London).

Mittelhammer, R. C., Judge, G. G., and Miller, D. J. (2000). *Econometric Foundations* (Cambridge University Press, Cambridge).

Mroz, T. A. (1987). The sensitivity of an empirical model of married women's hours of work to economic and statistical assumptions. *Econometrica 55,* 4 (July), 765–799.

Mundlak, Y. (1961). Empirical production function free of management bias. *Journal of Farm Economics 43,* 1 (February), 44–56.

Norris, J. R. (1997). *Markov Chains.* Cambridge Series in Statistical and Probabilistic Mathematics (Cambridge University Press, Cambridge).

Nummelin, E. (1984). *General Irreducible Markov Chains and Non-Negative Operators* (Cambridge University Press, Cambridge).

O'Hagan, A. (1994). *Bayesian Inference.* Kendall's Advanced Theory of Statistics, vol. 2B (Halsted Press, New York).

O'Hagan, A., Buck, C. E., Daneshkhah, A., Eiser, J. R., Garthwaite, P. H., Jenkinson, D. J., Oakley, J. E., and Rakow, T. (2006). *Uncertain Judgements: Eliciting Experts' Probabilities.* Statistics in Practice (John Wiley & Sons, Chichester).

Poirier, D. J. (1995). *Intermediate Statistics and Econometrics: A Comparative Approach* (MIT Press, Cambridge).

Poirier, D. J. and Tobias, J. L. (2003). On the predictive distributions of outcome gains in the presence of an unidentified parameter. *Journal of Business and Economic Statistics 21,* 2 (April), 258–268.

Press, S. J. (1972). *Applied Multivariate Analysis.* Quantitative Methods for Decision-Making (Holt, Rinehart and Winston, Inc., New York).

Priestley, M. B. (1981). *Spectral Analysis and Time Series.* Probability and Mathematical Statistics (Academic Press, London).

Ripley, B. D. (1987). *Stochastic Simulation.* Wiley Series in Probability and Mathematical Statistics (John Wiley & Sons, New York).

Robert, C. P. (1994). *The Bayesian Choice: A Decision-Theoretic Motivation.* Springer Texts in Statistics (Spring-Verlag, New York).

Robert, C. P. and Casella, G. (2004). *Monte Carlo Statistical Methods*, 2nd edn. Springer Texts in Statistics (Springer-Verlag, New York).

Rossi, P., Allenby, G., and McCulloch, R. (2006). *Bayesian Statistics and Marketing* (John Wiley & Sons, New York).

Rubinfeld, D. (1977). Voting in a local school election: A micro analysis. *Review of Economics and Statistics 59,* 1 (February), 30–42.

Rubinstein, R. Y. (1981). *Simulation and the Monte Carlo Method.* Wiley Series in Probability and Mathematical Statistics (John Wiley & Sons, New York).

Schervish, M. J. (1995). *Theory of Statistics.* Springer Series in Statistics (Springer-Verlag, New York).

Schott, J. R. (1997). *Matrix Analysis for Statistics.* Wiley Series in Probability and Statistics (John Wiley & Sons, New York).

Stigler, S. M. (1986). *The History of Statistics: The Measurement of Uncertainty Before 1900* (Belknap Press of Harvard University Press, Cambridge).

Tanner, M. A. and Wong, W. H. (1987). The calculation of posterior distributions by data augmentation. *Journal of the American Statistical Association 82,* 398 (June), 528–550.

Tierney, L. (1994). Markov chains for exploring posterior distributions (with discussion). *The Annals of Statistics 22,* 4 (December), 1701–1762.

Train, K. E. (2003). *Discrete Choice Methods with Simulation* (Cambridge University Press, Cambridge).

Vella, F. and Verbeek, M. (1998). Whose wages do unions raise? A dynamic model of unionism and wage rate determination for young men. *Journal of Applied Econometrics 13*, 2 (March–April), 163–183.

Winkelmann, R. (1997). *Econometric Analysis of Count Data*, 2nd edn. (Springer-Verlag, Berlin).

Wooldridge, J. M. (2002). *Econometric Analysis of Cross Section and Panel Data* (MIT Press, Cambridge).

Wooldridge, J. M. (2006). *Introductory Econometrics: A Modern Approach*, 3rd edn. (Thomson South-Western, Mason, OH).

Zellner, A. (1962). An efficient method of estimating seemingly unrelated regressions and tests for aggregation bias. *Journal of the American Statistical Association 57*, 298 (June), 348–368.

Zellner, A. (1971). *An Introduction to Bayesian Inference in Econometrics* (John Wiley & Sons, New York).

Zellner, A. (1997). The Bayesian method of moments (BMOM): Theory and applications. *Advances in Econometrics 12*, 85–105.

Author Index

Subject Index